The Jew and the Christian Missionary:

A Jewish Response
To Missionary Christianity

The Jew and the Christian Missionary:

A Jewish Response To Missionary Christianity

GERALD SIGAL

KTAV PUBLISHING HOUSE, INC.
NEW YORK
1981

Library of Congress Cataloging in Publication Data

Sigal, Gerald.
　The Jew and the Christian missionary

　Bibliography: p.
　Includes index.
　　1. Christianity—Controversial literature.
2. Judaism—Apologetic works. 3. Bible—Criticism,
interpretation, etc. I. Title.
BM590.S57　　220.7'7　　81-758
ISBN 0-87068-886-3　　　AACR2

MANUFACTURED IN THE UNITED STATES OF AMERICA

To the everlasting memory of my father,
Noach ben Yaʿaqov Levi Sigal

CONTENTS

BOOK II
THE NEW TESTAMENT

BIBLE TRANSLATIONS CONSULTED

The Holy Scriptures According to the Masoretic Text. Philadelphia: Jewish Publication Society of America, 1955.

New American Standard Bible. Carol Stream, Ill.: Creation House, 1971.

New World Translation of the Holy Scriptures. New York: Watchtower Bible and Tract Society of New York, 1970.

The Revised Standard Version Common Bible. Cleveland: Collins, 1973.

The King James Authorized Version. New York: International Bible Society, n.d.

The Jerusalem Bible. Garden City, N.Y.: Doubleday, 1966.

The Septuagint Version: Greek and English. Translated by Lancelot C. L. Brenton. Grand Rapids, Mich.: Zondervan Publishing House, 1979.

The R.S.V. Interlinear Greek-English New Testament. Literal translation by Alfred Marshall. Grand Rapids, Mich.: Zondervan Publishing House, 1979.

ACKNOWLEDGMENTS

The author wishes to thank Mrs. Lynda Sarnoff and Mrs. Gina Vega for their respective readings of the manuscript and for their many comments which improved the stylistic and grammatical form of this work. I would also like to thank my wife Frances for her invaluable help in the preparation of the index. A special word of gratitude must be reserved for Rabbi Norman Bronznick, whose patience, guidance, and wide range of scholarship, over the last half-dozen years, have in no small measure made this endeavor a fruitful one.

INTRODUCTION

Up-to-date information on the nature of the claims of the Christian missionary movement and how to respond to its arguments has generally been unavailable to Jews. The classical works in this area, such as the highly regarded *Faith Strengthened,* by Isaac ben Abraham Troki, are not fully suited to current needs in protecting the innocent and the uninformed against aggressive missionary groups.

The entire missionary view of the Jewish relationship to God is fundamentally wrong. This view is based upon a prejudiced Christian theological appraisal of Judaism, not on the nature of the covenantal relationship that exists between God and Israel. Misreading the essential meaning of the Torah, Christian theology developed along lines that are at variance with the message of the Hebrew Scriptures. As a result, missionary Christianity starts with the thesis that the Jewish Bible is the revealed word of God, but that Judaism went astray two thousand years ago. The missionaries claim that Christianity then became the true continuation of the Jewish spiritual past. To support that contention, they cannot attack the Hebrew Bible. Instead, in order to arrive at the theological concepts they desire, missionaries propose their own radically altered constructions of the meaning of biblical verses. These altered constructions bear no relation to any of the beliefs taught by priest and prophet, the authentic teachers in ancient Israel.

Few Jews are equipped with sufficient knowledge of their own Bible, let alone with that of Christian theology, to be able to discriminate between correct and incorrect interpretations of a biblical verse. Few Christians have any knowledge of the Jewish understanding of the Bible and the Jewish response to the claims made in the New Testament. To meet these needs, this book is designed to analyze, from a Jewish standpoint, the way the

xv

Hebrew Bible is used, and misused, by today's Christian missionary movement, providing a Jewish interpretation of the biblical passages commonly cited by missionaries. The basic theological differences involved in the dispute between Judaism and the missionaries are examined in detail, not in order to refute the beliefs of pious Christians but to demonstrate that the scriptural evidence does not substantiate the missionary claim that Christianity is the fulfillment of biblical prophecy.

This book represents the culmination of close examination of hundreds of missionary books and tracts over a period of some twenty-five years. In addition, countless hours were spent in serious discussions with various missionaries about the beliefs they espouse and preach. The result is a book which not only discusses the missionary interpretations of the Hebrew Scriptures but also offers new insights for all students of the Bible and comparative religion, whether Jewish or Gentile. Biblical passages are examined as they relate to the religious beliefs of both Judaism and Christianity, from a perspective rarely explored in theological studies of these religions.

The driving force behind the missionary movement's efforts against Judaism is the conviction that the validity of Christianity requires the withering away of ancient Jewish practice and belief (Hebrews 8:13). To accomplish this end, missionaries must undermine the foundation of Judaism. The missionary movement is mindful of the proclamation of the prophet Habakkuk that "the righteous shall live by his faithfulness" (Habakkuk 2:4), i.e., his steadfast loyalty to the Torah, the Law of God. The survival of the Jewish people is directly conditioned upon the observance of the Torah. During the course of Jewish history, faith, in its inner as well as its outer form, expressed itself in the strict observance of God's Law (cf. Daniel 1:8–21). Faith in God has never been an alien concept to Israel. The belief that God and Israel have a unique, trusting relationship has been the very core of the Jewish historic experience.

Uppermost in importance in the life of the Jew is the observance of the Torah, from which all else flows. Torah in Judaism expresses the will of God. By definition it requires no justification. It is God's prerogative that has determined what is right and what is wrong. The Torah does not deliver from sin; only God can do that. It does, however, reveal what God deems necessary to bring about deliverance. The Torah describes the intimate details of the covenantal bond between God and Israel. The quintessence of Judaism is the tenet that God has never ordained, nor will He accept, any other way for the Jew to enter into a personal loving relationship with Him than through the Torah. The Torah is the divinely mandated means to faith for the Jew. Through observance of its commandments, the Jew attains faith in the Creator, the Holy One, blessed be He, and is given spiritual strength in a lawless, ungodly world.

Since the Torah constitutes such a vital force in the relationship between God and Israel, the missionary movement has consistently sought to destroy any meaningful adherence to the Torah by contending that its observance is no longer required by God. This effort to undermine the normative function of the Torah is fundamental to the missionary effort to convert Jewish people to Christianity. The contention of the missionary movement that the Torah has been superseded by faith in Jesus, and that Jesus is thus the only means by which to approach God, has been refuted by the religious experience of the Jewish people. Through prayer and the faithful observance of the precepts of the Torah, the Jewish people have always enjoyed a direct and unmediated relationship with God. In the words of David: "The Lord is near to all that call upon Him, to all who call upon Him in truth" (Psalms 145:18).

The Christian missionary movement and most Christian denominational groups hold many beliefs in common. Since the main purpose of this work is to reply to the claims of the Christian missionary movement, it carries as a necessary concomitant a disputation of commonly held Christian beliefs. It is not, however, the aim of this book to direct criticism at Christians who do not seek to convert Jewish people and who are willing to abide by the view of the prophet Micah: "For let all the peoples walk each one in the name of its god, but we will walk in the name of the Lord our God forever and ever" (Micah 4:5). This book has been written neither with malice nor with intent to insult either Christians or Christianity, but with the purpose of setting aright those Jews who are being deluded into joining Christianity by out-and-out distortions of the Hebrew Bible.

The author does not utilize the works of those Christian scholars who, using the scientific approach to the New Testament, have, for more than a century, dismissed as unhistorical many of the traditional episodes in Jesus' life. The reasoning behind this approach is that Christian missionaries accept these traditions as literally factual. As a result, it is extremely important that one who wishes to challenge missionary claims be able to effectively counter their arguments through means other than the scientific. Perhaps of even greater value than the scientific approach is the effective use of the very sources considered valid by the missionaries themselves. Therefore, it is not unfamiliarity with modern New Testament study, but the conscious recognition that the problems engendered by the missionaries must be approached squarely through the very works the movement accepts as authoritative, that makes it necessary to investigate their assertions through these sources. Hence, we will examine the missionary claims on the basis of the Hebrew Scriptures and the New Testament, and these works alone. It would make little sense to approach the problem through the use of what is termed the scientific study of the New Testament when such scholarship would be simply dismissed as invalid by Christian missionaries and Christian converts from Judaism.

While occasional reference has been made to nonbiblical works, the use of the Hebrew Scriptures and the New Testament has been overwhelmingly emphasized. These are the fundamental texts upon which all missionary arguments are based. Since Christian missionaries do not accept the validity of the Oral Law, few references to it are made in the analysis of their assertions. Even so, those unacquainted with the Oral Law will learn that its views on certain subjects are supported by biblical proofs.

To facilitate the understanding of the material presented, each chapter is organized as an independent unit around the Bible verse used by missionaries for their arguments. Notes are kept to a minimum. Certain common points are restated rather than referring the reader from one section to another, with the result that each chapter can be read as a compact, self-enclosed unit.

Refutations of the claims of the missionaries are taken from the very books in which they profess to believe: the Hebrew and Greek Scriptures, often termed the Holy Bible. When the translations from the Hebrew Bible and the New Testament found in this book do not conform to the available standard translations, the former represent the more literal and correct renderings of the original text.

BOOK I
The Hebrew Scriptures

1

HER SEED

(Genesis 3:15)

And I will put enmity between you and the woman, and between your seed and her seed; he will strike at your head, and you will strike at his heel.

(Genesis 3:15)

From this verse Christian missionary theologians argue that the Messiah is to be born of the seed of a woman without a man's intervention. Yet there is absolutely no proof to assume that this verse is messianic or that the Messiah is to be born in a supernatural way. The Christian missionary claim of a direct and exclusive reference to Jesus is exegetically untenable.

The phrase "her seed" has nothing to do with the determination of the Messiah's lineage. The first mention of human "seed" in the Bible (Genesis 3:15) is used generically to include all of the future descendants of Eve. Since God was not addressing a man, but the serpent in the presence of the woman, it was not necessary nor would it have been grammatically correct for Him to have said: "I will put enmity between you and the woman, and between your seed and *his seed.*" It must read, in order to make sense, as found in Genesis: "I will put enmity between you and the woman, and between your seed and *her seed.*" Thus, the grammatical consistency of the sentence is upheld in reference to those addressed. In Genesis 16:10, God's message to Hagar states: "I will greatly multiply *your seed,* not "I will greatly multiply *his* [Abraham's] *seed.*" Since God's message concerning

Hagar's descendants is addressed directly to a woman, an occurrence not commonly found in the Bible, it is grammatically necessary to refer to these descendants as *her seed*. This was also the case concerning Eve. "Her seed" simply means her descendants, just as when addressed to a man, "his seed" means his descendants.

The pronouns "he" and "you" in "he will strike at your head, and you will strike at his heel" have been described by Christian missionary commentators as referring to Jesus and Satan respectively. The question of whether or not the verse is an allusion to Jesus and Satan is best answered by seeing whether Jesus fulfilled the prophecy. To prove fulfillment, Christian missionaries point to 1 John 3:8–9, Hebrews 2:14, and Romans 16:20.

1 John 3:8–9 states: "The Son of God appeared for this purpose, that he might destroy the works of the Devil. No one who is born of God practices sin, because His seed remains in him; and he cannot sin, because he is born of God" (see also 1 John 5:18). In Hebrews 2:14, it is stated that Jesus became flesh and blood so "that through death he might render powerless him who had the power of death, that is, the Devil." Have the works of Satan been destroyed? Did Jesus, by his death, render Satan, the cause of sin, powerless? If he did these things, there ought not to be any sinners among his believers, for "the one who practices sin is of the Devil" (1 John 3:8). But this is not the case, and sin abounds even among Christians (1 Timothy 1:15, 1 John 1:8). That Jesus did not fulfill the hoped-for deliverance from Satan is seen from the writings of Paul himself. In 1 Thessalonians 2:18, he says: "For we wanted to come to you, even I, Paul, once and a second time, but Satan hindered us." Furthermore, Paul says in Romans 16:20: "And the God of peace will crush Satan under your feet shortly." Since Satan is still at work, it is obvious that Paul's unfulfilled "shortly" is now two thousand years old and Jesus still has not crushed the head of the serpent identified by Paul as Satan. These passages show that, according to the New Testament, the power of Satan did not wane with the death of Jesus. In fact, the conclusion to be drawn is that Satan has more power in the world than Jesus.

It is obvious that "her seed" indicates no more of a miraculous birth than the "your seed" used in reference to Hagar. Moreover, we see that "he will strike at your head, and you will strike at his heel" does not refer to Jesus since he neither stopped the power of Satan "shortly" nor did he abolish sin among his followers, as Paul promised. It is, therefore, clear that the Christian missionary interpretation of Genesis 3:15 is yet another Christological dream that may be placed in the category of those prophecies unfulfilled by Jesus and which Christian missionaries hope will be fulfilled in what is called the "second coming."

2

THE FIRST HUMAN BIRTH

(Genesis 4:1)

I have acquired a man with [the help of] the Lord.

(Genesis 4:1)

Christian missionary exegetes interpret this verse to mean that Eve thought she had conceived in a supernatural way, with God as her consort, and had given birth to the Messiah, as the Christians claim happened to Mary. They claim prophetic power for Eve because, in accordance with Christian belief, she knew that the Messiah was to be born of the union of God with a female. However, they deny the mother of humanity the fundamental knowledge of the biological process of birth. Thus, according to them, Eve was not aware of the part played by Adam in the birth of her child. This is evidently not the case since the verse, as it reads in full, states: "And the man knew Eve his wife; and she conceived and bore Cain, and said: 'I have acquired a man with [the help of] the Lord.' " Adam is clearly acknowledged as the father of her child. This fact is not stated by the Bible merely for the edification of the reader. The knowledge of this fact is, first and foremost, attributed to the principals, Adam and Eve, themselves.

What Eve really means by her statement, and what the exegetes choose to ignore, is that she is grateful to the Almighty for His help in the process of birth. It should not be at all surprising for Eve to feel this way since divine aid is most essential in facilitating birth. This is implicit in Jacob's words to Rachel: "Am I in God's stead, who has withheld from you the

6

fruit of the womb?" (Genesis 30:2). This is explicitly stated in Ruth 4:13: "And he [Boaz] went in to her [Ruth], and the Lord gave her conception, and she bore a son." One might explain the interaction of God, man, and woman in the birth process as: God + Man + Woman = Child. The Rabbis have aptly phrased it by stating that: "There are three partners in man: The Holy One, blessed be He, his father, and his mother" (B. T. Kiddushin 30b, B.T. Niddah 31a). All in all, there is no messianic significance to be attached to the verse under discussion.

3

THE SEED OF ABRAHAM

(Genesis 13:15, 17:8)

. . . for all the land which you see, to you will I give it, and to your seed forever.

(Genesis 13:15)

And I will give to you, and to your seed after you, the land of your sojournings, all the land of Canaan, for an everlasting possession; and I will be their God.

(Genesis 17:8)

Commenting on the use of the word *zerʿa* ("seed") in Genesis 13:15 and 17:8, Paul says: "Now the promises were spoken to Abraham and to his seed. It does not say, 'And to seeds,' referring to many; but, referring to one, 'And to your seed,' who is Christ" (Galatians 3:16). Paul's claim that a single individual is meant by the term "seed" in Genesis 13:15 and 17:8 is fallacious. Nowhere in the Hebrew Bible do we find the plural of "seed" used with reference to human descendants. In all instances, the singular term "seed" is used in a plural sense (e.g., Genesis 13:16, 17:10, 22:17–18). This is clearly stated in Genesis 17:8: ". . . and I will be their God," where the third-person plural pronoun, "their," refers to "your seed."

8

4

UNTIL SHILOH COMES

(Genesis 49:10)

The scepter shall not depart from Judah, nor the ruler's staff from between his feet, until Shiloh comes; and to him shall be the obedience of peoples.

(Genesis 49:10)

Christian missionaries often use this verse as a proof-text for their messianic claims. But if this text is taken to mean that the scepter shall not depart from Judah until the Messiah comes, as the Christian missionaries assert, we are faced with an insoluble historical inaccuracy. The last king from the tribe of Judah, Zedekiah, was taken captive around 586 B.C.E. Following the return to Zion from the Babylonian exile, the Jews were continually subject to foreign domination—Persian, Greek, Roman— with only a brief interlude of independence during the Maccabean period (165 B.C.E. to 63 B.C.E.), whose rulers were members of the tribe of Levi. Thus, there was a period of some six hundred years, prior to the birth of Jesus, during which the scepter of leadership had departed from the tribe of Judah.

In view of this incontrovertible fact, we are compelled to interpret the verse under discussion somewhat differently from the interpretation imposed upon it by Christian missionary theology. What is meant by the phrase "the scepter shall not depart" is that the right to the scepter of leadership shall always remain within the tribe of Judah, regardless of who is actually exercising authority over Israel at any given time. What is meant by the phrase "until Shiloh comes" is not that at this time the

9

scepter of leadership will depart from Judah, but, on the contrary, from that time on, the scepter will remain in actuality within the tribe of Judah.

The adverb ʿad ("until") is used in a similar sense in a number of instances; for example: "For I will not leave you *until* I have done that which I have spoken to you" (Genesis 28:15), and "No man shall be able to stand before you *until* you have destroyed them" (Deuteronomy 7:24). Did God leave Jacob after doing all that He promised him? Were the enemies of Israel who were killed able to stand after they were destroyed? Even after the Messiah comes the scepter will still belong to Judah. The right to the scepter will never depart from Judah until the Messiah comes, at which time his scepter will be wielded over all nations (Isaiah 11); up to that time it was wielded over Israel alone. That this Messiah is not Jesus can best be seen through the investigation of the various messianic claims made by Christian missionaries on his behalf. As for Genesis 49:10, there is nothing in it to suggest that it applies to Jesus.

5

SIN AND ATONEMENT
(Leviticus 17:11)

There is a Christian missionary misinterpretation of the Scriptures according to which the Jewish people can have no assurance that their sins are forgiven, for it is written in Leviticus 17:11: "It is the blood that makes an atonement for the soul." Where there is no blood, it is claimed, there is no atonement. The fasting and repentance of Yom Kippur, it is contended, cannot give any assurance of sins forgiven. It is asserted that God will never accept something else in place of a blood sacrifice for the atonement of sins. Finally, this distortion culminates in the claim that Jesus, by his death and supposed sacrifice for humanity's sins, made atonement for all who believe in him, and so there is no longer any need for a Temple or a sacrifice or a priesthood. Within a few years of Jesus' death, it is claimed, God permitted the Temple to be destroyed, and the priesthood to be abolished, since they were no longer needed. Jesus was now to be the unblemished lamb that would bear away the sins of the world.

To fully comprehend how missionary Christianity has misinterpreted Leviticus 17:11, we must first understand the nature of the physical and spiritual ingredients of a Jewish sacrifice. The physical sacrifice was an unblemished clean animal. The spiritual sacrifice constituted a repentant mental attitude. Thus, the ceremonial service was an external symbolization of prayer, the service of the heart. The God of Israel has never left His people to wander in a spiritual vacuum, as our antagonists would have us believe. Let us briefly review some of the passages in Scripture which declare that prayer, without the shedding of blood, can and does provide a means for the

11

atonement and forgiveness of sin. Interestingly enough, in Solomon's prayer at the very dedication of the First Temple (1 Kings 8:44–52), prayer is given prominence as a means for remission of sin:

> If Your peaple go out to battle against their enemy, by whatever way You shall send them, and they pray to the Lord toward the city which You have chosen, and toward the house which I have built for Your name; then hear in heaven their prayer and their supplication, and maintain their cause. If they sin against You—for there is no man that does not sin—and You are angry with them, and deliver them to the enemy, so that they carry them away captive to the land of the enemy, far off or near; yet if they take thought in the land to which they are carried captive, and repent, and make supplication to You in the land of their captors, saying: "We have sinned, and have done iniquitously, we have dealt wickedly"; if they return to You with all their heart and with all their soul in the land of their enemies, who carried them captive, and pray to You toward their land, which You gave to their fathers, the city which You have chosen, and the house which I have built for Your name; then hear their prayer and their supplication in heaven Your dwelling place, and maintain their cause and forgive Your people who have sinned against You, and all their transgressions which they have transgressed against You, and give them compassion before those who carried them captive, that they may have compassion on them; for they are Your people, and Your inheritance, which You did bring out of Egypt, from the midst of the furnace of iron. Let Your eyes be open to the supplication of Your servant, and to the supplication of Your people Israel, to hear them whenever they cry to You.

And, indeed, Daniel did exactly as Solomon had said:

> He went into his house—now his windows were open in his upper chamber toward Jerusalem—and he kneeled upon his knees three times a day, and prayed, and gave thanks before his God, as he had done previously. Then these men came joined together, and found Daniel making petition and supplication before his God. (Daniel 6:11-12)

The idea that prayer takes the place of animal sacrifices is clearly expressed in Hosea 14:3: "So will we render for bullocks the offering of our lips." In fact, prayer is considered superior to animal offerings, as stated in Psalm 69:31–32: "I will praise the name of God with a song, and will magnify Him with thanksgiving. And it shall please the Lord better than a bullock that has horns and hoofs." And as Samuel said: "Has the Lord as great delight in burnt-offerings and sacrifices, as in obeying the voice of the Lord? Behold, to obey is better than sacrifice, and to hearken than the fat of rams" (1 Samuel 15:22). That forgiveness of sin can be achieved through prayer, the offering of the heart, rather than through an animal sacrifice, the offering of blood, is also seen in Psalm 32:5: "I acknowledged my sin to You, and I did not hide my iniquity; I said: 'I will make confession concerning my transgressions to the Lord'—and You, You forgave the iniquity of my sin."

It is a Christian missionary claim that the Temple was destroyed and the sacrificial system abolished only after Jesus offered himself as the supreme sacrifice. If that is so, what of the generations living in Babylonia during the first exile? Did God write them off as generations lost in sin with no means of atonement and forgiveness? Where was their blood atonement? But Jeremiah unequivocally told the exiles that they were not discarded by God, as even in the land of their exile they did not lack the means for achieving the atonement of their sins: "And you shall call upon Me, and go, and pray to Me, and I will hearken to you. And you shall seek Me, and find Me, when you shall search for Me with all your heart" (Jeremiah 29:12–13). Not by the blood of bullocks slain, but by the offerings of their lips, i.e., prayer, were they able to effect atonement. And so it is with us—by our prayers and repentance we make atonement for our sins, and God in His mercy forgives.

Prayer without blood sacrifice was recognized, among the ancient Israelites, as a means of atonement: "And the people came to Moses and they said: 'We have sinned, because we have spoken against the Lord, and against you; pray to the Lord, that He take away from us the serpents.' And Moses prayed for the people" (Numbers 21:7). There are cases where the holy incense, without the use of a blood sacrifice, could effect atonement: "And Aaron took as Moses spoke, and he ran into the midst of the assembly; and behold, the plague had already begun among the people; and he put on the incense, and he made atonement for the people" (Numbers 17:12). On returning from battle, the Israelites brought jewelry as an atonement offer for their sins: "And we have brought the Lord's offering, what every man has found, articles of gold, armlets, and bracelets, signet rings, earrings, and girdles, to make atonement for our souls before the Lord" (Numbers 31:50). In the preceding instances no shedding of blood was required for forgiveness of sin.

Isaiah also bears witness to the incorrectness of the claim that the only way for sin to be atoned for is through the shedding of blood: "Then flew one of the seraphim to me, having a live coal in his hand, which he had taken with the tongs off the altar; and he touched my mouth with it, and said: 'Behold, this has touched your lips; and your iniquity is taken away, and your sin forgiven' " (Isaiah 6:6–7). Despite the Christian missionary contention that there is no substitute for the shedding of blood, we find that Isaiah is forgiven his past misdeeds by means of a live coal that touched his lips. No shedding of blood is required, only the contrite heart and the will of God.

When David sinned against God by transgressing three of the Ten Commandments (the tenth, seventh, and sixth), in his affair with Bathsheba, he admitted to Nathan that he had sinned against the Lord, and Nathan answered him: "The Lord has put away your sin, you shall not die" (2 Samuel 12:13). Did David offer a blood sacrifice to achieve this? No! This is attested in Psalm 51, in which David's confession of his sin is expressed before God. This psalm shows explicitly that cleansing from sin may be achieved by the contrite heart:

> Deliver me from bloodguiltiness,
> O God, God of my salvation;

So shall my tongue sing aloud of Your righteousness.
O Lord, open my lips;
And my mouth shall declare Your praise.
For You have no delight in sacrifice, else I would give it;
You have no pleasure in burnt-offering.
The sacrifices of God are a broken spirit;
A broken and contrite heart,
O God, You will not despise.

(Psalms 51:16–19)

And what does the Torah say concerning a poor man who cannot afford the price of a blood sacrifice?

But if he cannot afford two turtledoves, or two young pigeons, then he shall bring his offering for that which he has sinned, the tenth part of an ephah of fine flour for a sin-offering; he shall put no oil upon it, neither shall he put any frankincense on it, for it is a sin-offering. And he shall bring it to the priest, and the priest shall take his handful of it as the memorial portion and make it smoke on the altar, upon the offerings of the Lord made by fire; it is a sin-offering. And the priest shall make atonement for him for his sin that he has sinned in any of these things, and he shall be forgiven; and the remainder shall be the priest's, as the meal offering.

(Leviticus 5:11–13)

Clearly, the poor man's meal offering is accepted by God as the equivalent of a blood sacrifice. There is thus sufficient evidence that blood sacrifice was not essential for attaining atonement.

Animal sacrifices are prescribed for unwitting sin, sins committed without intention, as stated in Leviticus 4:2, 13, 22, 27; 5:5, 15. The Torah, with one exception, does not decree any blood offerings for sins deliberately committed. The exception is for swearing falsely to acquit oneself of the accusation of having committed theft (Leviticus 5:24–26). Thus, the sacrificial system was virtually reserved for unwitting sins. The person who wittingly sins is "cut off" with no means of atonement prescribed (Numbers 15:30). The deliberate sinner, seeking atonement, had no other recourse but to come directly to God with prayer and contrition of heart.

It is clear from the Scriptures that sin is removed through genuine remorse and sincere repentance. A sinner fulfilling this requirement may expect the Almighty to forgive his sins and allow him to enter into fellowship with God. For what does God require "but to do justly, and to love mercy, and to walk humbly with your God" (Micah 6:8). God asks of the sinner: "Return to Me . . . and I will return to you" (Zechariah 1:3).

6

A PROPHET LIKE MOSES

(Deuteronomy 18:15, 18)

The Lord your God will raise up for you a prophet like me [Moses]
from among you, from your brethren, to him you shall listen. . . . I
[the Lord] will raise up for them a prophet like you from among their
brethren; and I will put My words in his mouth, and he shall speak to
them all that I shall command him.

(Deuteronomy 18:15, 18)

It is claimed by Christian missionaries that these verses constitute a prophetic reference to Jesus. There is absolutely no truth
to this contention. The noun *navi*ʾ, "prophet," is used generically here and does not at all refer to a particular prophet. In
these verses, the people of Israel are given the assurance that
God will raise up prophets for them, and that each of these
prophets will be similar to or like Moses. At no time is it
intimated that any of these prophets will be identical to Moses in
the quality of their prophecy. Certainly there is no indication in
the biblical text that there will ever be a prophet greater than
Moses. What is stated in these verses is that, following the
passing of Moses, God will continue to send prophets to Israel
who will be endowed with as genuine a prophetic spirit as that of
Moses. This is being told to Israel in order that they should be on
guard against the false prophets described subsequently in verse
20. These false prophets will presumptuously undertake to
subvert the teachings that God gave to Moses for delivery to
Israel. The mark of the true prophet is that he follows in the path
and tradition of Moses.

17

7

THE CURSE OF THE LAW

(Deuteronomy 27:26)

Cursed be he who does not establish the words of this law to do them.

(Deuteronomy 27:26)

Basing himself on Deuteronomy 27:26, Paul asserts that the individual who breaks any of the commandments is eternally cursed. Hence, his conclusion that one is actually cursed by the Law: "For as many as depend upon works of law are under a curse; for it is written: 'Cursed is everyone who does not abide by all the things written in the book of the Law, to do them'" (Galatians 3:10).

Paul gave verse 26 this unsubstantiated interpretation so that he would have a basis for his assertion that man is under "the curse of the Law" (Galatians 3:13).

The phrase "he who does not establish," does not refer to the breaking of the Law by an ordinary individual. It is, as the Rabbis explain, a reference to the authorities in power who fail to enforce the rule of the Law in the land of Israel (J. T. Sotah 7:4). The leadership of the nation is thus charged, under the pain of a curse, to set the tone for the nation and make the Law the operative force in the life of the nation.

Furthermore, had Paul properly evaluated verse 26, even in terms that it refers to the individual's compliance with the Law, he could never have arrived at his erroneous conclusion. Among the commandments of the Torah are those which teach man the ways to achieve atonement for his sins. These commandments

18

were given because God recognized that man is subject to error.

Thus, Deuteronomy 27:26 could declare as cursed only those who reject the means by which atonement for sins may be achieved. If one does not repent sincerely for his sins, he is cursed because he failed to save himself from the clutches of sin. It is only when a person refuses to avail himself of the means of atonement at his disposal that he brings down a curse on himself. Cursed is indeed the one who refuses to return to God with a contrite heart and insists, instead, on living a life of sin. In sum, not only is Paul's analysis of Deuteronomy 27:26 incorrect, but, contrary to his claim, the Law does indeed provide the necessary means for atonement from sin.

8

THE VIRGIN-BIRTH MYTH

(Isaiah 7:14)

In diluting Judaism so that it could meet the beliefs of the pagan world, the evangelists adopted a number of grotesque distortions of biblical belief. One of these is that a virgin has become pregnant, not by a man, but of the "Holy Spirit," and she has given birth to the Messiah. The belief in a Messiah was adopted by the Christians from the Jews, but the Jews never believed, nor did their Holy Scriptures teach, that the Messiah would be born of a virgin and a manifestation of God.

Many pagan religions believed in the idea of the impregnation of virgins by gods resulting in the birth of heroes. Stories of divine humans sired by the gods are told in several myths and legends. According to Greek and Roman legends, for example, Zeus and Apollo sired many distinguished men. Egypt produced the Hellenized cult of Isis with its adoration of the Mother and Child. By a simple change of names, Isis became mother Mary and Horus became the child Jesus. The pagan concept of divine birth, a concept alien to Judaism, entered Christianity through the Greco-Roman mythology then current in the western world. Seeking to substantiate the Christian-pagan concoction, the early Christians searched the Jewish Scriptures for justification of their claim of a virgin birth. They seized upon the word *'almah*, which they mistranslated in an attempt to give credence to their spurious claim that the birth of Jesus was foretold by the Bible.

This contention has made Judaism and Christianity forever incompatible, for Christians proceed to claim that this child, born of the union between God and a virgin, was conceived for

20

the purpose of bringing Judaism to an end. This would be in accordance with a divine plan which makes Jesus into a god-man, who, as part of the Trinity, is his own father.

This entire elaborate theological conception centers around the misinterpretation of Isaiah 7:14. This verse and the context from which it is taken must be closely examined here:

> And the Lord spoke again to Ahaz, saying: "Ask a sign of the Lord your God: ask it either in the depth, or in the height above." But Ahaz said: "I will not ask, neither will I try the Lord." And he said: "Hear now, house of David: Is it a small thing for you to weary men, that you will weary my God also? Therefore, the Lord Himself shall give you a sign: behold, the young woman shall conceive, and bear a son, and shall call his name Immanuel. Curd and honey shall he eat, when he knows to refuse the evil, and choose the good. For before the child shall know to refuse the evil, and choose the good, the land whose two kings you have a horror of shall be forsaken. (Isaiah 7:10–16)

This prophecy does not refer to the birth of Jesus. It refers to a situation which occurred at a different time in history and had nothing to do with him.[1] Isaiah tells of the troubles that befell the kingdom of Judah. Syria and Israel attacked Judah. The siege of Jerusalem brought fear to its inhabitants. Then came the prophet to comfort King Ahaz, and to assure him that the enemy would be defeated and would soon flee in rout. An era of prosperity in Judah would follow.

The importance of the sign was the assurance it gave that the child would be a male child. His very name, Immanuel, "God is with us," would evoke in the minds of the house of David and all the people of Judah the thought that God would fulfill His promise to protect the nation from its enemies. Verification of this interpretation is seen in Isaiah 8:8,10, where Immanuel is used as a rallying cry to call to mind the assurance of the prophet that God will protect His people. The fact that the purpose of the sign was to assure Ahaz of the fulfillment of the prophecy given to him, for his own day, rules out the Christological interpretation.

Isaiah does not identify the young woman who was to conceive or who was already pregnant (the Hebrew *harah* lends itself to either translation). While in Isaiah 7:14 the text says specifically *"the* young woman shall conceive," some Christian translations of Isaiah, e.g., the King James Version, change the definite article into the indefinite article and render this phrase as "*a* virgin shall conceive." If *ha-ʿalmah* ("the young woman") is taken in a general sense, i.e., "*a* young woman," with the indefinite article rather than with the definite article, it would lose its impact and significance as part of the sign given by God. The result would be to render Isaiah's words meaningless. The context indicates that the Hebrew noun *ʿalmah* ("young woman") is not used as a general and undefined term. Isaiah says *"the* young woman" using the definite article, referring to someone well known to both Isaiah and Ahaz.

There is no mention at all of a virgin giving birth to a child. When Isaiah says, "the young woman shall conceive," or "is conceived," he uses the word *ʿalmah*, which the Christians translate as "virgin." Such a rendering is unwarranted. We know from the Scriptures that a male youth may be called *naʿar* or *ʿelem*, the feminine forms of which are *naʿarah* and *ʿalmah* respectively, whether she be a virgin or not. *ʿAlmah* thus signifies a person of a certain age and not a state of virginity. In short, the meaning of *ʿalmah* is an adolescent female without any reference being made to her virginity.[2] This is obvious from a study of the word's use in Genesis 24:43, Exodus 2:8, Isaiah 7:14, and Proverbs 30:19.

Even if we were to presume, for the sake of argument, that *ʿalmah* specifically meant a virgin, it would simply show that the predicate *harah* should be taken as referring to the future, to be resolved in English as "she shall conceive." Her marriage could just as well have taken place immediately after the prophet spoke, with conception following shortly thereafter. There is nothing in this verse which indicates that "the young woman," if she is assumed to be a virgin, is going to give birth while in that physical state. Since the time of conception is not specified, this automatically precludes any necessity of her giving birth while still in a virgin state.

The Hebrew for "virgin" is *betulah*. The Torah clearly indicates the unequivocal meaning of *betulah* to be "a virgin" (Leviticus 21:14; Deuteronomy 22:15–19, 23, 28). The word *betulah* is used in an explicit legal sense leaving no question as to its meaning. While *'almah* does not define the state of virginity of a woman, *betulah*, by contrast, does. One would, therefore, reasonably expect that if Isaiah 7:14 refers specifically to a virgin, the prophet would have used the technical term *betulah* so as to leave no doubt as to the significance of his words. (See also Judges 11:37–38 concerning Jephthah's daughter, Judges 21:12, and 1 Kings 1:2.)

There are some Christian missionaries who argue that the verse "Lament like a *betulah* girded with sackcloth for the husband of her youth" (Joel 1:8) provides clear proof that *betulah* does not necessarily mean "virgin." But the argument is faulty since this verse may equally well refer to a young woman who is bereaved of the man to whom she had recently been betrothed and with whom she did not consummate her marriage before his death.[3] Such a loss is truly the height of tragedy, and hence the use of it as a simile for extraordinary lamentation.

According to some missionaries, proof that *betulah* does not necessarily always mean "virgin" can also be derived from the fact that Genesis 24:16 uses the qualifying words "neither had any man known her" in its description of Rebekah: "And the maiden was very fair to look upon, a virgin [*betulah*], neither had any man known her." Those who hold this view should read Rashi's commentary on this verse. Quoting from Bereshit Rabbah, Rashi states:

> "A virgin": [This refers to] the place of the virginity. "Neither had any man known her." [This refers to] an unnatural sexual act, since the daughters of the gentiles would guard the place of their virginity, but would act immodestly in another part [of their body]; [the text] attests concerning her that she was pure in every way.

Even leaving Rashi's interpretation aside, the Bible quite often adds an interpretive phrase to a word to emphasize the meaning. For example, Numbers 19:2: "Speak to the children of Israel, that they bring you a red heifer, faultless, in which there is no blemish." One could assume that anything which is faultless has no blemish in it. In 2 Samuel 14:5 it says: "Alas, I am an *ʾalmanah* [widow], my husband being dead." Will the Christian missionaries question the meaning of *ʾalmanah*? Surely we could assume that if she is a widow her husband is dead. Therefore, it should come as no surprise that the verse should say: "a virgin, neither had any man known her."

The Christian missionary contention that Proverbs 30:19—"And the way of a man with a young woman [*ʿalmah*]"—must refer to a virgin is without foundation. This verse does not describe virginity. It refers to age, i.e., "a *young* woman." Moreover, since *ʿalmah* refers to a young woman's age rather than her state of virginity, it is only through the context that one can see that the "young women" (*ʿalamot*) of Song of Songs 1:3 are also virgins. A clear indication of virginity, however, is used by Isaiah himself: "For as a young man marries a virgin [*betulah*] . . ." (Isaiah 62:5).

Christian missionaries who believe that the Septuagint's translation of the word *ʿalmah* as *parthenos* ("virgin") conclusively proves that an untouched virgin is spoken of, will have great difficulty explaining the connotation of the Septuagint's use of *parthenos* to translate the Hebrew word *yaldah* ("girl") in Genesis 34:3: "And his soul did cleave to Dinah the daughter of Jacob, and he loved the girl, and spoke comfortingly to the girl." Here there is no controversy as to Dinah's physical state. She was definitely not a virgin, yet the Greek word for "virgin" (*parthenos*) is used.[4]

We see further the extent of the Christian missionary misconceptions when we study the use of the word *ʾot* ("a sign"). Here, as in all other places where it is used in the Bible, *ʾot* pertains to the fulfillment of an event that is to take place in the near future. This rules out any interpretation that would identify the sign with Mary and Jesus, who lived more than seven hundred years after the events portrayed by Isaiah took place. The sign is not the manner of conception. It is, rather, as explained above, that the child would be a boy whose name would have a special meaning for the people of Judah at the time. The Book of Isaiah provides us with a number of examples of the use of names in this way. Isaiah 8:18: "Behold, I and the child whom the Lord has given me shall be for signs and for wonders in Israel from the Lord of hosts, who dwells in mount Zion." The name Isaiah means "God's help" or "God saves"; Shear-yashuv, "a remnant will return"; and Maher-shal-hash-baz, "the spoil speeds, the prey hastes." These names were designed to draw attention to the significance of the prophetic message contained therein. We see Shear-yashuv, the name given one of Isaiah's sons (7:3), as a sign and prediction which is fulfilled in Isaiah 10:21. The use of "the mighty God" (*ʾel-gibbor*) in Isaiah 10:21 is similarly a reference to the name given to the young Hezekiah in Isaiah 9:5. Hezekiah is called "A wonderful counselor is the mighty God, the everlasting Father, the ruler of peace." Similarly, the import of the name Immanuel, made up of ʿ*immanu* ("with us") and *ʾel* ("God")—"God is with us"—is resoundingly clear: God has not abandoned His people. As a result Hezekiah was able to declare: "Be strong and of good courage. Do not be afraid or dismayed because of the king of Assyria and before all the multitude that is with him; for there is a Greater with us [ʿ*immanu rav*] than with him. With him is an arm of flesh; but with us is the Lord our God to help us and to fight our battles" (2 Chronicles 32:7–8).

Certain Christian missionary commentators contend that if Immanuel had been conceived in the young woman in the same manner as other children, he could not be called Immanuel. This name, they claim, could apply only to Jesus, since, they allege, he was a compound of divine and human nature. Aside from the fact that it begs the question, the basis of the argument is patently fallacious. Names, both of men and inanimate objects, having as part of their composition a name of God, are common in the Bible. Thus, we have such names as Samuel, Zuriel, Uziel, Michael, Eliezer, Elijah, Isaiah, and Zurishaddai; altars are sometimes given such names as "God, the God of Israel"

(Genesis 33:20), "The Lord is my banner" (Exodus 17:15), and "The Lord is peace" (Judges 6:24). Jerusalem is called "The Lord is there" (Ezekiel 48:35).

Strangely enough, nowhere in the New Testament do we find that Jesus is called Immanuel. We only find that the angel purportedly informs Joseph in a dream that Mary will give birth to a son and that Joseph should call the child's name Jesus (Matthew 1:20–21). This information is followed by Matthew 1:23, which merely restates Isaiah 7:14 without actually applying the name Immanuel to Jesus. Matthew 1:25 states categorically: "and he [Joseph] called his name Jesus." In Luke 2:21, it says: "his name was called Jesus, the name called by the angel before he was conceived in the womb." All the evidence thus indicates that Immanuel was a different individual from Jesus since Jesus was never called Immanuel.

David Baron, an apostate Jew, in his book *Rays of Messiah's Glory: Christ in the Old Testament,* makes the following observation.

> An objection has been raised why Jesus, if Isaiah VII.14 was really a prophecy of Him, was not called Immanuel. But the truth is Immanuel was to be no more the actual name of Messiah than Wonderful, Prince of peace, Desire of all nations. Shiloh, or Jehovah Tsidkenu. All Messiah's titles were intended only as descriptions of His character, but his real name was, in the providence of God, concealed till his advent to prevent imposture on the part of pretenders, who would easily have taken advantage of it. . . . But Jesus is really the best commentary on Immanuel, Immanuel—"God with us;" Jesus—"Saviour." But how could God come near us except as Saviour? and how could Jesus be Saviour except as Immanuel, in Whom dwelt the fulness of the Godhead bodily?[5]

Upon closer analysis, however, Baron's argument does not stand up. While he may argue that Isaiah 9:5 and Jeremiah 23:6 are descriptions of character, Isaiah 7:14, "and she shall call his name Immanuel," implies that this is the exact name by which the child's mother was to call him. The name was, therefore, not to be merely descriptive. Since it is given to him at birth, it is the real and actual name of the child.[6] The same may be said of Baron's statement that "Jesus is really the best commentary on Immanuel." He disregards the fact that the sign in Isaiah 7:14 speaks specifically of a child named Immanuel and not of a name which will supposedly be a commentary on that name. His statements concerning God's ability to "come near us," and the Godhead dwelling in a body, must be dealt with in the context of a discussion on the false doctrine of the Trinity, with which this verse in Isaiah has no connection. Baron's contention that "his real name was, in the providence of God, concealed till His advent to prevent imposture on the part of pretenders, who would easily have taken advantage of it," glaringly exposes the shallowness of his belief. This is a claim made in desperation that not even the New Testament makes.

The question is not whether God could bring about a virgin birth, but rather whether He did as Christian missionaries contend. Would God have sexual relations with a betrothed woman (Matthew 1:18), thereby causing her to violate one of His commandments for which one is liable to receive the death penalty (Deuteronomy 22:23–24)? The claim that God transformed Himself into human flesh by implanting one-third of His alleged triune nature into the womb of a woman cannot be substantiated from the Scriptures.

To violently rip a verse out of context only leads to misunderstandings. Any verse must be studied within its context. Isaiah 7:13 proclaims: "Hear now, house of David." Where in the New Testament does it specifically say that Mary is of the house of David? All that we have is Joseph's genealogy repeated in two variant forms. Isaiah 7:14 states that the young woman herself "shall call his name Immanuel," whereas Matthew 1:23, allegedly quoting Isaiah, says "they shall call his name," thus distorting the divinely given text. What did Mary call her son? Surely not Immanuel, as required by Isaiah 7:14, since this would certainly have been mentioned by the evangelists. Isaiah 7:15 says: "Curd and honey shall he eat." When did Jesus eat curd and honey? And Isaiah 7:15 continues: ". . . when he knows to refuse the evil, and choose the good." Could Jesus as a sinless god-man choose "the evil" as opposed to "the good" and thereby change the Christological course of human events? Isaiah 7:16 says: "For before the child shall know to refuse the evil, and choose the good, the land whose two kings you have a horror of shall be forsaken." Where in the New Testament do we find the names of the two kings whose land was forsaken before the child-god Jesus knew "to refuse the evil, and choose the good"? The New Testament, which constantly endeavors to show scriptural fulfillment in the life of Jesus, becomes strangely silent concerning the complete fulfillment of Isaiah's words.

A tortured compilation of biblical verses, yanked overzealously from their contexts and interlarded with pagan mythology, became the basis for the notion known as the "virgin birth." Such is the shaky foundation on which has been erected the vast, imposing structure of missionary Christianity. An erroneous translation of a single word, a gross misconstruing of a lone phrase taken from the Scriptures, has led to this false belief. The Christian missionaries may claim, if it suits their needs, that Jesus is virgin-born, but they must look elsewhere for proof. Even the New Testament testifies against their renderings.

1. For the fulfillment of the prophecy, see 2 Kings 15:29–30 and 2 Kings 16:9.

2. It should be noted, however, that in biblical times females married at an early age.

3. In biblical times a betrothal was considered as binding as a marriage and there were formal ceremonies to celebrate it. (Cf. Deuteronomy 22:23–24, where such a woman is punished as an adulteress if she cohabits with another man.)

4. Regarding the unequal character of the Septuagint version of the Bible, Brenton writes in the introduction to his translation of the Septuagint that "The Pentateuch is considered to be the part best executed, while the book of Isaiah appears to be the very worst" (Lancelot C. L. Brenton, *The Septuagint Version: Greek and English* [Grand Rapids: Zondervan, 1979], p. iii).

5. David Baron, *Rays of Messiah's Glory: Christ in the Old Testament* (Grand Rapids: Zondervan), p. 38.

6. For the manner in which names were conferred upon a person during his lifetime, see 2 Kings 17:34 and Nehemiah 9:7. Nowhere in the New Testament does it say that Jesus was assigned the name Immanuel.

9

WHO IS THE CHILD?

(Isaiah 9:5–6)

For a child has been born to us, a son has been given to us; and the government is upon his shoulder; and his name is called A wonderful counselor is the mighty God, the everlasting Father, the ruler of peace; that the government may be increased, and of peace there be no end, upon the throne of David, and upon his kingdom, to establish it, and to uphold it through justice and through righteousness from henceforth even forever. The zeal of the Lord of hosts does perform this.

(Isaiah 9:5–6)

Isaiah is known for the method by which he presents many of his messages through the use of prophetic names (Isaiah 7:3, 14; 8:3). In the verse under study, the prophet expounds his message by formulating a prophetic name for Hezekiah. The words of this name form a sentence expressive of God's greatness which will become manifest in the benefits to be bestowed upon the future king in his lifetime. Thus, the name, though borne by the king, serves, in reality, as a testimonial to God.

Hezekiah is called "a wonderful counselor" because this name is a sign which foretells God's design for him.

The Lord of hosts has sworn, saying: "As I have thought, so shall it be, and as I have purposed, so shall it stand, that I will break Asshur in My land, and upon My mountains trample him under foot; then shall his yoke depart from off them, and his burden depart from off their shoulder." This is the purpose that is purposed upon the whole earth; and this is the hand that is stretched out upon all the nations.

29

For the Lord of hosts has purposed, and who will annul it? And His hand is stretched out, and who shall turn it back? (Isaiah 14:24–27)

Be not afraid of the words that you have heard, with which the servants of the king of Assyria have blasphemed Me. Behold, I will put a spirit in him, and he shall hear a rumor, and shall return to his own land; and I will cause him to fall by the sword in his own land. (Isaiah 37:6–7)

Hezekiah is called "the mighty God" because this name is a sign which foretells God's defense of Jerusalem through the miraculous sudden mass death of Sennacherib's army.

Therefore thus says the Lord concerning the king of Assyria: He shall not come to this city, nor shoot an arrow there, neither shall he come before it with shield, nor cast a mound against it. By the way that he came, by the same shall he return, and he shall not come to this city, says the Lord. For I will defend this city to save it, for My own sake, and for My servant David's sake. (Isaiah 37:33–35)

Hezekiah is called "the everlasting Father" because this name is a sign which foretells that God will add years to his life. "Go, and say to Hezekiah: Thus says the Lord, the God of David your father: I have heard your prayer, I have seen your tears; behold, I will add to your days fifteen years" (Isaiah 38:5).

Hezekiah is called "the ruler of peace" because this name is a sign which foretells that God would be merciful to him. Punishment for lack of faith in the Almighty will be deferred and peace granted during the last years of his rule. "Then said Hezekiah to Isaiah: 'Good is the word of the Lord which you have spoken.' He said moreover: 'If but there shall be peace and security in my days' " (Isaiah 39:8).

The fulfillment of the above-stated declarations is foretold in Isaiah 9:6, when, after the Assyrian defeat, Hezekiah's glory increased and peace reigned for the rest of his life (2 Chronicles 32:23). Archaeologists have found that there was a sudden expansion of Judean settlements in the years following the fall of the northern kingdom. This indicates that many refugees fled south, thus giving added significance to the statement "that the government may be increased."

Hezekiah's kingdom is declared to be forever, for through his efforts to cleanse the Temple ritual of idolatry, even though apostasy followed under his son Menasseh, the Davidic dynasty was once more confirmed as the only true kingly rule that God would accept over his people "from henceforth and forever." The greatness of Hezekiah lies in his setting the stage for Israel's future. Hezekiah was a true reformer. He cleansed religious worship of foreign influence, purged the palace and the Temple of images and pagan altars, and reestablished pure monotheistic religion. In the long run Hezekiah's achievements would outlive him, leaving an everlasting, indelible impact on the history of his people. Thus, God, through Isaiah, bestows upon Hezekiah this name which honors the king by proclaiming the great things God will do for him, and, through him, for the people of Israel.

Christian missionary theologians argue that the name "A wonderful counselor is the mighty God, the everlasting Father, the ruler of peace" refers to Jesus, who they allege combined human and divine qualities. They mistakenly believe that such a name can only be applied to God Himself. Moreover, the Christians incorrectly translate the verbs in verse 5 in the future tense, instead of the past, as the Hebrew original reads. Thus, the Christians render verse 5 as: "For a child will be born to us, a son will be given to us; and the government will rest on his shoulders; and his name will be called Wonderful Counselor, Mighty God, Eternal Father, Prince of Peace."

While admitting that "wonderful counselor" and "ruler of peace" can be applied to a man, Christian missionary theologians argue that the phrases "mighty God" and "everlasting Father" cannot be incorporated as part of a man's name. Thus, they contend that Isaiah teaches that the Messiah has to be not only a man, but God as well. That this entire reasoning is incorrect may be seen from the name Elihu, "My God is He," which refers to an ordinary human being (Job 32:1, 1 Samuel 1:1, 1 Chronicles 12:21, 26:7, 27:18). A similar Christian missionary misunderstanding of Scripture may be seen in the missionary claims revolving around the name Immanuel, "God is with us." The simple fact is that it is quite common in the Bible for human beings to be given names that have the purpose of declaring or reflecting a particular attribute of God, e.g., Eliab, Eliada, Elzaphan, Eliakim, Elisha, Eleazar, Tavel, Gedaliah.

The fact remains that Jesus did not literally or figuratively fulfill any of Isaiah's words. A wonderful counselor does not advise his followers that if they have faith they can be agents of destruction (Matthew 21:19–21; Mark 11:14, 20–23). A mighty God does not take orders from anyone (Luke 2:51, Hebrews 5:8), for no one is greater than he is (Matthew 12:31–32; John 5:30, 14:28). Moreover, he does not ask or need to be saved by anyone (Matthew 26:39, Luke 22:42), for he cannot die by any means (Matthew 27:50, Mark 15:37, Luke 23:46, John 19:30). He who is called the Son of God the Father (John 1:18, 3:16) cannot himself be called everlasting Father. One cannot play simultaneously the role of the son and the Father; it is an obvious self-contradiction. He who advocates family strife (Matthew 10:34–35, Luke 12:49–53) and killing enemies (Luke 19:27) cannot be called a ruler of peace.

10

THE MESSIANIC AGE

(Isaiah 11)

In chapter 11, Isaiah gives us an insight into the Messianic Age. Speaking of the Messiah he states in the opening verse: "And there shall come forth a shoot out of the stock of Jesse, and a branch out of his roots shall bear fruit." Undoubtedly, the phrase "out of the stock of Jesse" signifies the Davidic dynasty, from which will come forth a fresh, strong "shoot."

Christian missionaries, applying this chapter to Jesus, were forced to divide his career into what is called his first and second comings. To have any relationship to Jesus' life, Isaiah's prophecy must refer to the first coming because Isaiah speaks specifically of the "shoot" coming "out of the stock of David," which can only refer to the Messiah's ancestry at the time of his birth. In addition, when the prophet describes the dynamic appearance of the Messiah as "a shoot out of the stock of Jesse," he is portraying the latter's glorious nature from its very inception. This glowing portrayal provides a glaring contrast to the one in Isaiah 53:1–2, where the suffering servant, whom the missionaries also identify with Jesus, is portrayed in somber terms. Since both prophecies of Isaiah's (11:1 and 53:1–2), if they are to apply to Jesus, must refer to his first coming, we are faced with an irreconcilable contradiction, because the two accounts stand in stark contrast to each other. It takes a feat of missionary exegetical acrobatics to harmonize these two prophecies so as to make them appear to be applicable to one individual.

There is no justification for the interpretation that the prophet's words are to be divided into two separate periods, one during the Messiah's lifetime, and the other after some future return following his death. That the account of this chapter can only apply to a single coming of the Messiah is verified by verse 10. In this verse, where all the events enumerated in verses 2–9 occur, he is given what can only be a human title, "the root of Jesse." Missionaries attempt to solve the problems inherent in their explanation of this chapter by claiming that Jesus appeared the first time to provide a means of salvation for mankind, whereas in the second coming, he will come to judge and rule the world. This, however, is simply not in accord with Isaiah's prophetic message. The Messiah is not portrayed as a part of a triune godhead returning to earth as judge and king.

Specific mention must also be made of the Christian missionary contention that the statement in verse 2 that "The spirit of the Lord shall rest upon him" was fulfilled at Jesus' baptism (Matthew 3:16, Mark 1:10, Luke 3:22). This is a claim which is, at best, selective fulfillment, and which, upon closer analysis, is devoid of any validity. According to the missionary comprehension of this verse, we must assume that Jesus, part of a triune deity, needed the "Spirit of God," another one-third of the deity, to descend upon him by permission of still another one-third of this godhead: "God anointed him [Jesus] with the Holy Spirit and with power" (Acts 10:38; see also John 3:34). The author of Acts indicates that Jesus' ability to do wonders stemmed from God's annointing and that "God was with him." However, if Jesus was God, he would not need to be anointed by God and have God be with him in order to perform miracles. Moreover, if Jesus was God, he could stand in no relationship with God.

Missionaries cannot legitimately dismember this chapter in order to choose those verses which they believe to have been fulfilled in the first coming and leave the remainder to be fulfilled during a second coming. Isaiah 11 is to be taken as a homogeneous unit. There is no evidence to suggest a division within the chapter.

11

THE SUFFERING SERVANT OF THE LORD

(Isaiah 52:13–53:12)

1. Who would have believed our report? And to whom has the arm of the Lord been revealed?
2. For he grew up before Him as a tender plant, and as a root out of a dry land; he had no form nor comeliness, that we should look upon him, nor appearance that we should delight in him.
3. He was despised, and rejected of men, a man of pains, and acquainted with disease, and as one from whom men hide their face: he was despised, and we esteemed him not.
4. Surely our diseases he did bear, and our pains he carried; but we considered him stricken, smitten of God, and afflicted.
5. But he was wounded as a result of our transgressions, he was crushed as a result of our iniquities. The chastisement of our welfare was upon him, and with his stripes we were healed.
6. All we like sheep did go astray, we turned every one to his own way; and the Lord has visited upon him the iniquity of us all.
7. He was oppressed, though he humbled himself and did not open his mouth; as a lamb that is led to the slaughter, and as a sheep that before her shearers is dumb; and he did not open his mouth.
8. From dominion and judgment he was taken away, and his life's history who is able to relate? For he was cut off out of the land of the living; as a result of the transgression of my people he has been afflicted.
9. And his grave was set with the wicked, and with the rich in his deaths; although he had done no violence, neither was there any deceit in his mouth.
10. And it pleased the Lord to crush him—He made [him] sick. If he would offer himself as a guilt-offering, he shall see seed, he

35

shall prolong days. And the purpose of the Lord will prosper by his hand.

11. *From the labor of his soul he shall see; he shall be satisfied. With his knowledge, the righteous one, my servant, shall cause many to be just. And their iniquities he shall bear.*

12. *Therefore will I divide him a portion with the great, and he shall divide the spoil with the mighty; because he has poured out his soul to death: and he was numbered with the transgressors; and he bore the sin of many, and made intercession for the transgressors.*

(Isaiah 53:1–12)

Introduction

Christian missionaries have often wondered why Jews do not accept their contention that the fifty-third chapter of Isaiah is a prophecy of the life and death of Jesus. What Jews find even more amazing and mystifying is how any person who studies this chapter critically can possibly believe it alludes to Jesus. Based on what they thought the Hebrew Scriptures said concerning the Messiah, the New Testament authors restructured the life of the historical Jesus to make it conform to their preconceived ideas. However, neither figurative nor literal fulfillment of all that the New Testament authors claim holds up upon close examination of the text of Isaiah 53. In fact, by investigating their assertions, it will be found that the New Testament unintentionally provides evidence that refutes the notion that the prophet's words refer to Jesus.

No contrived resemblance between Isaiah 53 and the life of Jesus will suffice. Only a careful analysis will establish the truth concerning the messianic qualifications of Jesus of Nazareth. Let it be stated from the outset that although we believe Isaiah 53 speaks of the nation of Israel, our main concern here is not with the exegetical problem of whom Isaiah is referring to—whether it is one of the prophets, the people of Israel as a whole, or the Messiah—but with the investigation of the Christian missionary claim. Ignoring the fact that Israel is often spoken of as the servant of the Lord (e.g., Isaiah 41:8–9; 44:1–2, 21; 45:4; 48:20; 49:3), Christian missionaries often argue that this chapter does not refer to the people of Israel. This, however, is sidestepping the issue. Even if such were the case, it would not prove that Isaiah's prophecy in chapter 53 has any reference at all to Jesus.

Isaiah's prophecy does not begin with chapter 53, but with chapter 52:13–15, which serves as an introduction and summary. There, Isaiah prophesies that at a specific juncture in history, the Gentiles will begin to realize the vital part the servant played in their national history.

> Behold, My servant shall prosper, he shall be exalted and lifted up, and shall be very high. According as many were appalled at you—so marred was his appearance unlike that of a man, and his form unlike that of the sons of men—so shall he startle many nations, kings shall shut their mouths because of him; for that which had not been told them shall they see, and that which they had not heard shall they perceive.

Isaiah 53:1–8 finds the prophet quoting the astonished exclamations of the Gentile spokesmen as they describe their bewilderment at the unfolding events surrounding the life of the suffering servant of the Lord. In verse 9 and the first half of verse 10, he reflects upon the tribulations suffered by the servant and states that if the servant remains faithful to God, despite all adversity, God will amply reward him. In the latter part of verse 10 through verse 12, the prophet records the blessings with which God will reward His faithful servant for all the abuse and injury he endured for the sanctification of the Name of God.

Isaiah 53

53:1–2. *Who would have believed our report? And to whom has the arm of the Lord been revealed? For he grew up before Him as a tender plant, and as a root out of a dry land; he had no form nor comeliness, that we should look upon him, nor appearance that we should delight in him.*

The verse above speaks of the suffering servant of the Lord as he is growing up (i.e., the historical development of the Jewish people). It is a continuation of Isaiah 52:14, where the prophet states that the servant seems, in the eyes of his enemies, the Gentiles, to have a repulsive appearance. Judging him merely on his outward features, they can find nothing positive to say about him. Suddenly, the Gentile nations and their rulers will be startled by the glorious transformation that will come about in the servant's fortunes. In amazement they will exclaim: "Who would have believed our report? And to whom has the arm of the Lord been revealed?" They then reflect upon their earlier reaction to him, attributing to God what was really their own lack of insight as to the true nature of the servant. Accordingly, they speak of the servant as one who "grew up before Him [God] as a tender plant, and as a root out of a dry land" which is stunted and withered and does not produce fruit or distinguish itself in any way, being both unproductive and unsightly. They further state their opinion that the servant did not possess any physical attribute which should draw people to him.

Does this description fit the one of Jesus as depicted by the evangelists? Was he a frail, unsightly child? Was he a repulsive adult? According to them, he was, throughout his entire lifetime, greatly desired by an ever growing multitude of people, as is strikingly illustrated in Luke's summation of Jesus' formative years: "And Jesus kept increasing in wisdom and in physical growth [*helikia*, cf. Luke 19:3], and in favor with God and men" (Luke 2:52). In this statement, it is asserted that Jesus was tall, wise, and enjoyed popularity even in the years prior to his active ministry. His handsome appearance and charismatic personality, it is intimated, attracted so many followers that the few negative reactions to his teachings that he encountered early in his career were of no consequence. This is contrary to the description of the suffering servant of the Lord found in Isaiah 53:2. There are simply no indications in the Gospels that Jesus, as he grew up, could in any way be likened to a "tender plant," i.e., stunted, or to a "root out of a dry land," i.e., withered, or that he was extremely repulsive to look at, as the servant was said to be by his many enemies. We are thus compelled to conclude that the life of Jesus, as portrayed in the Gospels, does not at all fit that of the suffering servant of the Lord as portrayed in Isaiah.

53:3. He was despised, and rejected of men [אישים: *"men of high status"*], *a man of pains, and acquainted with disease, and as one from whom men hide their face: he was despised, and we esteemed him not.*

This verse, continuing the theme of the previous one, speaks of the servant as being generally despised. He is described as suffering from pains and diseases with which he is well acquainted. Terms having to do with wounds, sickness, pain, and disease are often used in the Scriptures to describe the humiliations and adversities suffered by the nation of Israel (Isaiah 1:5–6; Jeremiah 10:19, 30:12). The prophet quotes the Gentiles as saying that the suffering servant of the Lord "was despised and rejected" by their leaders, the "men of high status." They then indicate that this rejection was even more widespread, as implied in the words: "He was despised and we esteemed him not." The "we" includes a wider range of enemies than is expressed by the term "men of high status." Contrary to this verse, the evangelists insist that Jesus was greatly admired by large segments from every level of society. True, the evangelists claim that the Jewish rulers condemned Jesus, but, nevertheless, they assert that Jesus had many followers from among the ruling class. The evangelists speak of Jesus as one who, while losing, at times, many of his followers, always had, even at the end of his life, a great many adherents. What is extremely significant is that these adherents came from every segment of society.

When the news about Jesus spread through all the districts surrounding Galilee, he began teaching in the synagogues and was "glorified by all" (Luke 4:14–15). "And the news about him went out into all Syria" (Matthew 4:24). As his fame grew, "a great crowd came together with those that went to him from the various cities" (Luke 8:4). "And great crowds followed him from

Galilee and Decapolis and Jerusalem and Judea and from the other side of the Jordan" (Matthew 4:25). The press of the crowds was tremendous (Luke 7:11; 8:19, 45). In the city of Nain, a large part of the populace calls Jesus a great prophet and says that God has visited His people (Luke 7:12, 16). Nor was it just the poor masses that followed him; we find that the wife of Herod's steward and other women contributed to the needs of Jesus and his disciples (Luke 8:3). Mark 5:36 informs us how Jairus, ruler of the synagogue, became a believer. John states that many of the Jews believed in Jesus (John 12:11), and that among them were many of the rulers who secretly believed in him (John 12:42). In Luke 13:31, we are told that even some of the Pharisees warned Jesus that Herod was planning to kill him and urged him to escape. Matthew 21:46 and Mark 12:12, 37, inform us that Jesus taught the crowds in the Temple and that his enemies were afraid to arrest him because they feared the multitudes who listened to him enthusiastically. Moreover, when his enemies made their final plans to arrest him, they decided: "Not during the festival, lest there be an uproar of the people" (Mark 14:1–2). When Jesus entered Jerusalem, it was to the accompanying shouts of "Hosanna" coming from the crowds (Matthew 21:9) that declared: "This is the prophet Jesus from Nazareth of Galilee" (Matthew 21:11).

Lest anyone think that all abandoned Jesus in his last hours, we are told that Nicodemus, a Pharisee and "a ruler of the Jews" (John 3:1), helped Joseph of Arimathaea, a rich man, to prepare the body for burial (John 19:39). We are told that Joseph of Arimathaea was not only a disciple of Jesus (Matthew 27:57, John 19:38), but as a counselor, i.e., member of the Sanhedrin, "had not consented to their plan and action" (Luke 23:50–51). Helpless though Joseph and Nicodemus may have been to bring about Jesus' freedom, they, contrary to Peter, did not deny knowing him. Indeed, Joseph of Arimathaea's asking Pilate for the body was a bold, albeit dangerous, move on his part. Nor should we forget Mary Magdalene and the "other women" who came to the tomb (Matthew 28:1, Mark 16:1, Luke 24:10, John 20:1), and the alleged multitude who, throughout it all, it is claimed, believed in Jesus despite his sentence and crucifixion. As he went to be crucified, "there were following him a great multitude of people, and of women who were beating themselves and bewailing him" (Luke 23:27). According to the evangelical accounts, in addition to this "multitude," there must have been, throughout Judea and the surrounding territories, countless people from every level of society who did not know of events in Jerusalem and who still looked to Jesus as the Messiah.

Can such a person be described as one who "was despised and rejected," from whom people fled? The words: "He was despised and rejected of men . . . and as one from whom men hide their face . . . and we esteemed him not" cannot be applied to Jesus if one is to believe the New Testament report of the popularity that Jesus enjoyed during his lifetime among the upper class as well as among the common people. Moreover, the evangelists claim that the chief priests and the scribes sought to take Jesus "by craft" but "not during the festival" because they feared a popular demonstration against them if the people learned of Jesus' arrest (Mark 14:1–2). Mark has these plans for the arrest of Jesus take place two days before Passover: "After two days was the Passover and Unleavened Bread" (Mark 14:1). Hence, very shortly before his death, Jesus' enemies expressed fear of the wrath of the people if they should arrest him. This confirms that even at that crucial point, just before the end of his life, Jesus had a significant following among the people, regardless of social class. Even if we accept that a crowd actually stood outside the judgment hall demanding that Pilate execute Jesus (Matthew 27:22; Mark 15:13; Luke 23:21, 23; John 18:39–40), it would have constituted only an extremely small fraction of the people then in Jerusalem. Clearly, in this incident, the evangelists have distorted developments in order to condemn the entire Jewish people for their rejection of the messianic pretensions of Jesus. However, the major thrust of their writings argues for popular support, not only in the country as a whole, but even in those last hours in Jerusalem (Luke 23:27).

Present-day Christian missionaries argue that Jesus died

without any significant following. This, however, is only an argument of Christian missionary apologists necessitated by theological needs. In contrast to Isaiah's statement, which includes the high-born as well as the common folk rejecting the suffering servant of the Lord, the evangelical record argues that Jesus had a significant following among the well-born as well as among the common people even at the time of his crucifixion. According to the Gospels, this faithful following was not composed of ignorant masses following a mere miracle-working prophet. The Gospels allege that the masses adhered to a messianic belief that Jesus, who was believed to be the son of David (Matthew 9:27), was not only the prophet promised in Deuteronomy 18:15 (John 7:40), but was in fact, the very Messiah himself (John 7:41). Even though there was a division among the crowd over the validity of his claim (John 7:43), and many of his disciples left him (John 6:66), we must assume, the Gospels not telling us otherwise, that besides Joseph of Arimathaea and Nicodemus, men such as Jairus, along with thousands of others throughout the country, still believed in him as the Messiah at the time of the crucifixion. To whatever reason one may attribute the belief in Jesus among his followers, the fact still remains that, according to the Gospels, he was not generally rejected by the members of the various social strata of society. On all accounts, there is little resemblance between the life of Jesus as portrayed in the Gospels and the life of the servant of the Lord as depicted by Isaiah 53. Any attempt to assert the contrary is fallacious, and forced at best.

53:4–6. *Surely our diseases he did bear, and our pains he carried; but we considered him stricken, smitten of God, and afflicted. But he was wounded as a result of our transgressions, he was crushed as a result of our iniquities. The chastisement of our welfare was upon him, and with his stripes we were healed. All we like sheep did go astray, we turned every one to his own way; and the Lord has visited upon him the iniquity of us all.*

In verse 4, the Gentile spokesmen depict the servant as bearing the "diseases" and carrying the "pains" which they themselves should have suffered. At the time of the servant's suffering, the Gentiles believed that the servant was undergoing divine retribution for *his* sins. Now, when the servant has attained glory, the Gentiles come to the realization that the servant's suffering stemmed from *their* actions and sinfulness. It is not that the servant is without sin, but that the Gentiles speak here of their own treatment of the servant, not God's. Seeing events unfold, the Gentiles confess, as recorded in verse 5, that they were the cause of the servant's distress and are more deserving of his afflictions than he was. In the verse: "But he was wounded from our transgressions, he was crushed from our iniquities," the preposition "from" is used with the meaning "as a result of," which furnishes the idea that the servant suffered as a result of the evil deeds perpetrated against him by the Gentiles. Both king and commoner persecuted the servant for their own ends. They used him as a scapegoat to hide such things as corruption in government and incompetence in battle, and, in general, to distract the masses from the difficulties of daily life. Through the persecution of the servant, the Gentiles created the illusion of national unity and the means by which to cover up their own misdeeds. Hence the exclamation: "And with his stripes we were healed." In verse 6, the Gentiles acknowledge that each of their respective nations had gone after its own selfish interests and desires. However, even the evil Gentile nature served the divine purpose. The servant's suffering, inflicted upon him by the Gentiles, was used by God to test the moral and spiritual fiber of the servant vis-à-vis the Gentile nations. As we shall see, verse 10 further illuminates this point, indicating that it was God's plan to test the servant to see whether he would offer himself to any fate ordained for him in order to sanctify the Name of God.

53:7. *He was oppressed, though he humbled himself and opened not his mouth; as a lamb that is led to the slaughter, and as a sheep that before her shearers is dumb; and opened not his mouth.*

To understand why Jesus could not be the fulfillment of the above verse, we must sift through the various accounts of his trial. We must first dispense with the notion that Jesus' refusal to answer the statements of what are called the "false witnesses" constitutes a fulfillment of the verse under study. The only two evangelists who mention this event are Matthew and Mark (Matthew 26:59–66, Mark 14:55–64). According to their accounts, the actual charge leveled against Jesus by the high priest concerned his claim to be the Christ, i.e., the Messiah. He was not charged with threatening to destroy and rebuild the Temple, as he had been accused by the "false witnesses."

Therefore, the statements of the alleged "false witnesses" and the subsequent silence by Jesus cannot be construed as a fulfillment of Isaiah 53:7. According to Jewish law, the statements attributed to Jesus by the witnesses constituted no punishable offense whatsoever and therefore could not be considered real accusations. The witnesses did not present evidence concerning his messianic pretensions but mentioned an incident having no bearing on the actual charge. Claiming to be able to perform miracles was not punishable by law. Accordingly, the appearance of these witnesses was inconsequential and with no real significance in relation to the actual accusation. Jesus' lack of response to their specific statements was equally inconsequential in relation to the fulfillment of Isaiah's prophecy. That the claim to be the Messiah was the focus of the inquiry is seen from the way the high priest, according to the evangelists, dispensed with the need for witnesses once Jesus admitted to the charge.

The proceedings against Jesus did not constitute a formal trial. Rather, they were an inquiry aimed at learning the details of Jesus' activities as a messianic claimant. Although a number of charges were leveled against Jesus (Luke 23:2, 5), fundamentally each one of them focused, as we shall soon see, on the messianic authority arrogated by Jesus for himself and its ancillary implication of seditious activity against the Roman hegemony over Judea. Jesus' claim to be the Messiah was the accusation placed against him before the Sanhedrin and Pilate. For the Jews, this was not a claim deserving of death, but to the Romans, the charge was tantamount to sedition. To the charge of his messianic claim, Jesus answered both the Jews and Pilate in a forceful manner.

Interest in Jesus as a messianic claimant is further illustrated by the alleged encounter between Jesus and Annas, which John, in contrast to the Synoptic Gospels, insists took place before Jesus was sent to Caiphas.

> The high priest therefore questioned Jesus about his disciples, and about his teaching. Jesus answered him: "I have spoken openly to the world; I always taught in a synagogue and in the Temple, where all the Jews come together; and I spoke nothing in secret. Why do you question me? Question those who have heard what I spoke to them; behold these know what I said." When he had said these things, one of the officers standing by gave Jesus a slap, saying: "Is that the way you answer the high priest?" Jesus answered him: "If I have spoken wrongly, bear witness of the wrong; but if rightly, why do you strike me?" (John 18:19–23)

These accounts illustrate the evangelical emphasis on the purported Jewish and Roman interest in the "teaching" of Jesus, which can only refer to his self-conception as the destined Messiah. "Are you the Christ?" was the question allegedly asked by his Jewish interrogators, and this he answered in the affirmative. From this answer derives the list of accusations to be found in Luke.

> Then the whole multitude of them arose, and brought him before Pilate. And they began to accuse him saying: "We found this man misleading our nation and forbidding the paying of taxes to Caesar, and saying that he himself is Christ, a king." And Pilate asked him, saying: "Are you the King of the Jews?" And he answered him and said: "You are saying so." And Pilate said to the chief priests and the multitudes: "I find no fault in this man." But they were insistent, saying: "He stirs up the people, teaching throughout all Judea, starting from Galilee to here." (Luke 23:1–5)

Concerning this same event Matthew and Mark testify as follows:

When morning came, all the chief priests and the elders of the people took counsel against Jesus to put him to death; and they bound him, and led him away, and delivered him to Pilate the governor. . . . Now Jesus stood before the governor, and the governor questioned him, saying: "Are you the King of the Jews?" Jesus said: "You yourself are saying it." But while he was being accused by the chief priests and the elders, he made no answer. Then Pilate said to him: "Do you not hear how many things they testify against you?" But he did not answer him, not even to a single charge, so that the governor wondered very much. (Matthew 27:1–14)

And as soon as it was morning the chief priests with the elders and scribes, and the whole council held a consultation; and they bound Jesus and led him away and delivered him to Pilate. And Pilate questioned him, saying: "Are you the King of the Jews?" And he answered him: "You yourself are saying it." And the chief priests accused him of many things. And Pilate again questioned him, saying: "Have you no answer? See how many charges they bring against you." But Jesus made no further answer, so that Pilate wondered. (Mark 15:1–5)

Comparing the three preceding versions we find a number of differences. According to Matthew and Mark, Pilate first asks Jesus if he is the King of the Jews and then the Jewish officials offer their accusations, which are not recorded. Luke, by contrast, has the Jewish officials first accuse Jesus, then list the accusations, and finally has Pilate ask if he is the King of the Jews. Only Luke actually lists the accusations: "misleading our nation," "forbidding the paying of taxes to Caesar," and claiming that "he himself is Christ, a king." In the other Gospels the charges are implied. The first two accusations are expressions of the political aim of the messianic movement to reestablish the kingdom of Israel. These two accusations center around the assertion that Jesus claimed to be the Messiah. Indeed, this messianic accusation would attract Pilate's special attention for its apparent danger to Roman authority. Clearly, the Sanhedrin, in this instance, functioned only as a grand jury. It merely presented evidence of Jesus' seditious behavior against Rome.

The Gospel of John provides us with alternate information concerning the trial proceedings, while illuminating certain features mentioned by the Synoptic Gospel writers. John says:

> They led Jesus therefore from Caiphas into the judgment hall. It was early. But they themselves did not enter the judgment hall, in order that they might not be defiled, but might eat the passover. Therefore Pilate went out to them and said: "What accusation do you bring against this man?" They answered and said to him: "If this man were not a evildoer, we would not have handed him over." Therefore Pilate said to them: "Take him yourselves and judge him according to your own law." The Jews said to him: "It is not lawful for us to kill anyone." This was in order that the word of Jesus might be fulfilled, which he spoke, signifying what sort of death he was about to die. Therefore Pilate entered the judgment hall again and called Jesus, and said to him: "Are you the King of the Jews?" Jesus answered: "Do you say this of your own accord, or did others say it to you about me?" Pilate answered: "I am not a Jew, am I? Your own nation and the chief priests have handed you over to me; what did you do?" Jesus answered: "My kingdom is not of this world. If my kingdom were of this world, my servants would fight, that I might not be handed over to the Jews; but as it is, my kingdom is not from here." Therefore Pilate said to him: "So you are a king?" Jesus answered: "You are saying that I am a king. For this I have been born, and for this I have come into the world, to bear witness to the truth. Everyone who is of the truth hears my voice." Pilate said to him: "What is truth?" And when he had said this, he went out again to the Jews, and said to them: "I find no guilt in him." (John 18:28–38)

John agrees with Luke, in opposition to Matthew and Mark, that Pilate heard the charges from the Jewish officials before interrogating Jesus. They inform Pilate that Jesus has been brought to him because Jesus is an "evildoer." Pilate then asks Jesus: "Do you not hear how many things they testify against you?" (Matthew 27:13). "Have you no answer? See how many charges they bring against you" (Mark 15:4). No, Jesus did not hear the charges against him. As a result, he did not answer his accusers. John explains that the reason Jesus did not answer the Jewish accusers before Pilate (Matthew 27:12, Mark 15:3) was because Jesus was in the judgment hall and the accusers were outside the building (John 18:28, 29, 33, 38). This view is further strengthened by Jesus' comment to Pilate: "Do you say this of your own accord, or did others say it to you about me?" (John 18:34). This shows that he could not hear what was going on outside, where the Jews were.

The statement: "Therefore Pilate entered the judgment hall again and called Jesus, and said to him: 'Are you the King of the Jews?' " makes it clear that claiming to be the King Messiah was the Jewish accusation against Jesus. Matthew and Mark comment that Jesus did not answer the Jewish accusations when questioned by Pilate: "But he did not answer him, not even to a single charge" (Matthew 27:14); "But Jesus made no further answer" (Mark 15:5). However, the list of charges made by the Jews, which is found in Luke's Gospel (Luke 23:2), is answered by Jesus. The charges are answered in his defense before Pilate, as found in John's Gospel. There he claimed to head a peace-loving, nonmilitary, otherworldly group which would not countenance revolt against the Roman Empire. The evangelists argue, with the help of alleged quotations from the trial, that Jesus claimed to be King of the Jews but not one who sought power in this world, i.e., at the expense of the Roman Empire.

Luke contends that Jesus was also questioned by Herod Antipas, the Jewish ruler of Galilee.

But when Pilate heard it [that Jesus had worked in Galilee], he asked whether the man was a Galilean. And when he learned that he belonged to Herod's jurisdiction, he sent him to Herod, who was himself also in Jerusalem at that time. When Herod saw Jesus he was very glad, for he had wanted to see him for a long time, because he had heard about him and he was hoping to see some sign done by him. Also he questioned him at some length; but he answered nothing. And the chief priests and the scribes were standing by vehemently accusing him. And Herod together with his soldiers, after treating him with contempt and mocking him; dressed him in a bright garment and sent him back to Pilate. And Herod and Pilate became friends with each other on that very day; for before they had been at enmity with each other. (Luke 23:6–12)

This event, it is claimed, took place as an interruption in the trial before Pilate. Pilate, it is argued, broke off his own prosecution of Jesus in order to send him to Herod Antipas, continuing with his own trial proceedings upon Jesus' return. This sequence of events is not only logically unlikely but is not found in any other Gospel. Obviously, this episode is an addition to the trial events and is unknown to the other evangelists. They leave no time for this incident in their description of the trial, which was, according to them, conducted in its entirety before Pilate. The other Gospels would certainly not have omitted the story if it had been known.

Luke makes Herod Antipas one of Jesus' interrogators. He is depicted as joining with his soldiers in abusing Jesus. The inclusion of this story in the narrative is obviously an attempt to involve a Jewish ruler in the trial events. The blame for the execution is thereby shifted further away from the Romans and closer to the Jews.

The entire episode before Herod Antipas is spurious. Luke's description of the rough treatment suffered by Jesus is taken from the trial before Pilate. Luke omits completely the harsh treatment Jesus received at the hands of Pilate's soldiers, as mentioned by the other Gospels, and attributes the administration of this abusive treatment to Herod's soldiers. The conclusion to be drawn from the New Testament evidence is that Luke's narrative of the Herodian trial is patterned after the account of the trial before Pilate. There is no justification for believing that Luke's unique reference, thrust suddenly into the middle of the trial before Pilate, represents an actual event in Jesus' prosecution. Accordingly, even though Jesus is portrayed as not answering Herod Antipas, this obviously contrived scene cannot be classified as a fulfillment of Isaiah 53:7.

As we have seen, both the Jewish officials and Pilate, when questioning Jesus, directed their inquiry to his messianic pretensions. Far from showing the humility and silence with which Isaiah describes the servant in verse 7, the encounter between the high priest, the elders, and Jesus is highlighted by a vigorous verbal exchange. In addition, Jesus did not show humility and silence during his confrontation with Pilate. At their meeting, Jesus is depicted as skillfully defending himself. Jesus at no time humbled himself, but, on the contrary, presented a clever verbal defense before Pilate (the one man who could condemn him to death), pleading shrewdly that his messianic teaching was a nonviolent, "not of this world" movement, one which the Romans need not fear. Since Pilate was concerned with messianic movements, which posed a political and military threat to the Roman Empire, he would not be interested in a movement which was not of "this world" and which would not be in conflict with the Empire. Jesus was obviously defending himself by presenting a shrewd verbal response when he tried to convince Pilate that he was not the head of a seditious movement but that his intentions were peaceful.

Thus, in summation, we may say that contrary to what many Christian missionary theologians would have us believe, Jesus presented a strong defense before the Jewish officials and Pilate. Jesus was not "dumb" before his accusers, Jewish or Gentile, and it is simply not true to say of Jesus that "he humbled himself and did not open his mouth." Despite the evangelical distortions, made to curry favor with the Romans, Jesus' movement must have appeared to Pilate like any of the other messianic movements which confronted the Roman procurators. He reacted accordingly.

53:8 From dominion and judgment he was taken away, and his life's history who is able to relate? For he was cut off out of the land of the living; as a result of the transgression of my people he has been afflicted.

Generally, the beginning of this verse is rendered: "By oppression and judgment he was taken away." It is meant to indicate that, by means of persecution and judicial decision, the servant was exiled, not only from his own homeland but from the lands of his dispersion as well. The manner in which the early Christians treated this verse affords an example of how they seized on anything in the Hebrew Scriptures that had even the slightest resemblance to the life of Jesus. But, at best, the prophet's words have no particular application to Jesus, since they could, in actuality, be applied generally to many people who suffered persecution.

However, the general context of this verse indicates that the word *may-ʿotser* should not be translated as "by oppression" but in accordance with its derivation from *ʿetser*, denoting "dominion, sovereignty," and thus the beginning of the verse should read: "From dominion and judgment. . . ." Accordingly, the verse does not refer to *how* the servant was taken away but to *what* he was taken away from. It thus reflects critical events in Jewish history: Taken from "dominion and judgment," i.e., rulership and the right to judge, who can relate Israel's history which followed after "he was cut off out of the land of the living," i.e., the Land of Israel? Israel's life was filled with innumerable sufferings because of the misdeeds of the Gentiles who afflicted him unjustly. Driven into exile, the servant was deprived of his right to rule and judge. Can this be applied to Jesus? From what dominion and judgment was Jesus taken away? He never had any power as a ruler to lose. He was never deprived of any office. According to the New Testament, Jesus' "first coming" was not as a ruler or judge, but as one who would bring salvation. The New Testament further claims that Jesus will be coming back a second time and it is only then that he will reign as king and judge of the world. Jesus is quoted as saying: ". . . the Son of Man did not come to be served, but to serve, and to give his life a ransom for many" (Matthew 20:28) and "My kingdom is not of this world" (John 18:36). It is further stated in the Gospel of John: "For God did not send the Son into the world to judge the world; but that the world should be saved through him" (John 3:17). The preceding quotations illustrate that Jesus did not lose any dominion or right to judge during his lifetime, since he never had these rights in the first place. Considering verse 7 in its entirety, within the context of the entire chapter, it becomes clear that, no matter which rendering one might prefer, Isaiah did not refer to Jesus.

"And his life's history who is able to relate?" The translation of *dor,* which is generally rendered as "generation," is to be understood here as meaning "life's history" or "life's cycle." What is involved here is not just the servant's life-span but the entire spectrum of events contained within those years. This is similar to the use of *dor* in Isaiah 38:12, where Hezekiah speaks of how he felt about what was believed to be his imminent passing: "My life's cycle [*dori*] is pulled up and carried from me as a shepherd's tent." He bewails not just his expected loss of life but all that he could still accomplish if allowed to live. Isaiah 53:8 quotes the repentant Gentiles as asking, in effect, the rhetorical question: Who is able to properly relate all the trials and tribulations suffered by the servant during his passage through history?

"For he was cut off out of the land of the living" is not to be taken literally. This is explained in detail in our discussion of verse 9.

"As a result of the transgression of my people he has been afflicted." The literal translation of this verse is: "From the transgression of my people there has been affliction to him." On the basis of studying Isaiah 53 *in toto,* and comparing it to the life of Jesus, we must conclude that this statement, made by the enemies of the suffering servant of the Lord, does not refer to Jesus, who, it is alleged, suffered as an atonement for mankind's sins. There is no indication in this verse that the servant of God suffered to atone for the sins of others. What this verse states is that he suffered as a result of the misdeeds of others, who treated him unfairly and unjustly. Hence, the conclusion of the verse, in which the enemies of the servant admit responsibility for the cruel treatment they had meted out to him. This is the confession of the Gentile spokesmen, who now realize that it was they and their people who deserved to suffer the humiliations inflicted on the servant of the Lord, as they stated in verses 4–6. In short, his enemies admit that the servant's suffering stemmed from their own sinful imposition of hardships upon him.

As for Jesus, his afflictions came about, not because of the sins of other men, but because he pressed his messianic claims. The

Gospels relate that he entered Jerusalem and proceeded to disrupt the peace of the Temple area in a manner which was openly defiant of the Roman hegemony over Judea. These events, it is said, occurred just before Passover, the very time of year the Romans considered the most volatile in rebellion-prone Judea. By arousing Roman ire, he brought upon himself, not a religious, but a distinctly political death, i.e., crucifixion. In shifting the blame for Jesus' death to the Jews, the New Testament writers were seeking to curry favor with the Romans at Jewish expense.

53:9. And his grave was set with the wicked, and with the rich in his deaths; although he had done no violence, neither was there any deceit in his mouth.

The Christian missionary interpretation of Isaiah 53 posits that such phrases as "for he was cut off out of the land of the living" (verse 8), "his grave was set" (verse 9), and "in his deaths" (verse 9) refer to the death and burial of Jesus, with subsequent verses indicating his postresurrection glorification. Actually, these phrases are not to be taken literally. The metaphor "his grave was set," describing an event in the life of God's suffering servant, is similar to the statement, "for he was cut off out of the land of the living" (verse 8). Metaphors of this type, used to describe deep anguish and subjection to enemies, are part of the biblical idiom. Similar metaphorical language is used, for example, in Ezekiel 37 to express the condition preceding relief and rejuvenation following the end of exile. Ezekiel provides the clues needed for understanding the phraseology used by Isaiah. The metaphorical images employed by Isaiah—"cut off out of the land of the living" and "grave"—are also used in Ezekiel's description of the valley of the dry bones, where the bones symbolize the exiled Jewish people. Lost in an apparently hopeless exile, the Jewish people exclaim: "we are clean cut off" (Ezekiel 37:11). In reply, God promises: "And I will put My spirit in you, and you shall live, and I will place you in your own land" (Ezekiel 37:14). It is now clear that Isaiah's phrase, "for he was cut off out of the land of the living," refers to the deadly condition of exile. Similarly, the term "grave" in Isaiah—"And his grave was set with the wicked"—refers to life in exile as used in Ezekiel: "I will open your graves, and cause you to come up out of your graves" (Ezekiel 37:12), where "graves" is a metaphor for the lands of exile.

The messages of these two prophets are addressed to God's suffering servant. Although "cut off out of the land of the living" and now living in the lands of exile, the "grave set with the wicked," God will free the servant from this fate and restore him to the "land of the living," the Land of Israel. That Isaiah speaks in the singular and Ezekiel in the plural is of no consequence, for the people of Israel may be spoken of in both forms, e.g., Exodus 14:31, Psalms 81:12–14.

If Christian missionaries insist that Jesus went to his death voluntarily, the phrase "And his grave was set with the wicked" cannot refer to Jesus, because it describes an imposed fate and not something accepted voluntarily by the servant. Furthermore, this was not a literal death, as the servant was alive when "his grave was set" (cf. Genesis 30:1; Exodus 10:17; Numbers 12:12; 2 Samuel 9:8, 16:9; Jonah 4:9 for examples of figurative death). With the servant representing Israel, this verse informs us that despite the imposed fate of exile, Israel continued to be faithful to God. Accordingly, Israel is to afterwards enjoy the fruits of his sacrifice. The phrase "in his deaths" signifies that the suffering servant of the Lord experienced figuratively many "deaths" in exile. His anguish was multiplied exceedingly by the constant harassment of his enemies. Jewish history shows us how often Israel, hounded by its enemies, seemed to be in its last throes only to rise again.

"Although he had done no violence, neither was there any deceit in his mouth." Violence may be defined as causing injury or damage by rough or abusive treatment. If the New Testament account is true, Jesus did commit certain acts of violence. Whip in hand, he attacked the merchants in the Temple area, causing a fracas (Matthew 21:12, Mark 11:15–16, Luke 19:45, John 2:15). He caused the death, by drowning, of a herd of swine by allowing demons to purposely enter their bodies (Matthew 8:32, Mark 5:13, Luke 8:33) and destroyed a fig tree for not having fruit out of season (Matthew 21:18–21, Mark 11:13–14).

The evangelists agree that Jesus attacked the commercial activity in the Temple courtyard by violent means. He over-turned the tables of the moneychangers and the seats of those selling doves, and drove out of the Temple courtyard not only those who sold, but even those who were buying animals, along with the sheep and oxen. Jesus' action was a direct assault, planned in advance, and accompanied by a determined show of force. It appears that Matthew and Luke attempted to suppress the information concerning the extent of Jesus' actions so as to minimize the impression that Jesus was a man of violence. However, Mark writes that Jesus took such complete control of the Temple courtyard that he prevented its use as a thoroughfare (Mark 11:16).[1]

Jesus must have been in quite a mean mood that day. Earlier, while on the road to Jerusalem, he became hungry (Matthew 21:18, Mark 11:12), and seeing a fig tree with leaves, he ap-proached it but found no fruit on it, "for it was not the time of figs" (Mark 11:13), so he cursed it, and it withered either instantly (Matthew 21:20) or by the next morning (Mark 11:20–21). Whatever the reason for Jesus' action, it was an act of violence, which is not in conformity with the picture of the nonviolent suffering servant of the Lord as portrayed in Isaiah 53:9.[2]

By allowing the demons to enter and take possession of the herd of swine, Jesus was at fault for causing the death of the swine. Since the demons, unlike humans, had no free will, but were subject to Jesus' will, he was culpable for the wanton death of the swine by reason of his giving permission for the demons to enter and take possession of them. We must, thus, accept the inescapable conclusion that Jesus was indeed responsible for the violent death of the swine.[3]

Whether Jesus was right or wrong in attacking the merchants, or cursing a tree for not bearing fruit out of season, or permitting demons to enter the swine herd, causing their death, is of little consequence, because violence is violence. Admittedly, the use of violence is not always an act of evil, but Isaiah speaks of one who "had done no violence." If this is not taken literally, then it may fit others even more aptly than Jesus, e.g., the people of Israel personified. Furthermore, if Jesus was truly the submissive servant of the Lord depicted by Isaiah, he could not have uttered his call to family strife and devisiveness. Jesus proudly avows that his is a mission which will cause discord, disturb the universal peace, and bring war to the world. (Matthew 10:34–35, Luke 12:49–53). In addition, he called for his opponents to be brought before him for summary execution: "But these enemies of mine who did not want me to reign over them, bring them here, and slay them in my presence" (Luke 19:27). This is the love, compassion, and nonviolence that Jesus taught.[4]

The portrayal of God's suffering servant as one who had no "deceit in his mouth" belies Jesus' ambiguous behavior. When Jesus appeared before the high priest and the elders of Israel he declared: "I have spoken openly to the world; I always taught in a synagogue and in the Temple, where all the Jews come together; and I spoke nothing in secret. Why do you question me? Question those who have heard what I spoke to them; behold, these know what I said" (John 18:20–21). However, the fact remains that Jesus did not want the masses to understand him. Jesus uttered parables whose meanings were deliberately hidden from those who heard them. He claimed that he revealed the meanings of those esoteric declarations only to his disciples (Matthew 13:10–11; Mark 4:10–12, 34). Yet even that was not true. Jesus, as the all-knowing god-man, knew very well that the disciples did not understand everything he told them (Mark 9:32, Luke 9:45, 18:34). The people who heard Jesus were often misled by him into believing things which were completely opposite to what he really meant. Jesus, speaking in a deceitful manner, had declared: "Destroy this temple, and in three days I will raise it up" (John 2:19). The people were led to believe that he meant the Temple in Jerusalem when he actually "spoke of the temple of his body" (John 2:21). According to John 18:36, Jesus said to Pilate: "If my kingdom were of this world, my servants would fight, that I might not be handed over to the Jews." He implies that his followers knew his kingdom was not of this world and would not use violence. The truth is that they expected Jesus to restore the kingdom of Israel in a terrestrial sense. Even after his death, Jesus' followers looked forward to a speedy return which would usher in the overthrow of the Roman Empire: "Lord, will you at this time restore the kingdom to Israel?" (Acts 1:6). Moreover, just a few hours before his meeting Pilate, Jesus had ordered the disciples to buy swords if they had none (Luke 22:36), and the disciples responded by saying that two swords were available (Luke 22:38). Soon after this, Peter cut off the ear of Malchus, the servant of the high priest, who came to seize Jesus (Matthew 26:51, Mark 14:47, Luke 22:50, John 18:10). Obviously, contrary to Jesus' statement that "these know what I said" (John 18:21), Peter did not know that since the kingdom was not of this world he should not fight (John 18:36). Jesus knew, at his trial, that Peter had used violence. Nevertheless, he lied and said that his followers would not feel the necessity of acting violently since his kingdom was not of this world. Jesus knew very well that his followers did not understand him and that they would, indeed, use violence. Yet he persisted in his lie, saying: "I spoke nothing in secret." If he spoke openly we should at least expect his disciples to have known the meaning of his words.

Shortly after undertaking his messianic role, Jesus is quoted as having predicted that success would follow within a short period of time: "Truly I say to you, there are some of those who are standing here who shall not taste death until they see the Son of Man coming in his kingdom" (Matthew 16:28). Jesus' disciples must have accepted this statement at face value and thus mistakenly believed his false assurance that the messianic kingdom was about to be established. When Jesus assured his disciples that the end of the world order and his own triumphant return to judge all men would occur before the generation then living had passed away (Matthew 24:34, Mark 13:30, Luke 21:32), he used deceit, for he knew that this was not true.

Knowing that Elijah must precede the Messiah (Malachi 3:1,

23), Jesus claimed that John the Baptist was Elijah (Matthew 11:10–14, 17:10–13) even though John himself denied any connection with that prophet (John 1:21).[5] Did not Jesus deliberately mislead the thief when he said: "Today you will be with me in Paradise" (Luke 23:43)? Jesus did not go to Paradise on that day. Did he not instruct the parents of the girl he allegedly revived (Luke 8:56) that they should not inform anyone of what was done? Did he not instruct his disciples not to mention that he was "the Christ" (Matthew 16:20)? Yet he declared: "I have spoken openly to the world . . . I spoke nothing in secret" (John 18:20). Jesus' actions say otherwise.

Matthew 26:55 has Jesus saying: "Day after day I sat in the Temple teaching, and you did not seize me." On the contrary, John says that on one occasion they wanted to stone him while he was in the Temple, but he "hid and went out of the Temple" (John 8:59). Did Jesus lie? Did he falsely imply that they never attempted to apprehend him? Or did the evangelist lie?

Jesus' avowal that the Law will exist "until heaven and earth pass away" (Matthew 5:18) is meant to be misleading since, according to the New Testament, it only applies to a period of a mere three and one half years at most, i.e., the duration of his ministry. In the same verse, Jesus emphasizes that the whole Law would remain completely intact "until all should take place." In Matthew 5:17 Jesus declares: "Do not think that I came to destroy the Law, or the Prophets: I came, not to destroy, but to fulfill." Having fulfilled the Law and the Prophets, what is the need for the second advent? If he truly brought about all that was promised concerning the peaceful society the Messiah will bring, as stated in the Law and the Prophets (Isaiah 2:1–4, chap. 11; Jeremiah 23:5–6; Ezekiel 34:23–31; Amos 9:13–15), there should be no reason for a second advent. Surely Jesus has fulfilled all the Law and the Prophets in the first advent, for Paul says: "For Christ is the end of the Law for righteousness to everyone that believes" (Romans 10:4), and in Hebrews 8:13 it says: "In that he says, a new covenant, he has made the first obsolete. Now that which is made obsolete and growing old is near to vanishing away." According to the New Testament, the

Law is over, yet not all has been fulfilled, for, as stated, if it were accomplished, a second advent would not be necessary. If Jesus secretly meant that the Law was to be carried out now in a spiritual sense, he deluded not only the Jews, but even his own followers, by not explaining what he really meant. This is from one who said: "I spoke nothing in secret."

53:10. *And it pleased the Lord to crush him—He made [him] sick. If he would offer himself as a guilt-offering, he shall see seed, he shall prolong days. And the purpose of the Lord will prosper by his hand.*

In this verse, the prophet reiterates, in bold terms, a basic biblical concept. In suffering there is purification. Thus, there are times that God presents crushing personal challenges to His most loyal followers in order to strengthen their spirit. The lives of the patriarchs, with all their vicissitudes and tribulations, exemplify this process of purification through suffering. The righteous person is frequently confronted with painful experiences, not as a punishment for sins committed, but as a means of refinement. Indeed, suffering has been compared to a refining fire (Zechariah 13:8–9, Malachi 3:2–3).

No person is born pious or righteous. The potential for piety and righteousness can be actualized only through wrestling, over a period of time, with the vexing problems of life, and emerging, not only unscathed, but even strengthed by the experience. Facing adversity and cruel challenges, the individual must overcome all obstacles by nurturing and developing his inner faith and unswerving belief in God's justice. By remaining steadfast in his convictions and commitments, he will emerge, in the end, a truly pious and righteous person. His piety and righteousness will then be an essential part of his actual being.

The words of Isaiah, "If he would offer himself as a guilt-offering," do not mean that the servant offers himself vicariously as a guilt-offering for others. The message contained here is that the servant must feel that the suffering he has been experiencing is part of his burden and task in life in order to strengthen him inwardly. Viewing it from this perspective, he will be able to bring out his inner potential, fortify his moral fiber, and, in the end, become spiritually transformed. After having reached this state, the prophet assures him, he will then be the recipient of the most coveted of biblical rewards, namely, having many children and a long life.

Such a task is inappropriate for Jesus, the all-knowing god-man. There would have been no reason for Jesus to prove himself, since he began as perfection incarnate. Furthermore, there was no reason to reward one who is said to be an equal part of the triune god with having children and prolongation of days. Satan's temptation notwithstanding (Matthew 4:1–11, Mark 1:13, Luke 4:1–13), the outcome of Jesus' earthly life was assured, since he was incapable of committing a sinful act. Knowing that there was a divine timetable of events, i.e., Daniel's seventy weeks, and knowing God's purpose, Jesus, being aware of his divine origin, could not have done other than what was expected of him. Jesus could not freely go against the will of God and join forces with Satan, thereby abandoning the Trinity, which would then be reduced to a duet. Since he did not have free will, he could not really have been tempted.

Can it honestly be said that Jesus, who, in his final statement on the cross, is quoted as saying: "My God, my God, why have you forsaken me?" (Matthew 27:46, Mark 15:34), willingly offered himself as a guilt-offering? The evidence points to the contrary. Yet, because Jesus died at the time of the Passover festival, Christian missionaries often refer to him as the paschal lamb (1 Corinthians 5:7) who, by his voluntary sacrificial death, takes our sins away. To use the paschal lamb as a typology of Jesus' death (as the paschal lamb represented the redemption of Israel from bondage in Egypt, so Jesus' death represents the redemption of humanity from bondage to sin) is at best an arbitrary assumption without a secure basis in the biblical text. In fact, a closer look at the text should convince any objective student that the annual sacrifice of the paschal lamb is not treated, in any way, as referring to a guilt-offering intended to bring about forgiveness of sin. It was instituted as part of the celebration commemorating the redemption from Egyptian bondage (Exodus 12:14, 26, 27), and in no honest way can it be used in conjunction with a typological redemption from sin. There are several sacrifices whose purpose is the atonement of sin, and there is no need to misappropriate the paschal lamb for this purpose. Certainly the sacrifice offered on Yom Kippur, the Day of Atonement, affords a more logical symbol of redemption from sin. If the New Testament is a continuation of what Christians call the Old Testament, it must harmonize with the Old Testament. False comparisons will not do. Christian missionaries cannot pick and choose what suits them in order to make it seem as if Jesus willingly offered himself as a guilt-offering. Either Jesus is complete fulfillment of Scripture or none at all—and the verdict, clearly, is none at all.

According to the words "He shall see seed, he shall prolong days," the suffering servant of the Lord is to be rewarded for his selflessness in the service of the Almighty by being blessed with children and prolongation of life. These two promises must be treated as a unit, as described in greater detail in Isaiah 65:20–23. Each promise complements the other, highlighting the ancient Hebraic ideal of viewing children and a long life as the two greatest rewards God gives to man here on earth. This is further illustrated in Job 5:25–26: "You shall know also that your seed shall be great, and your offspring as the grass of the earth. You shall come to your grave in ripe age, as a shock of corn in its season."

From the manner in which the Hebrew word *zer'a* ("seed") is used in the Scriptures, there can be no doubt that actual physical offspring is meant here. Christian missionary exegetes have interpreted certain verses in the Scriptures (Genesis 3:15, 38:8; Isaiah 1:4, 57:4; Malachi 2:15; Psalms 22:31; Proverbs 11:21) as referring only symbolically to "bodily seed." But such an interpretation is unwarranted, since in each of these verses, the term "seed" can be taken in a literal and physical sense. Yet Christian missionaries would like us to believe that the term "seed" is used metaphorically, meaning, in the verse under discussion, "disciples." Generally, the Hebrew word *bayn* ("son") may be employed metaphorically with the meaning "disciples," but never is the term *zer⁢a* ("seed") used in this sense. Hence, the latter must be taken literally, which rules out the possibility that it refers to Jesus since he had no children of his own.

Neither can the second part of the promise, ". . . he shall prolong days," be applied to Jesus, who died at a young age. To apply these words, as Christian missionary exegetes do, is not only evasive but meaningless. How can such a promise have any meaning for Jesus, who is viewed as being of divine substance and whose existence is believed, by Christian missionaries, to be eternal? There would be no need for God to assure a fellow member of the Trinity eternal life. Obviously, there is a difference in meaning between the concept of prolongation of days and that of gaining eternal life. The concept of a prolonged life cannot be treated as the equivalent of eternal life because in an eternal context, time of any duration is of no consequence. Consequently, one cannot speak of an eternal being as having his days prolonged: "Are Your days as the days of man, or Your years as a man's days?" (Job 10:5). God must be referred to as eternal: "The number of His years is unsearchable" (Job 36:26). He is the first, He is the last, He cannot be anything else. Prolonging the days of one who is already supposed to be eternal would make his life longer than eternity. That obviously is an impossibility. If the promise of prolonged days is applied to Jesus, he could not be of divine origin.

Prolongation implies mortality, a cut-off date in the future, while the term "eternal life" refers to immortality. Therefore, the phrase "prolonged life" can only relate to the limited bodily existence in this world, and not to the endlessness of eternal life. We are compelled to conclude that since the blessings of seeing children and prolonging life are only appropriate when applied to a mortal man and not to an immortal being, these blessings cannot be applied to the Jesus of Christian missionary theology. Jesus died young and childless. If, after his alleged resurrection, he returned to heaven to become an eternal heavenly being again, prolongation of days cannot be appropriately applied to this stage of his existence. Thus, Isaiah 53:10 cannot and should not be applied to Jesus.

"And the purpose of the Lord will prosper by his hand." This refers to a time when true religion will prosper. Under the leadership of a kingdom of priests (Exodus 19:6), all nations will acknowledge and accept God's unity, sovereignty, and commandments (Zechariah 8:20–23).

53:11. From the labor of his soul he shall see; he shall be satisfied. With his knowledge, the righteous one, my servant, shall cause many to be just. And their iniquities he shall bear.

This verse indicates the abundant rewards that God will bestow upon His faithful servant. No longer will he suffer humiliation at the hands of the other nations (Ezekiel 34:28–29). In the past, the servant was physically mistreated by the nations and used as a means of covering up their own sins. At the time indicated in this verse, the servant will still bear the iniquities of the nations. However, he will bear them spiritually, not physically. This will take place through the servant's sacrifices in the reconstructed Temple on behalf of the nations, and through the instruction of the nations in God's laws (Isaiah 2:3–4, Micah 4:2–3, Zechariah 14:16–21).

Christian missionaries claim that the life's work of Jesus is reflected in this verse. However, there is a wide gap between asserting and proving one's claim. Certainly, the New Testament Jesus was not "satisfied" with what he accomplished during his lifetime, as is indicated by what he said on the cross: "My God, my God, why have you forsaken me?" (Matthew 27:46, Mark 15:34). The argument that verse 11 refers to the heavenly Jesus, following his death, becoming increasingly satisfied as his following grew, is of little help since this verse deals with an earthly being. Furthermore, if Jesus was an equal partner in the Trinity, he would not have had to ask his "Father" to "forgive them, for they do not know what they are doing" (Luke 23:34). He himself should have been able to bear iniquities and forgive sins without invoking the assistance of God, the Father.

> *53:12. Therefore will I divide him a portion with the great, and he shall divide the spoil with the mighty; because he has poured out his soul to death: and he was numbered with the transgressors; and he bore the sin of many, and made intercession for the transgressors.*

As part of the servant's reward for faithful service to God and mankind, "God will divide him a portion with the great." His exile over, the ingathering of the exiles complete, the servant, Israel, formerly despised by the nations, will now attain a place of honor and recognition among "the great," the sovereign nations of the world (Zechariah 8:13, Isaiah 61:9). Indeed, Israel will be recognized as the greatest of all the world's nations (Deuteronomy 4:6–8). The servant, as the true possessor of God's word, assumes a position of leadership among the nations of the world (Zechariah 8:20–23), who now turn to righteousness (Zechariah 14:16).

Parallel with God's promise to "divide him a portion with the great" is the phrase, "he shall divide the spoil with the mighty." The term "the mighty," or "the mighty ones," refers to the mighty nation, the descendants of Abraham (Genesis 18:18). The entire nation of Israel will share the spoils of war (Zechariah 14:14). It will not just be those who actually fought that will partake in the division of the spoils, but the spoils will be equally shared among all Israel (cf. Numbers 31:27, Joshua 22:8, 1 Samuel 30:24–25).

How is a Christian missionary theological interpretation of Isaiah 53:12 to be reconciled with Daniel 9:26: "And after the sixty-two weeks an anointed one shall be cut off, and he shall have nothing"? Certainly the phrase "he shall have nothing" cannot be reconciled with verse 12, where God divides, for his servant, "a portion with the great." From their respective contexts, it is clear that, if applied to the Jesus of Christian missionary theology, both Daniel 9:26 and Isaiah 53:12 would have to apply to a postresurrection period, and thus cancel each other out. According to Christian missionary theology, Jesus came into his greatest rewards only after his earthly death, and, indeed, as a result of that death. Thus, if verse 12 applies to Jesus, then Daniel's statement, "he shall have nothing," cannot refer to him, for Jesus' rewards could only have been actually guaranteed from the moment he was "cut off." To apply these two verses to one individual would be self-contradictory.

As a human being, Jesus certainly had very little. Yet, because he was allegedly God, he could expect, on reassuming his heavenly role, to exercise his power as God. So what did he, in the final accounting, give up in dying a human death? Christian missionary theology is saying that Jesus gave up a temporary earthly life as a god-man to return to his role in heaven, where, as part of the Trinity, he reigns as God. In Isaiah 53:12, God speaks of the suffering servant of the Lord, who, as a result of his selflessness, is willing to give up all that he possesses in the service of God. Clearly, it is unreasonable to say that Jesus sacrificed himself for the redemption of mankind when, by his actions, he knowingly gained more than he lost. There is a gross misuse of the concept of "sacrifice" where one who is alleged to be divine knows that by giving up a flesh-and-blood existence, something essentially unimportant to him, he will receive in return a position of eternal exaltation and power. This cannot be called sacrifice. On leaving his transitory human life-span behind him, Jesus, it is alleged, returned to heaven to once more become part of the eternal Godhead. Why should Jesus be rewarded for his alleged sacrifice, for doing what he himself, as God, wanted done? There is no point for God, of whom Jesus is allegedly a part, to say: "I will divide him a portion with the great" as an actual reward to Himself. Such reward can be properly given to one who is all human and not one who is at the same time divine. The suffering servant is promised "a portion with the great" and that "he shall divide the spoil with the mighty," but if Jesus is God, who can be great enough to share the spoil with him? Is it conceivable that one who is God could possibly have only "a portion" comparable to that of mere earthly rulers, or that "he shall divide the spoil" with anyone? Even if this could be rationalized, it would then run counter to what is stated in Psalm 2, which Christian missionaries claim refers to

Jesus. In that psalm, God offers, to the person in question, the entire earth for a possession (verse 8), and all rulers are told to give homage to that person (verse 10–12). Christian missionary commentators will often try to explain away these irreconcilable contradictions with arguments that have no basis even in their own New Testament. It is for the reader to be vigilant and to be wary of such vain attempts that are based on distortions.

The phrase "because he has poured out his soul to death" cannot refer to Jesus. According to the evidence presented in the Gospels, Jesus "poured out his soul," i.e., died, on the cross unwillingly, saying at the last moment: "My God, my God, why have You forsaken me?" (Matthew 27:46, Mark 15:34). This final statement from the cross contradicts the assertion that Jesus "learned obedience through what he suffered" (Hebrews 5:8) and that he submitted to God's will (Matthew 26:39, 42; Mark 14:36; Luke 22:42). In those last moments of life, Jesus expressed himself in such a way that his death cannot be considered a voluntary sacrificial death made in response to a call from God. Jesus went to his death feeling abandoned by God. His last words from the cross expressed a sense of frustration, not obedience.

"And he was numbered with the transgressors; and he bore the sin of many, and made intercession for the transgressors." The servant was considered to be numbered with the transgressors because living among the Gentile nations he suffered their fate, and worse, when adversity struck. Furthermore, Isaiah's prophecy describes the servant as one who bore the sins of the Gentile nations in that he was blamed for their misdeeds. Yet "he made intercession" for the transgressions of those nations by praying for their well-being (Jeremiah 29:7).

It is well known that much of what the New Testament claims concerning Jesus was added after his death, as his followers began combing the Scriptures in search of proof-texts. They seized upon Isaiah 53 and built the claims of their faith around it. Stories concerning Jesus were adjusted to agree with Isaiah 53, but, as we have seen from a thorough study of the chapter, they did not really succeed. The inability to fulfill all that is stated regarding the suffering servant indisputably disqualifies Jesus from any claim to this title.

The suffering of Israel, as visualized by various rabbinic sages, is epitomized in the suffering of a messianic person who, leading Israel in battle, would die. Such is their understanding of the situation described in Zechariah 12:10, where the surviving Israelites will mourn for those killed by the nations and especially for their leader, the fallen warrior Messiah (B. T. Sukkah 52a). But soon thereafter, the nations of the world will, by virtue of the Israelite triumphs, become aware of God's special relationship to Israel. This will have the effect of causing, first, shock and disbelief, and then, an acknowledgment of the special rewards that God will grant Israel, as is described in the latter part of Isaiah 53. What is described by the prophet in this chapter refers to Israel as a whole, not to every individual Israelite. Not every Jew will have to undergo every aspect of suffering to be worthy of eventually partaking in the rewards God promises.

If one is to insist, however, that Isaiah 53 refers to a single individual, this person could not be Jesus. He would have to fulfill all the elements in the account of the suffering servant of the Lord. Any individual who fails to fulfill even one aspect cannot be considered the servant. Judged from this vantage point, Jesus is clearly disqualified.

Early Christianity filled in certain elements in the life of Jesus so that Jesus could fulfill all the biblical passages that the early church considered to contain messianic prophecies. The events of Jesus' life have been arranged and amplified to accord with early Christian doctrines and to serve apologetic needs. Yet for all the early church's efforts, a careful scrutiny of the texts will reveal that Jesus cannot be considered the embodiment of the biblical Messiah.

In the New Testament, arguments are presented to show fulfillment of this chapter of Isaiah in the life and death of Jesus. Yet what is the proof? Is there any reason to believe that the Gospel presentation conforms to the historical facts? If we are to evaluate the New Testament proof honestly, we must treat and interpret Isaiah's prophecy in all its parts, and as a whole, to see whether Jesus actually fulfilled all that it contains. What is called for is verification on the basis of actual fulfillment of the Scripture rather than an imaginary verification based on blind faith. The New Testament record itself contains far too many inconsistencies vis-à-vis this chapter for anyone to honestly take the Christian missionary claim seriously. Christian missionaries will find answers, rationalize wherever possible, and relegate what cannot be explained away to the realm of unanswerable mysteries. When all is said and done, one important fact remains: the events of the life of Jesus are simply not in harmony with the whole tenor of Isaiah 53.

1. See below Chapter 41, "Violence in the Temple."
2. See below Chapter 42, "The Cursing of the Fig Tree."
3. See below Chapter 37, "The Drowning of the Herd of Swine."
4. See below Chapter 38, "Jesus' Outlook on Violence."
5. Despite Luke's claim that John came "in the spirit and power of Elijah" (Luke 1:17), Jesus asserted that John was actually Elijah without qualifying his physical and spiritual characteristics as Luke did. Indeed, what need would there have been for Elijah to ascend to heaven bodily (2 Kings 2:11) if only his "spirit and power" were going to return?

12

A WOMAN ENCOMPASSES A MAN

(Jeremiah 31:22)

For the Lord has created a new thing on the earth: a woman encompasses a man.

(Jeremiah 31:22)

As is not uncommon, Christian missionary exegetes, in their zeal to find proof for their doctrines, read more into this verse than is really there. The noun *neqevah* ("woman") does not at all mean a virgin, nor does the verse deal with conception. That the word *neqevah* is used in the Bible to denote any woman, virgin or not, can be seen from the following verses: Leviticus 27:4–7; Numbers 5:3, 31:15; Deuteronomy 4:16. In no way can this word be twisted to mean a virgin, nor can this verse be made to refer to conception by a virgin. Therefore, the claim that this verse alludes to the birth of Jesus from a virgin is completely unfounded. Any such claim is the work of an overzealous imagination. Making use of a verse whose meaning lends itself to various interpretations does not justify assigning meanings to words which have absolutely no basis in fact. Neither context nor language usage justifies the Christian missionary position.

13

JEREMIAH'S NEW COVENANT

(Jeremiah 31:31–34)

Behold, the days come, says the Lord, that I will make a new covenant with the house of Israel, and with the house of Judah; not according to the covenant that I made with their fathers in the day that I took them by the hand to bring them out of the land of Egypt; forasmuch as they broke My covenant, although I was a lord over them, says the Lord. But this is the covenant that I will make with the house of Israel after those days, says the Lord, I will put My law in their inward parts, and in their heart I will write it; and I will be their God, and they shall be My people; and they shall teach no more every man his neighbor, and every man his brother, saying: "Know the Lord"; for they shall all know Me, from the least of them to the greatest of them, says the Lord; for I will forgive their iniquity, and their sin will I remember no more.

(Jeremiah 31:31–34)

Christian missionaries insist that the term "new covenant" found in Jeremiah 31:31 means the promulgation of a new religious orientation, i.e., Christianity. By any objective reading of the text, one fails to see any reference to a substitution of a new covenant which will supersede the old. There is nothing in Jeremiah's statement to suggest that the new covenant will contain any changes in the Law.

What we are told by Jeremiah is that God will enter into a new covenant with Israel which, unlike the old, will for all time be faithfully observed by the Jews, because it will be inscribed in their hearts. As a result, God will embrace his chosen people again and will lead them to independence from their subjection to the Gentiles (Leviticus 26:44). God is to bestow upon Israel a

70

new covenant of protection, a covenant which will never be violated, when Israel will be restored to their land. Viewed from this perspective, the "new covenant" constitutes a reaffirmation of the covenant that has already been given to the Jewish people.

It is important to remember, in this connection, that Israel viewed itself not only as a religious community but also as a political and national entity. Consequently, as far as the Jewish people were concerned, based on the teachings of the Scriptures, the task of the Messiah is not to free them from sin, but to help liberate them from foreign domination (Isaiah 11:10–12). Freeing man from sin is within the sole domain of God. When God helps His people, it implies that He has already forgiven their sins.

Jeremiah prophesies that, unlike in the past, Israel will henceforth remain faithful to God, while He in turn will never neglect or forsake them. As such, Jeremiah is not foreseeing the issuance of a new law. Rather, the ancient divine law will be renewed by becoming everlastingly impressed upon their hearts, never to be forgotten.

The identical prophecy is also found in Ezekiel expressed in similar words:

> And I will give them one heart, and I will put a new spirit within you; and I will remove the stony heart out of their flesh, and will give them a heart of flesh; that they may walk in My statutes, and keep My ordinances, and do them; and they shall be My people, and I will be their God. (Ezekiel 11:19–20)

That the covenant of old is of eternal duration, never to be rescinded or to be superseded by a new covenant, is clearly stated in Leviticus 26:44–45.

> And yet for all that, when they are in the land of their enemies, I will not reject them, neither will I abhor them, to destroy them utterly, and to break My covenant with them; for I am the Lord their God. But I will for their sakes remember the covenant of their ancestors, whom I brought forth out of the land of Egypt in the sight of the nations, that I might be their God: I am the Lord.

And this is forcefully reasserted by Jeremiah.

> Behold, I will gather them out of all the countries, to which I have driven them in My anger, and in My fury, and in great wrath; and I will bring them back to this place, and I will cause them to dwell safely; and they shall be My people, and I will be their God; and I will give them one heart and one way, that they may fear Me forever; for the good of them, and of their children after them; and I will make an everlasting covenant with them, that I will not turn away from them, to do them good; and I will put My fear in their hearts, that they shall not depart from Me. Yea, I will rejoice over them to do them good, and I will plant them in this land in truth with My whole heart and with My whole soul. For thus says the Lord: Just as I have brought all this great evil upon this people, so will I bring upon them all the good that I have promised them. (Jeremiah 32:37–42)

The covenant between God and Israel is frequently referred to as everlasting (e.g., Genesis 17:7, 13, 19; Psalms 105:8, 10; 1 Chronicles 16:13–18). To Jeremiah, God speaks of the covenant being "in their inward parts, and in their heart will I write it" (Jeremiah 31:33). In Leviticus 26:41–42, God speaks of remembering the covenant that He made with the patriarchs if the people's "uncircumcised heart is humbled." Both references are, in any case, to the original covenant made with Abraham, Isaac, and Jacob.

The Christian missionary position concerning Jeremiah's covenant is found in Hebrews 8:13: "In that he says, a new covenant, he has made the first obsolete. Now that which is being made obsolete and growing old is near to vanishing away." In stark contrast to this statement, the Scriptures state: "The works of His hands are truth and justice; and His precepts are sure. They are established forever and ever, they are done in truth and uprightness" (Psalms 111:7–8); "The grass withers, the flower fades; but the word of our God shall stand forever" (Isaiah 40:8). The Scriptures convey the message that God's enactments are eternally valid and immutable.

The term "new covenant" would be meaningless unless what

Jeremiah meant by it was the renewing of the old covenant, which will thereby regain its full original vigor. Jeremiah is thus able to speak of a "new covenant," and still remain a true prophet among his people because there was absolutely no difference between the new and old. His prophetic message accords with the words of Isaiah 65:17: "For, behold, I create new heavens and a new earth," which cannot be considered a contradiction of Ecclesiastes 1:4: "And the earth abides forever," because Isaiah obviously speaks metaphorically of the reordering of that which already exists. If the Christian missionary theological fiction of a literal "new covenant" to supersede the "everlasting covenant" is to be taken seriously, then why not say a literally new heaven and earth are to be created? Obviously, Jeremiah's "new covenant" is not to be viewed as a replacement of the existing covenant, but merely as a figure of speech for the reinvigoration and revitalization of the old covenant.

Elsewhere Jeremiah says (11:3–4):

> And you shall say to them: Thus says the Lord, the God of Israel: Cursed be the man that does not hear the words of this covenant, which I commanded your fathers in the day that I brought them forth out of the land of Egypt, out of the iron furnace, saying: Listen to My voice, and do them, according to all which I commanded you; so shall you be My people, and I will be your God.

He is our God and we are His people. We possess an old covenant yet a new covenant, truly an everlasting covenant.

14

HOSEA AND THE SECOND COMING OF JESUS

(Hosea 5:15)

I will go and return to My place until they feel guilt and seek My face; in their trouble they will earnestly seek Me.

(Hosea 5:15)

Ignoring the context, some missionaries interpret this verse as prophesying the second coming of Jesus. However, this conception is belied by the setting of the prophecy. Hosea is speaking of an altogether different event. In the course of his message, Hosea emphasizes that Ephraim and Judah must first return to God through their own conscious decision before He will give them relief from their affliction.

The missionary understanding of Hosea's words is incorrect, as may even be seen from the New Testament. Paul declares that Israel as a nation will be converted to belief in Jesus, not through their own efforts but through the direct intervention of Jesus after his return. To prove his view he cites, with significant variations, Isaiah 59:20–21: ". . . and thus all Israel will be saved; just as it is written: 'The Deliverer will come from Zion, he will remove ungodliness from Jacob. And this is My covenant with them, when I take away their sins' " (Romans 11:26–27).[1] Thus, even if we disregard the context of the verse in Hosea, it does not agree with Paul's view that Jesus will bring about the conversion of Israel as a nation *through direct intervention*. Hosea clearly declares that Israel must by their own initiative return to God before He will intervene to alleviate their affliction. There is no

74

direct divine intervention indicated by the prophet to initiate the process of repentance—it must begin with the sinner. It is obvious that even according to the New Testament, Hosea's words do not apply to a second coming of Jesus. Interestingly enough, the Hebrew text of Isaiah 59:20 agrees with Hosea that the people must first repent. Isaiah indicates that the final redemption will come to those who have first turned away from transgression: "And a redeemer will come to Zion, and to those that turn from transgression in Jacob." This is contrary to Paul's interpretation, based on the changes he made in the text, which states that Jesus will initiate the process of repentance.[2]

1. The Hebrew text of Isaiah 59:20–21 reads in translation: "And a redeemer will come to Zion, and to those that turn from transgression in Jacob, says the Lord. And as for Me, this is My covenant with them, says the Lord; My spirit that is upon you, and My words which I have put in your mouth, shall not depart out of your mouth, nor out of the mouth of your seed, nor out of the mouth of your seed's seed, says the Lord, from henceforth and forever."

2. Paul changed Isaiah's "a redeemer will come *to* Zion" to "a Deliverer will come *from* Zion" and Isaiah's "*and to those that turn* from transgression in Jacob" to "*he will remove* ungodliness from Jacob." The latter wording agrees with the Septuagint. However, see above, n. 4, p. 28.

15

BETHLEHEM EPHRATAH

(Micah 5:1)

But you, Bethlehem Ephratah, who are little to be among the thousands of Judah, out of you shall one come forth to Me that is to be ruler in Israel; whose goings forth are from of old, from ancient days.

(Micah 5:1)

This verse refers to the Messiah, a descendant of David. Since David came from Bethlehem, Micah's prophecy speaks of Bethlehem as the Messiah's place of origin. Actually, the text does not necessarily mean the Messiah will be born in that town, but that his family originates from there. From the ancient family of the house of David will come forth the Messiah, whose eventual existence was known to God from the beginning of time.

Christian missionaries allege that Jesus fulfilled Micah's prophecy in that he was supposedly born in Bethlehem. Matthew's claim that Jesus was born in Bethlehem (Matthew 2:1) is supported by Luke 2:4–7. Mark is silent on the matter. John relates that some people believed the Messiah will come from Bethlehem (John 7:42), but does not take advantage of the opportunity to demonstrate that Micah's prophecy was fulfilled by claiming that Jesus was actually born there. This is highly unusual and leads one to suspect that John did not agree with the assertion that Jesus was a Bethlehemite. He lets stand the opposing assertion that Jesus was really of Galilean origin (John 1:46, 7:41).

Except for the birth references found in Matthew and Luke, all indications, even in the writings of these two evangelists, point to the fact that Jesus was from Nazareth. In any case, being born in Bethlehem is of dubious value in establishing messianic credentials for Jesus. So many essential messianic qualities, as found in the Prophets, were not fulfilled by Jesus, that having been born in Bethlehem would be of no consequence whatsoever.

16

ONE ASS OR TWO?

(Zechariah 9:9)

Rejoice greatly, O daughter of Zion, shout, O daughter of Jerusalem; behold, your king is coming to you, he is just and has been saved, humble, and riding upon an ass, even upon a colt the foal of a she-ass.

(Zechariah 9:9)

The Synoptic Gospels inform us that, in fulfillment of prophecy, Jesus sent two of his disciples to get the animal he was to ride into Jerusalem (Matthew 21:2–7, Mark 11:2–7, Luke 19:30–35). At variance with this, the author of the Gospel of John states that Jesus found the animal all by himself: "And Jesus, finding a young ass, sat on it; as it is written: 'Fear not, daughter of Zion; behold, your King comes sitting on a she-ass's colt' " (John 12:14–15).

The Gospel narratives present the reader with still another mystery. Did Jesus enter Jerusalem riding on one animal, as Mark, Luke, and John tell it, or on two, as Matthew relates?

[Jesus said] to them: "Go into the village opposite you, and immediately you will find a she-ass tied and a colt with her; untie them, and bring them to me. And if anyone says something to you, you shall say, 'The Lord needs them'; and immediately he will send them." Now this took place that what was spoken through the prophet might be fulfilled, saying: "Say to the daughter of Zion, behold your King is coming to you, gentle, and mounted upon a

78

she-ass, and upon a colt, the foal of a beast of burden." And the disciples went and did as Jesus had directed them, and brought the she-ass and the colt, and put upon them their garments, and he sat upon them. (Matthew 21:2–7)

Matthew, in his eagerness to use Zechariah 9:9 as an example of how Jesus fulfilled prophecy, misses the point that biblical poetry makes frequent use of synonymous parallelism. Reading Zechariah correctly, we see that the prophet is not speaking of someone riding two animals. As is common in biblical poetry, which is based on parallel structure, the repetition of an idea or fact does not indicate its duplication in reality. Parallelism is a poetic device to create a thought rhythm and is not to be taken literally as a repetition in fact. The prophet's statement, "riding upon an ass, even upon a colt the foal of a she-ass," describes the same event in different words. Matthew sought compliance with a prophecy that did not exist. The evangelist assumes that two different animals are involved and so has the disciples bring two, a she-ass and its colt. He writes: "Behold your King is coming to you, gentle, and mounted upon a she-ass, and upon a colt, the foal of a beast of burden. And the disciples . . . put upon them their garments, and he sat upon them."

According to Matthew, Jesus came to Jerusalem riding astride both animals, one being male and the other female. Each animal was covered by the garments of Jesus' disciples. Contrary to Matthew's record, Zechariah mentions only the riding of one male animal. Although more subdued in their claim, the other Gospels give us no reason to believe they are based on traditions any more trustworthy than Matthew's. These narratives, describing Jesus' entry into Jerusalem, are fabrications suggested by Zechariah's prophecy. Using such methodology, it is no wonder that the New Testament is able to make so many claims of prophetic fulfillment by Jesus. Christian missionaries must accept these alleged fulfillments of prophecy on unquestioning faith alone, as they lack a basis in historical fact.

17

WHO WAS PIERCED?

(Zechariah 12:10)

And they shall look to Me whom they have pierced; then they shall mourn for him, as one mourns for an only son.

(Zechariah 12:10)

Misconstruing this verse as a Christological reference, Christian missionary theologians become entangled in needless exegetical difficulties. While the sentence structure may appear confusing, it must be remembered that we are dealing here with an English reproduction of biblical Hebrew with its peculiar usages. Actually this verse is not difficult to understand, if we look at it within the context of Zechariah 12, where we are told that God will defend His people and destroy their enemies. On that day, "they [the nation of Israel, i.e., the house of David and the inhabitants of Jerusalem, mentioned at the beginning of verse 10] shall look to Me [God] whom they [the nations, spoken of in verse 9, that shall come up against Jerusalem] have pierced; then they [Israel] shall mourn for him [the slain of Israel as personified by the leader of the people, the warrior Messiah who will die in battle at this time]."

Of course, God cannot literally be pierced. The idea of piercing God expresses the fact that Israel stands in a very special relationship to God among all the nations of the earth. God identifies with His people to the degree that He takes part figuratively in the nation's destiny. To attack (pierce) Israel is to attack God. That is why God says: "Me whom they have pierced" even though it is the people of Israel and not God who is actually "pierced." Accordingly, Isaiah says of God's relationship to Israel: "In all their affliction He was afflicted" (Isaiah 63:9), and in Psalm 83:2–6 we see that the nations which hate God manifest that hatred by seeking to destroy the Jewish people.

O God, do not keep silent; do not hold your peace, and be not still, O God. For, lo, Your enemies are in an uproar; and they that hate You have lifted up the head. They hold crafty converse against Your people, and take counsel against Your hidden ones. They have said: "Come, and let us cut them off from being a nation; that the name of Israel may be remembered no more." For they have consulted together with one accord; against You they make a covenant.

There are many biblical passages which show that God identifies Himself with Israel. This is illustrated by the following:

Thus says the Lord: "Concerning all My evil neighbors that touch the inheritance which I have caused My people Israel to inherit, behold, I will pluck them up from off their land, and I will pluck up the house of Judah from among them." (Jeremiah 12:14)

But thus says the Lord: "Even the captives of the mighty shall be taken away, and the prey of the oppressor shall be delivered; and I will contend with him that contends with you, and I will save your children." (Isaiah 49:25)

But if you shall indeed hearken to his voice [the angel in the desert], and do all that I speak, then I will be an enemy to your enemies and an adversary to your adversaries. (Exodus 23:22)

For thus says the Lord of hosts who sent me [Zechariah] after glory to the nations which plundered you: "Surely, he that touches you touches the apple of His eye [actually "My eye" before the emendation of the Scribes]. For, behold, I will shake My hand over them, and they shall be plunder for those who served them." Then you shall know that the Lord of hosts has sent me. (Zechariah 2:12–13)

The Christian missionaries, in their confusion, equate the "Me" with the "him" of verse 10 and refer both to Jesus. Grammatically, the "Me" and the "him" cannot refer to the same individual. The only admissible interpretation is, as stated above, that the Gentile nations shall look to God, whom they have attacked by the persecution, death, and general suffering they inflicted on the nation of Israel ("him"), whose dead will be mourned by the surviving Jewish people. The rabbis of the Talmud saw this suffering personified in the leader of the people, the warrior Messiah, the son of Joseph, who will be slain at this time (B. T. Sukkah 52a). All of the nation's dead will be mourned, but the mourning over the death of the warrior Messiah symbolizes the collective grief as the people mourn for the fallen of Israel. The author of the Gospel of John realized the untenability of the claim that Zechariah's prophecy referred to Jesus. John, perplexed by Zechariah's prophecy, changed the wording of verse 10 to make it conform to his belief. Thus, he wrote: "They shall look upon *him* [not "Me" as in the Hebrew text] whom they have pierced" (John 19:37). Emending a text may be a convenient way of demonstrating one's theological beliefs, but has nothing to do with biblical authenticity.

18

ELIJAH THE PROPHET

(Malachi 3:1, 23–24)

Behold, I send My messenger, and he shall clear the way before Me; and the Lord, whom you seek will suddenly come to His temple; and the messenger of the covenant, whom you delight in, behold, he comes, says the Lord of hosts.

(Malachi 3:1)

Behold, I will send you Elijah the prophet before the coming of the great and terrible day of the Lord. And he shall turn the heart of the fathers to the children, and the heart of the children to their fathers; lest I come and smite the land with utter destruction.

(Malachi 3:23–24)

Some Christian missionary theologians, realizing that Elijah did not appear prior to the coming of Jesus, put off the event described by the prophet Malachi to the alleged second coming of Jesus. Others have attempted to disassociate Malachi's two statements from each other. However, it is obvious from reading the Synoptic Gospels that Jesus considered these verses very much connected, and he applied them both directly to John the Baptist. According to the Synoptic Gospels, Jesus considered Malachi's prophecies concerning Elijah, the harbinger of the Messiah, as completely fulfilled in John. For Jesus, Elijah had come in the person of John. When asked: "Why then do the scribes say that Elijah must come first?" (Matthew 17:10), Jesus replied: "Elijah, indeed, is coming and will restore all things," i.e., before the Messiah comes (Matthew 17:11). He then con-

83

tinues: "But I am saying to you Elijah has already come" (Matthew 17:12). This claim is restated in Mark 9:13: "But I say to you Elijah, also, has come." Jesus did not say Elijah would come in the future. Jesus explained Malachi's prophecy as indicating that "Elijah, indeed, does come first and restore all things" (Mark 9:12). He understood the prophet's message to mean that Elijah must come prior to the coming of the Messiah.

In Matthew 11:10–11 and Luke 7:27–28, Jesus connects John the Baptist with Malachi 3:1. In Matthew 11:13–14, 17:12 and Mark 9:13, Jesus declares Elijah has already come in the actual person of John, thus fulfilling Malachi 3:23. Accordingly, Jesus led his disciples to believe that John was the fulfillment of Malachi's prophecy, paving the way for Jesus' own messianic claims. But the identification of John the Baptist with Elijah is emphatically rejected, according to the Gospel of John (John 1:21), by John the Baptist himself. When asked: "Are you Elijah?" he answered: "I am not." To the question: "Are you the Prophet?" his answer was: "No."

Did John the Baptist only represent Elijah in respect to Elijah's "spirit and power" (Luke 1:17) instead of actually being the prophet? If such were the case, Malachi would have used terms as "like Elijah," or "similar to Elijah." Instead, the Hebrew text reads, *hinay 'anochi sholayach lachem 'et 'Ayliya hanavi'* ("Behold, I will send you Elijah the prophet"). *'Et* is placed before the direct object of a verb if the object it indicates is definite. Elijah is a proper noun and is regarded as definite. The participle *'et* emphasizes that the individual who is to appear will be Elijah. Certain Christian missionary exegetes, using the alleged declaration of the angel found in Luke—"And it is he who will go before him in the spirit and power of Elijah" (Luke 1:17)—claim that John the Baptist only represents Elijah in spirit and power. However, viewing John the Baptist as representing Elijah in spirit and power does not satisfy Malachi's prophecy, as it does not agree with the plain meaning of the text in its use of the participle *'et*. Furthermore, as we have already seen, Jesus himself considered John the Baptist to be Elijah in the flesh and not merely in the spirit. While John was still alive Jesus said:

"And if you care to accept it, he is Elijah who is intended to come," i.e., was destined by the prophet to come (Matthew 11:14). After John was executed, Jesus said of him: "But I am saying to you Elijah has already come, and they did not recognize him" (Matthew 17:12). Jesus made no distinction whatsoever between Malachi 3:1 and 3:23 but used them together. To Jesus, John was not only the "messenger" but also "he is Elijah." That Elijah is to return in body, and not only in spirit, is implicit in the fact that Elijah, in departing from this world, ascended bodily.[1] Furthermore, nowhere do we find John claiming that he is Elijah in spirit. On the contrary, when he was asked who he was, John replied: "I am a voice of one crying in the wilderness, 'Make straight the way of the Lord,' as said the prophet Isaiah" (John 1:23). By this claim, he does not identify himself with Elijah since the prophecy of Isaiah, from which the verse comes, speaks of the Jewish people's returning from exile and bears no relation to the purported mission of John as the forerunner of the Messiah. No exile was terminated during John's lifetime.

Only superficial comparisons between Isaiah's prophecy and the life of John, not true to the contexts of either Isaiah's or Malachi's prophecies, can and will be made by Christian missionary theologians. The shallowness of such claims is easily recognizable to the careful reader. In view of John's emphatic denial of having any connection with Elijah (John 1:21), it becomes obvious that either Jesus or John was in error about the role of the latter.

If John was that prophet, in any form, he failed to carry out God's commission to Elijah. The forerunner of the Messiah is expected to usher in an era of perfect peace and harmony between fathers and their children, ending all discord and strife between them. Thus, Malachi states: "And he shall turn the heart of the fathers to the children, and the heart of the children to their fathers." John's mission was supposed to be "to turn the hearts of the fathers back to the children, and the disobedient to the attitude of the righteous; so as to make ready a people prepared for the Lord" (Luke 1:17). This John the Baptist failed to do. For his part, Jesus explains his own function as the exact opposite not only of Elijah's mission but of John's as well. For Jesus said:

> Do not think that I came to bring peace on earth; I did not come to bring peace, but a sword. For I came to set a man against his father, and a daughter against her mother, and a daughter-in-law against her mother-in-law. (Matthew 10:34–35)

> I have come to cast fire upon the earth; and how I wish it were already kindled! But I have a baptism to undergo, and how distressed I am until it is accomplished! Do you suppose that I came to grant peace on earth? I tell you, no, but rather division; for from now on five members in one household will be divided, three against two, and two against three. They will be divided, father against son, and son against father; mother against daughter, and daughter against mother; mother-in-law against daughter-in-law, and daughter-in-law against mother-in-law. (Luke 12:49–53)

There is no doubt that Malachi says Elijah is the forerunner of the Messiah and that Malachi 3:1 and 3:23–24 refer to the actual person of Elijah. These verses relate to his coming immediately preceding the Messiah's arrival. Since Elijah has not come beforehand, we are compelled to conclude that Jesus could not be the Messiah.

---

1. There would have been no need for Elijah to ascend to heaven bodily (2 Kings 2:11) if only his "spirit and power" were going to return.

19

YOU ARE MY SON

(Psalms 2)

In the Christian missionary search for biblical proof of the belief in Jesus as the Son of God, proof has often been found where none exists by violating the integrity of the plain meaning of many scriptural passages. Prominent among these is Psalm 2:7, wherein it is stated: "The Lord said to me: 'You are My son, this day I have begotten you.' " An examination of the context will show that this verse refers to the father-and-son relationship between God and David. A similar relationship later existed between God and Solomon (2 Samuel 7:14; 1 Chronicles 22:10, 28:6). This special relationship is not to be taken in a literal sense. The adoption of an individual or a whole people by God is called, in the Scriptures, "to beget" (Deuteronomy 32:18). David, on his ascension to the throne, was declared to be begotten of God. The title of son is given to all those who enjoy a special relationship with God (Exodus 4:22, Hosea 2:1). Christian missionaries may argue that the references to sonship are typologies pointing to the existence of an actual divine sonship embodied in Jesus. But this argument is obviously based on purely subjective reasoning, with no facts from the Hebrew Scriptures to give it support.

Psalm 2:7 could not at all refer to Jesus. The verse says: "The Lord said to me: 'You are My son . . .' " Why would God have to inform Jesus, a fellow member of the Trinity, of the exact nature of their relationship? The verse then continues: ". . . this day I have begotten you." If Jesus is God, how can he be begotten? Are we to presume that this statement was made on the day of Jesus' conception, and that God spoke to the fertilized egg? Moreover, should we presume that this fertilized egg had the ability to answer God, as is implied in verse 8? There God states: "Ask of Me, and I will give the nations for your inheritance, and the ends of the earth for your possession." Would Jesus, if he was a member of the Trinity, with all its implications, have to make this request of God? Did Jesus have to ask for these or any other possessions? If he were God, the heavens and the earth and all that they contain are already his possessions. Furthermore, if Jesus had the ability to understand God's statement on the very day of his conception, it would seem incongruous for the New Testament to describe him as "increasing in wisdom and in physical growth with both God and men" (Luke 2:52). This offer by God would have had no meaning since Matthew 20:28 and Mark 10:45 say Jesus came to serve, not to be served. Did God make an empty offer? If the statement "This day I have begotten you" was made to Jesus at a date later than the day of his conception, and is thus figurative in meaning, he is then not distinguished from all the others who are in the "sonship of God."

According to the New Testament accounts, Jesus certainly did not have an earthly kingdom during his lifetime. If this is supposed to occur during a second coming, then we come to a further problem. It is alleged that at that time Jesus would be coming back not in an earthly state, but exalted and as God. That being the case, he would not have to ask for either "inheritance" or "possession." Actually, verse 7 does not mean that David was to inherit literally "the ends of the earth." It is an obvious hyperbole, the true meaning of which is, a large expanse of territory, and can only apply to a human being who, unlike God, or allegedly Jesus, does not possess all of creation. Similar hyperboles can be found in the Scriptures, i.e., "There was *no end* to his treasures . . . and there was *no end* to his chariots" (Isaiah 2:7), and David, who never left the vicinity of the Land of Israel, says: "From the end of the earth I will call you" (Psalms 61:3).

A related statement parallel to that of Psalm 2:7 is found in Psalm 89:28: "I will also appoint him firstborn, the highest of the kings of the earth." Since the latter verse clearly refers to the actual person of David, and not to any typological Messiah, as is evident from verses 4, 21, 27, 36, and 37, there is good reason to assume that Psalm 2:7 refers to King David.

There is no doubt that when the true Messiah comes he will rule the nations, as can be seen from Isaiah 11, and we do not have to seek out references where none exist. Psalm 2 is an historical psalm and does not speak about the messianic age.

In Psalm 2:12 it is stated: "Do homage in purity [*nash-ku bar*], lest He be angry, and you perish in the way...." The Christian translation of the Hebrew phrase *nash-ku bar* as "kiss the son" is based on a misinterpretation. The meaning of the Hebrew word בר (*bar*) is "pure" or "clear." Only in Aramaic does it have the meaning of "son." However, in Aramaic, *bar* is used only as a construct "son of" (Proverbs 31:2; Ezra 5:1–2, 6:14), whereas the absolute form of "son" in Aramaic (which would have to be used in verse 12) is ברא (*ber᾽a*), Thus, according to the Christian conception, the verse should have read *nash-ku ber᾽a*, "kiss the son," not *nash-ku bar*, "kiss the son of." Even though "son" could refer to David in verse 12, it is not the proper translation. There is no compelling reason to employ an Aramaism in view of the use of the Hebrew noun *bayn*, "son," in verse 7. The phrase is best rendered as, "do homage in purity," because kissing is generally an expression of homage, as found, for example, in 1 Samuel 10:1: "Then Samuel took the vial of oil, and poured it upon his head, *and kissed him.*" *Bar*, meaning "purity," occurs in the phrase "pure in heart" (Psalms 24:4, 73:1). The intention implied in verse 12 is: with sincerity of heart, acknowledge me, David, as God's anointed, and thereby avoid incurring God's anger. Thus, the Hebrew phrase *nash-ku bar* simply means "do homage in purity," and superimposing any other interpretation will distort the meaning of this psalm.

20

THE PSALMIST AND THE RESURRECTION OF JESUS

(Psalms 16:9–10)

Therefore my heart is glad, and my glory rejoices; my flesh also dwells in safety. For You will not abandon my soul to the nether-world; neither will You allow Your faithful one to see the pit.

(Psalms 16:9–10)

The author of Acts claims that this is a foreshadowing of the resurrection of Jesus. Thus, he has Peter state:

He [David] saw beforehand and spoke concerning the resurrection of the Christ, that neither was he forsaken in Hades nor did his flesh see corruption. (Acts 2:31)

The author then quotes Paul as stating:

That He raised him up from the dead, no more to return to corruption, He has stated in this way: "I will give you the loving-kindnesses and faithful things of David." Therefore He also says in another psalm: "You will not allow Your loyal one to see corruption." For David, after he had served the purpose of God in his own generation, fell asleep, and was laid among his fathers, and did see corruption; but he whom God raised did not see corruption. (Acts 13:34–37)

The application of David's words to explain the disappearance of Jesus' body is without foundation. These verses were seized upon as proof-texts by desperate men attempting to explain the disappearance of Jesus' body to his followers. However, even the New Testament does not provide any concrete proof for the allegation that the physical or spiritual resurrection of Jesus ever took place. Although Peter states: "This Jesus God resurrected, of which we are all witnesses" (Acts 2:32), absolutely no one saw the alleged resurrection take place, in any form whatsoever. At best, the only statement that can be made is that the body was missing. Nothing definite can be said concerning its final disposition at the time of the alleged resurrection. All the information concerning this alleged event is derived from the New Testament. The New Testament, while not a contemporary document, is the earliest and only source of information on the subject of the resurrection of Jesus. However, it lacks the necessary factual information to allow one to learn about the final disposition of the physical remains of Jesus. Moreover, the New Testament writers often explicitly indicate that the alleged postresurrection appearances were sightings of individuals who did not look or sound like Jesus. Jesus' disciples and the early Christian community simply did not really know what had happened to the remains of their crucified leader.

If the psalmist's words are to be used as an explanation of what happened to the entombed physical remains of Jesus, there is no reason for not applying the statement: "My flesh also dwells in safety" to his entire lifetime as well. The Hebrew verb *yishkon*, "dwells," appears in the imperfect tense, which denotes incomplete action. It is used to express a continuation of an action that starts at a point in time and continues on into the future. Did Jesus' body "dwell in safety," never seeing any form of "corruption," i.e., decay, as implied by the statements attributed to Peter and Paul in Acts? If we apply the words, "my flesh also dwells in safety," to Jesus the god-man, then what happened to his foreskin after his circumcision (Luke 2:21)? Did it ascend to heaven, or did it decompose as with any human piece of flesh? During his lifetime what happened to his hair, nails, and blood shed from wounds? Did the cells of his body die as in ordinary human beings? If his body did not function in a truly human way, he could not be truly human as well as truly God. Yet if his body functioned exactly in a human way, this would nullify any claim to divinity. It would be impossible for any part of God, even if incarnate, to decompose in any way and still be considered God. By definition, not mystery, the everlasting, one God, in whole or in part, does not die, disintegrate, or decompose: "For I the Lord do not change" (Malachi 3:6).

The New Testament writers are ambivalent on the subject of whether Jesus was resurrected with a physical body or only as a spirit. For our discussion, the crucial time period is at the moment the alleged resurrection took place. However, we must take into consideration the nature of the alleged later appearances as well. Luke and John write in their respective Gospels that Jesus appeared, on occasion, after the resurrection in a physical body. John illustrates this by having Jesus order Mary Magdalene to stop touching him (John 20:17). By this he wishes to show that the body of Jesus was, after the resurrection, a tangible object. John continues in this manner when he writes that Thomas was instructed by the resurrected Jesus to touch him. While nothing is mentioned of his actually touching Jesus, the reader is left with the impression that what Thomas discerned was the physical nature of Jesus.

> And after eight days again his disciples were inside, and Thomas with them. Jesus came, the doors having been shut, and stood in the midst, and said: "Peace be to you." Then he said to Thomas: "Put your finger here, and see my hands, and take your hand and thrust it into my side. . ." (John 20:26–27)

The author of John does not indicate whether the apparition actually looked like Jesus.

In his Gospel, Luke states emphatically that Jesus was not a spirit. He claims that Jesus appeared in an actual physical body, without clearly indicating whether it was the same body as he had before his death: " 'See my hands and my feet, that it is I myself; touch me and see, for a spirit does not have flesh and bones as you see that I have.' And when he said this he showed them his hands and his feet" (Luke 24:39–40). The evangelist then states that Jesus requested food from the disciples which he proceeded to eat (Luke 24:41–43). Luke suggests that a definite physical resurrection took place. The implication of his words is that whereas a spirit is not a tangible object, which one is able to touch, the postresurrection Jesus was an actual physical being that could be touched and was even capable of consuming food. Luke, the purported author of Acts, put this same viewpoint into the mouths of Peter (Acts 2:31) and Paul (Acts 13:34–37). Whatever Luke or John may have believed about the tangibility of Jesus' body when he allegedly appeared to his followers, the respective epistles attributed to Peter and Paul state emphatically that Jesus did not rise in a physical body. In Paul's explanation of the nature of the body at the time of the resurrection, he denies the physical resurrection, saying that the "natural body" is buried, but what is raised is a "spiritual body" (1 Corinthians 15:44). This he applies not just to ordinary human beings, but even to Jesus. Although Paul refers to the postresurrection Jesus as a "man" in 1 Timothy 2:5, he obviously does not mean that Jesus is a physical man. Paul emphatically declares the risen Jesus to be spirit, not flesh: "The last Adam [literally "man" in Hebrew] became a life-giving spirit" (1 Corinthians 15:45). Accordingly, Paul's resurrected Jesus was not a man in the physical sense, but rather, a spiritual man. The author of the First Epistle of Peter states that the change from flesh to spirit occurred at the moment of resurrection. He states that Jesus was "put to death in the flesh, but made alive in the spirit" (1 Peter 3:18). The epistles attributed to Peter and Paul provide information which is in direct contradiction to the claim that Jesus rose in a physical body from his tomb. According to Luke 24:39, cited above, "a spirit does not have flesh and bones," but in the same verse Luke declares that Jesus did have flesh and bones. Obviously, Luke does not believe Jesus was a spirit, as Peter and Paul claim in the writings attributed to them.

Some Christian missionary exegetes attempt to harmonize the differences of opinion among the New Testament writers by conjecturing that Jesus had a "glorified" physical body. Therefore, they claim, he could enter locked rooms, appearing and disappearing at will. Others take the view that God disposed of the physical body of Jesus without resorting to the process of decay. Both Peter and Paul propagate a belief that Jesus' physical body was not preserved for use by the resurrected Jesus. While they do not speculate as to how the physical body was disposed of, neither do they mention a "glorified" physical body. In fact, what they teach is quite contrary to this belief. Paul believes that Jesus had a "body of glory" (Philippians 3:21) but does not state that it was a physical body. Paul definitely rules out a physical resurrection in any form for Jesus when he states: "Flesh and blood cannot inherit the kingdom of God" (1 Corinthians 15:50). Obviously, even according to the New Testament, Jesus did not fulfill the psalmist's statement, "My flesh dwells in safety."

The psalmist's words can only make sense if they are a poetic reference to David's gratitude to God for watching over him throughout his life, rather than to the allegedly resurrected body of a divine being.

21

THE PSALMIST AND THE CRUCIFIXION OF JESUS

(Psalms 22)

The early Christians, in interpreting and expanding the accounts of Jesus' death, sought confirmation of their claims in the Hebrew Scriptures. Believing Jesus to be the fulfillment of biblical prophecy, they proclaimed him the Messiah. The Scriptures were searched for evidence which could be used to demonstrate the truth of their hypotheses. This was especially true for the crucifixion since such a fate does not easily fit into the prophetic visions of a triumphant Messiah. That is why early Christianity inserted many scriptural references within the account of the crucifixion, altering at the same time some of the details of the crucifixion story in order to coordinate them with these scriptural references. In this effort, Psalm 22 played a crucial role. Indeed, it has become, for Christianity, a major proof-text for the most important elements of the several crucifixion accounts.

There are several versions recorded by the evangelists as to what were Jesus' last words from the cross. Mark, followed in the main by Matthew, gives this account:

> And at the ninth hour Jesus called out with a loud voice: "Eloi, Eloi, lama sabachthani?" which is translated: "My God, my God, why have you forsaken me?" And some of the bystanders having heard it were saying: "Behold, he is calling for Elijah." And someone ran and filled a sponge full of sour wine, put it on a reed, and gave it to him to drink, saying: "Let us see whether Elijah will come to take him down." And Jesus uttered a loud cry, and expired. (Mark 15:34–37)

Jesus' cry of anguish: "My God, my God, why have you forsaken me?" is the open sentence of Psalm 22. But why should Jesus have expressed this sentiment? Why should he have thought of himself as separated from God at the very moment when, according to Christian missionary theology, he was fulfilling God's plan? Luke and John omit this cry in their crucifixion accounts, and instead, imply that Jesus himself was in complete control of the event. According to Luke the final cry of Jesus was: "Father, into your hands I commit my spirit" (Luke 23:46), words taken from Psalm 31:6. John also views the crucifixion not as an abandonment by God, but as the conclusion of Jesus' divine mission, in which he peacefully surrenders his soul to God: "He bowed his head and gave up his spirit" (John 19:30).

Christian missionary interpreters, in their attempt to explain Jesus' feeling of abandonment, as recorded by Matthew and Mark, claim that in reality Jesus had in mind, not only the despairing words with which Psalm 22 opens, but also the trusting words with which this psalm ends. But this amounts to putting words in Jesus' mouth. That Jesus knew the theme of the entire psalm is of no consequence. What matters is that he made use only of the opening words of the psalm, expressing despair, and failed to continue with the concluding words of the psalm, which are expressive of hope and trust in God. Furthermore, it makes little sense to see in Psalm 22, prophecies depicting the agony felt by Jesus at his crucifixion. Are we to believe that Jesus, who is supposed to be God's equal, and His only begotten son, fell into deep depression and anguish because God refused to help him in his hour of need? Besides, why should he offer prayers to be saved from a fate that he is knowingly supposed to endure in order to redeem mankind from the power of sin. How could Jesus have entertained the thought that he was forsaken by God, if by his death mankind was given the only means of attaining salvation? If, as the Gospels assume, Jesus knew and predicted long in advance the events surrounding his death, and if these events were neither a surprise nor a defeat, but a working out of a divinely designed plan, what sense does it make for Jesus to complain: "My God, my God, why have you forsaken me?" Earlier, in Gethsemane, Jesus is alleged to have prayed that God should spare him from having to undergo his bitter fate. However, Jesus added that not his will, but God's will, should be done (Matthew 26:36–45, Mark 14:32–41, Luke 22:41–44). Why did Jesus give vent to feelings of despair and failure while supposedly knowing that he was really acting out a preordained cosmic plan? "After this, Jesus, knowing that all things had already been accomplished, in order that the Scripture might be fulfilled, said: 'I am thirsty' " (John 19:28). Despite John's claim, Jesus obviously had neither foreknowledge nor control of events. We must conclude that in those last agonizing minutes he truly felt personally abandoned, his mission coming to grief. Such being the case, Jesus could not be the Messiah that Christian missionaries believe him to be. In sum, if he was the Messiah, as envisioned by Christian missionaries, he would have known that the crucifixion was essential to his mission; on the other hand, if we are to assume that he knew this, then his words of despair were deceiving, something unbefitting the true Messiah.

Psalm 22 cannot be made to apply to the life of Jesus. Jesus' life ends on a note of disappointment, whereas the psalmist, after describing metaphorically his trials and tribulations, concludes on a positive note. No such positive position is taken by Jesus. If he fulfilled literally all of Psalm 22, instead of selective parts, the logical order of development would be for depression to give way to joy as he realizes God's purpose has been attained through his act of sacrificial death.

Christian missionary apologists assert that the Hebrew word כארי *(ka-ʾari)* in verse 17 (16 in some versions) should be translated as "pierce." They render this verse as: "They pierced my hands and my feet." This follows the Septuagint version, used by the early Christians, whose error is repeated by the Vulgate and the Syriac. This rendering contains two fallacies. First, assuming that the root of this Hebrew word is *krh* (כרה), "to dig," then the function of the *ʾaleph* in the word *ka-ʾari* is inexplicable since it is not part of the root. *Karah* consists only of the Hebrew letters *kaph, resh,* and *he,* whereas the word in the Hebrew text, *ka-ʾari,* consists of *kaph, ʾaleph, resh,* and *yod.* Second, the verb *krh,* "to dig," does not have the meaning "to pierce." *Karah* generally refers to the digging of the soil, and is never applied in the Scriptures to the piercing of the flesh (cf. Genesis 26:25, Exodus 21:33; Numbers 21:18; Jeremiah 18:20; 22; Psalms 7:16, 57:7). There are a number of words which are used in Hebrew for piercing the body: *ratsʿa,* "to pierce," "to bore with an anvil" (Exodus 21:6); *dakar,* "to pierce" (Zechariah 12:10, Isaiah 13:15); *nakar,* "to pierce," "to bore," "to perforate" (2 Kings 18:21). This last word is used in a very significant sense in the last verse cited: "It [the reed] will go into his hand and pierce it." Any of these words would be far better suited for use in this passage than one which is generally used to denote digging the soil.

The correct interpretation of the verse must be based on the elliptical style of this particular psalm. The text should read, in effect: "Like a lion [they are gnawing at] my hands and my feet." Ellipsis (the omission of words) is an apt rhetorical device for a composition in which suffering and agony is described. A person in agony does not usually express his feelings in complete round sentences. Such a person is capable of exclaiming only the most critical words of his thoughts and feelings. In this case: "Like a lion . . . my hands and my feet!" Similarly, in verse 1 we find broken phrases rather than whole sentences: "Far from helping me . . . the words of my roaring."

Examining Psalm 22, we find that verses 17, 21, and 22 express parallel thoughts. In verse 17, the psalmist speaks of "dogs" and "a lion," which are metaphoric representations of his enemies, and in verses 21 and 22 respectively, he beseeches the Almighty to save him "from a dog's paw" and "from a lion's mouth." Thus, in verse 17, where he complains of the lion, the missing words are understood, and it is to be read: "Like a lion [they are gnawing at] my hands and my feet." This is the most plausible interpretation of the text. Rashi's interpretation of the verse—"As if crushed by the mouth of a lion are my hands and my feet"—is similar in thought to the one we have offered though differently stated. While these interpretations fit with the diction of the entire psalm, the Christian translation—"They pierced my hands and my feet"—does not.

Grammatical proof of the correctness of the Masoretic text is seen by the use of the *qamatz* under the *kaph* in *ka-ʾari*, which is the result of an assimilated definite article. Thus, the literal translation would be "Like the lion . . ." While in English, a noun used in a general sense is recognized by having no article, either definite or indefinite, in Hebrew, as well as in many other languages, such nouns take the definite article. For example, "Work is good for man" in Hebrew would be *"The* work is good for man." (Cf. Amos 5:19 with the English translation.)

The metaphorical terminology used by the psalmist to express in physical terms his mental anguish is comparable to similar usage found in Jeremiah 23:9, where the prophet exclaims: "My heart within me is broken, all my bones shake; I am like a drunken man, and like a man whom wine has overcome."

Psalm 22:19 (18 in some versions) reads: "They divide my clothes among them, and for my garment they cast lots." A misunderstanding by the author of the Gospel of John influenced the way he applied this verse to his version of the division-of-the-clothing incident (John 19:24; cf. Matthew 27:35, Luke 23:34). He misinterpreted the Hebrew parallelism as referring to two separate acts. In biblical poetry, which is based on parallel structure, the repetition of an idea does not indicate its duplication in reality (cf. Zechariah 9:9). Seeking to harmonize this crucifixion event with the psalm, John states that the soldiers divided Jesus' garments among themselves, but that they could not divide the inner garment, which was seamless, so they cast lots for it. "They said therefore to one another: 'Let us not tear it, but let us decide by lot whose it will be'; that the Scripture might be fulfilled: 'They divided my outer garment among themselves, and for my apparel they cast lots' " (John 19:24). Evidently, John created this legendary crucifixion event to meet what he believed to be a messianic requirement of Psalm 22. In this way, the crucifixion tradition was rounded out to agree with what John thought was the prophetic message of this psalm.

22

A FAMILIAR FRIEND

(Psalms 41:10)

Even my own familiar friend, in whom I trusted, who did eat of my bread, has lifted his heel against me.

(Psalms 41:10)

Utilizing the last half of this verse, the Gospel of John has Jesus predict Judas' betrayal: "He who eats my bread has lifted up his heel against me" (John 13:18). John thus infers that Psalm 41 alludes to events in the life of Jesus. However, one cannot legitimately pick and choose only those parts of a verse that seem to refer to a future event while totally disregarding the rest. There is no reasonable justification for taking a verse out of context, then fragmenting it to make it apply to a particular individual, while treating the rest of the psalm as being inapplicable. The full verse and, in fact, the entire psalm should be treated as one integral unit.

It was a theological necessity for John to fragment verse 10 (verse 9 in some versions), because the full verse, and indeed the whole psalm, would otherwise interfere with his concept of a sinless, all-knowing, god-man. Jesus, as an all-knowing god-man, would know the meaning this psalm had in his life. He would also know what Judas' function would ultimately be. John's Jesus had the specific foreknowledge that Judas would eventually be a traitor; therefore, he could not say, in all honesty, that Judas was a "familiar friend" or, as poignantly put in the literal Hebrew, "the man of my peace." Moreover, if Jesus could tell no lie, Judas certainly would not be referred to as one "in whom I trusted." Obviously, John's Jesus would have to know that Judas could not be trusted and that it was inevitable that he would be a traitor.

Psalm 41:10 concerns a betrayal by one who was trusted and ate at the table of the betrayed. The psalmist expresses feelings of dismay and hurt at being betrayed by a person extremely close to him, one whom he never thought would betray him. By contrast, the all-knowing god-man, Jesus, must have known the heart of Judas even long before he met him. Indeed, John's Jesus knew when Judas was about to betray him: "What you do, do quickly" he says as Judas leaves to inform Jesus' enemies of his whereabouts (John 13:27).

As already stated, this psalm is an integral unit, and it thus must apply in its entirety to the same individual. With this in mind let us study verse 5 (verse 4 in some versions): "As for me, I said: O Lord, be gracious to me, heal my soul; for I have sinned against You." Applied to Jesus, it would mean that Jesus admits to being a sinner against God. There is no way to consider this psalm, in whole or in part, as a prophecy of the betrayal of Jesus without considering that he was also a sinner.

23

MIXED-UP DRINKS

(Psalms 69:22)

In order to justify faith in Jesus as the Messiah, the evangelists scanned the Hebrew Scriptures for verses they might employ in their writings. The evangelists sought to legitimatize their declarations by taking verses out of context. However, their attempts to subtly delude the Gospel reader into believing their arguments do not succeed when one studies these verses in context. For example, Psalm 69:22 (verse 21 in some versions) states: "They put poison into my food; and in my thirst they gave me vinegar to drink." Taking these words out of context, the evangelists sought to prove that Jesus fulfilled this verse. Matthew writes that when Jesus was on the cross, "They gave him wine to drink mingled with gall, and after tasting it, he was unwilling to drink" (Matthew 27:34). Matthew employed the Greek word *khole* ("gall"), the same term found in the Septuagint version of Psalm 69:22 and which he obviously applied directly from that source.

The veracity of Matthew's claim to scriptural fulfillment is seemingly verified by the testimony of Mark 15:23: "And they tried to give him wine mixed with myrrh; but he did not take it." However, Mark's account differs from Matthew's in that it mentions myrrh. This has given rise to the opinion, among some Christian missionaries, that in this case the "poison" or "gall" was myrrh. This, of course, disregards the fact that there was no reason for the psalmist to employ the word ראש *(roʾsh)*, "poison" or "gall", when he could have easily used the word מור *(mor)*, "myrrh." *Roʾsh*, the word used by the psalmist and variously translated as "poison" or "gall," may perhaps mean more

102

specifically either hemlock, colocynth, or the poppy (opium). No certain identification of this poisonous plant is now possible. In many instances, *ro'sh* refers to either a poisonous plant (Lamentations 3:5, 19); poison or venom (Deuteronomy 32:33, Job 20:16), or poisonous water (Jeremiah 8:14, 9:14, 23:15). It is used figuratively for the perversion of justice (Hosea 10:4, Amos 6:12) and for describing apostasy (Deuteronomy 29:17). To resolve the discrepancy as to whether gall or myrrh was used, some Christian missionaries suggest that the drink may have contained both gall and myrrh. The fact remains that *ro'sh* is not *mor*. Myrrh, although bitter tasting, is not poisonous and is even used in medicine. Luke and John do not even mention the alleged incident.

Christian missionaries, agreeing with the evangelists, claim that Psalm 69:22 refers to Jesus. However, verse 22 cannot pertain to Jesus. When was poison (gall) put into Jesus' food? Where is there mention of Jesus eating food at the crucifixion? It is doubtful that the psalm is referring to wine as food. How were the Hebrew Scriptures fulfilled on the cross?

"Wine mingled with gall"; "wine mixed with myrrh"! Because we Jews refused to accept their misunderstandings and misinterpretations of the Scriptures, the followers of Jesus have mingled our blood with the dust of the earth. To any Jew who entertains the idea that Jesus is the Messiah, the words of the true God spoken to Cain come to say: "What have you done? the voice of your brother's blood cries to Me from the ground" (Genesis 4:10).

24

MY LORD

(Psalms 110:1, 4)

A psalm concerning David. The Lord says to my lord: "Sit at My right hand, until I make your enemies your footstool." . . . "You are a priest forever after the manner of Melchizedek."

(Psalms 110:1, 4)

The early Christians believed that Psalm 110 contained material to bolster their belief that Jesus was greater than David and was not only the Messiah but a divine being as well (Matthew 22:42–45, Mark 12:35–37, Luke 20:41–44, Acts 2:34–36, Hebrews 1:13). Yet a careful examination finds their hypothesis to be totally without merit.

Since *le-David* does not always mean "written by David," but sometimes "concerning David" or "in the style of David," it cannot be said with certainty that the preposition *le*, often translated "of," actually indicates "composed by," David. Further investigation is necessary in order to understand its meaning as militated by the context of this psalm.

Psalm 72 was written by David "for," or "concerning," Solomon (cf. verses 1 and 20), yet the Hebrew contains an introductory phrase similar to the one found in Psalm 110. The introductory statement, *li-Shlomo*, stresses that the psalm is "concerning" Solomon rather than that it is by Solomon. Even more significant is 2 Samuel 22:51 and Psalm 144:10, where David speaks of himself in the third person. Accordingly, there is every indication that the proper translation of Psalm 110:1 is: "A Psalm concerning David. The Lord says to my lord: 'Sit at My right hand, until I make your enemies your footstool.'" David is writing this psalm from the perspective of the individual who is going to recite it. From this perspective, David, as king, is appropriately referred to as "my lord." Perhaps David wrote this psalm in the third person out of humility, not wishing to boast of the exalted position granted him by God. However, the claim that David is referring to Jesus by the phrase "my lord" is invalid (see below p. 141).

The privilege of sitting at the right hand is a mark of distinction (1 Kings 2:19). When God invites David to "sit at My right hand," it is to show the privileged position enjoyed by David in his relationship with God. It is not to be taken as literally indicating sitting at God's right hand. The terminology "right hand" is here used as an expression of God's favoritism toward David.

"You are a priest forever after the manner of Melchizedek" (verse 4). David was not a priest in the manner of the priesthood of Aaron, but rather a priest of God, "after the manner of Melchizedek." Genesis 14:18 describes Melchizedek as "king of Salem" and "priest of God Most High." Melchizedek and David each ruled his people in accordance with God's will as priest-king. The Hebrew term le'olam, commonly rendered in English as "forever," is not necessarily always synonymous with "eternal." It is frequently used with the meaning "for a very long time," or "for an indefinite period," or, as in the verse under discussion, to indicate the normal life-span of an individual (cf. Exodus 21:6). Thus, "You are a priest forever" means that David discharged certain priestly functions during his lifetime. We are informed that, on occasion, David wore the sacerdotal ephod (2 Samuel 6:14) and "offered burnt-offerings and peace-offerings before the Lord" (2 Samuel 6:17–18).

In his interpretation of Psalm 110 the author of Hebrews makes statements concerning Melchizedek which have no basis in fact: "Without father, without mother, without genealogy, having neither beginning of days nor end of life, but having been made like the Son of God, he remains a priest perpetually" (Hebrews 7:3). The Scriptures contain no such distorted information. The absence of any reference to his descent does not justify the extreme statement that Melchizedek had "neither beginning of days nor end of life." There is absolutely no biblical foundation for such a conclusion. Moreover, Melchizedek cannot be identified as an earlier manifestation of Jesus. If he was "made like the Son of God," he could not actually *be* "the Son." However, "having been made like the Son of God, he remains a priest perpetually" is asserting that Melchizedek did not just typify Jesus, but was something more than a mere mortal. It appears that the writer of Hebrews gives Melchizedek an existence not possible for a human being. If Melchizedek, without father, mother, or genealogy, has "neither beginning of days nor end of life" and has "been made like the Son of God," he must be an eternal being.[1] Elevated to the status of a divinity, Melchizedek is lifted to a level equal to the members of the Trinity. Thus, he becomes a fourth member of the Christian godhead, thereby replacing the Trinity with a Quaternity. This addition of Melchizedek to the Christian godhead to form a Quaternity, rather than a Trinity, is the only conclusion to be drawn from the information provided by the author of Hebrews (see below 284–285).

The New Testament writers have misconstrued Psalm 110 as a reference to Jesus. The biblically unsound arguments they present are vain attempts to prove that Jesus was more than a mere mortal.

---

1. According to Hebrews, Melchizedek could not have been an angel since angels are created beings and, as such, have a "beginning of days."

25

WHAT IS HIS SON'S NAME?

(Proverbs 30:4)

In an attempt to prove the divine origin of Jesus, Christian missionary theologians have pointed to this proverb as a proof-text for their claim. However, an examination of what the text actually says will dispel any attempt at such a forced interpretation.

After informing us that he does not have all the wisdom and understanding that he should possess, Agur, the son of Jakeh, poses a series of rhetorical questions, the answers to which he realizes all men who seek knowledge should possess:

> Who has ascended up into heaven, and descended?
> Who has gathered the wind in his fists?
> Who has bound the waters in his garment?
> Who has established all the ends of the earth?
> What is his name, and what is his son's name, if you know?
> (Proverbs 30:4)

Knowing the answers to these questions is to know the fundamentals of all knowledge.

The answer to the question "What is his name?" is given in the Scriptures, where we are informed that only God, the creator of heaven and earth, is in complete control of the forces of nature. Following this question a second question is asked: "What is his son's name?" As the first question is readily answered through a reading of the Scriptures, the source of all true knowledge, so, too, the second question is to be answered by studying the same source. We thus obtain the answer by studying such verses as

Exodus 4:22: "Israel is My Son, My firstborn"; Deuteronomy 14:1: "You are the children of the Lord your God"; and Hosea 2:1: "It will be said to them: 'You are the children of the living God.' " Consequently, it is Israel that is the name of His son, His firstborn. True, we find elsewhere in the Bible that David and Solomon stand in a filial relationship with God (Psalms 89:27–28, 1 Chronicles 22:10, 28:6). Indeed, this will also be true of the future Messiah. But the right to this title is due, in the final analysis, to the fact that they are the representatives or personifications of Israel as a whole. Hence, it is Israel which is the sole bearer of the august title of the "son" or "firstborn" of God.

Christian missionary theology may argue that any reference to Israel's relationship with God only points to an allegedly greater relationship between God and Jesus, but this argument remains unproved, having no basis in the Hebrew Scriptures. It is an argument based on misguided motives, trying to prove the preconceived by forced interpretation. Only in a figurative sense will the future Messiah, when he comes, enter into the "sonship" of God, a position he will share with all of God's chosen servants.

26

DANIEL'S SEVENTY WEEKS

(Daniel 9:24–27)

Seventy weeks are decreed upon your people and upon your holy city, to finish the transgression, and to make an end of sin, and to forgive iniquity, and to bring in everlasting righteousness, and to seal vision and prophet, and to anoint the Holy of Holies. Know therefore and understand that from the going forth of the word to restore and to build Jerusalem until an anointed one, a prince, shall be seven weeks; then for sixty-two weeks it shall be built again, with broad place and moat, but in troubled times. And after the sixty-two weeks an anointed one shall be cut off, and he shall have nothing; and the people of a prince that shall come shall destroy the city and the Sanctuary; but his end shall be with a flood; and to the end of the war desolations are determined. And he shall make a strong covenant with many for one week; and for half of the week he shall cause sacrifice and offering to cease; and upon the wing of detestable things shall be that which causes appalment; and that until the extermination wholly determined be poured out upon that which causes appalment.

(Daniel 9:24–27)

The King James Version of the Bible renders Daniel 9:24–27 as follows:

Seventy weeks are determined upon thy people and upon thy holy city, to finish the transgression, and to make an end of sins, and to make reconciliation for iniquity, and to bring in everlasting righteousness, and to seal up the vision and prophecy, and to anoint the most Holy. Know therefore and understand, that from the going forth of the commandment to restore and to build Jerusalem unto the Messiah the Prince shall be seven weeks, and threescore and two weeks: the street shall be built again, and the wall, even in troublous times. And after threescore and two weeks shall Messiah be cut off, but not for himself: and the people of the prince that shall come shall destroy the city and the sanctuary; and the end thereof shall be with a flood, and unto the end of the war desolations are determined. And he shall confirm the covenant with many for one week: and in the midst of the week he shall cause the sacrifice and the oblation to cease, and for the overspreading of abominations he shall make it desolate, even until the consummation, and that determined shall be poured upon the desolate.

Our objections to various Christian missionary interpretations of Daniel 9:24–27 are based on the missionaries subscribing in whole or in part to the following incorrect suppositions (the King James Version of the Bible will be used as the main example since it contains the grossest errors, which are, in whole or in part, duplicated by other Christian versions of the Bible):

1. The King James Version puts a definite article before "Messiah the Prince" (9:25).
   a. The original Hebrew text does not read "*the* Messiah the Prince," but, having no article, it is to be rendered "a *mashiach* ("anointed one," "messiah"), a prince," i.e., Cyrus (Isaiah 45:1, 13; Ezra 1:1–2).
   b. The word *mashiach* is nowhere used in Scripture as a proper name, but as a title of authority of a king or high priest.
   c. Therefore, a correct rendering of the original Hebrew should be: "an anointed one, a prince."
2. The King James Version disregards the Hebrew punctuation:
   a. The punctuation mark *ʾatnaḥ* (⅄) functions as the main pause within a sentence. The *ʾatnaḥ* is the approximate equivalent of the semicolon in the modern system of punctuation. It thus has the effect of separating the seven weeks from the sixty-two weeks: ". . . until an anointed one, a prince, shall be seven weeks; then for sixty-two weeks it shall be built again. . ." (9:25).

    b. By creating a sixty-nine week period which is not divided into two separate periods of seven weeks and sixty-two weeks respectively, Christian missionaries reach an incorrect conclusion, i.e., that the Messiah will come 483 years after the destruction of the First Temple.[1]

3. The King James Version omits the definite article in Daniel 9:26, which should read: "And after *the* threescore and two weeks. . ." By treating the sixty-two weeks as a distinct period, this verse, in the original Hebrew, shows that the sixty-two weeks mentioned in verse 25 are correctly separated from the seven weeks by the *ʾatnaḥ*. Hence, two anointed ones are spoken of in this chapter, one of whom comes after seven weeks, and the other after a further period of sixty-two weeks.

4. The words *vʾayn lo* (9:26) are incorrectly translated by the King James Version as "but not for himself." It should be translated as "he has nothing" or "he shall have nothing." How can Christian missionaries apply this verse and Isaiah 53:12, where God's servant receives "a portion with the great," to Jesus? Moreover, *vʾayn lo* cannot refer to Jesus' situation at or after death, for, unlike mere mortal bodies which decay after death, Christian missionaries claim that Jesus rose bodily into heaven, where he sits at the "right hand of the throne of the Majesty." It certainly could not refer to a lack of wealth or followers, for this would not distinguish Jesus from the great majority of the world's population. One who "has nothing" (Daniel 9:26) does not receive "a portion with the great" (Isaiah 53:12), does not rise bodily to heaven (Acts 1:9), and does not sit at the "right hand of the throne of the Majesty" (Hebrews 8:1). It is precisely with his death that Jesus was allegedly able to attain his rewards. Therefore, "he shall have nothing" cannot refer to the Jesus of Christian missionary theology.

5. After covering sixty-nine consecutive weeks, most Christian missionary apologists are compelled to separate the seventieth week from the rest of the time period. This last

week is relegated to some future period of time, with no agreement among the Christian missionary exegetes on how to explain this last week as a direct continuance of the preceding sixty-nine weeks. They are in effect turning the ninth chapter of Daniel into a "prophecy of sixty-nine weeks."

6. Daniel asks divine guidance in determining the meaning of God's words to Jeremiah concerning the end of desolation and the restoration of Jerusalem (Daniel 9:2). He is obviously referring to Jeremiah 25:11–12, 29:10, 30:18, and 31:37–39, where the promise of restoration appears. Therefore, "the going forth of the word to restore and to build Jerusalem" (Daniel 9:25) dates from the time when God related His message to Jeremiah. That the reckoning of the seventy years dates from the time of Jeremiah is attested to by the prophet Zechariah (ca. 519 B.C.E.). He relates a vision in which God's message comes to him in the form of a dialogue between God and an angel: "Then the angel of the Lord spoke and said: 'O Lord of hosts, how long will You not have compassion on Jerusalem and on the cities of Judah, against which You have had indignation these seventy years' " (Zechariah 1:12). The number is a round one, corresponding to the years during which the Temple, which was to be completed in approximately three more years, lay desolate. In responding to the angel, God declares: ". . . I return to Jerusalem with compassions: My house shall be built in it, says the Lord of hosts, and a line shall be stretched forth over Jerusalem" (Zechariah 1:16). Thus, the seventy years of desolation must refer to the period of Temple desolation. Only by manipulating the figures can one arrive at 483 years between the destruction of the Temple (ca. 586 B.C.E), when the seventy-week period began, and Jesus' death (ca. 33 C.E.). In a desperate attempt at reconciling a period of 483 years with its terminus at the death of Jesus, other starting dates are proposed. However, all these interpretations hinge upon the incorrect renderings mentioned above.

7. The claim that the seventy-week period and, therefore, the rebuilding of Jerusalem begins during the time of Nehemiah (444 B.C.E. alternately 455 B.C.E.) is erroneous. Artaxerxes' permission to Nehemiah was not in the form of a proclamation or decree. The letters given Nehemiah were for safe conduct through the various Persian provinces on his way to Judah (Nehemiah 2:7) and a letter of permission to use lumber from the royal forests for the specific building program he wished to carry out (Nehemiah 2:8). Nehemiah never possessed a royal proclamation specifically allowing him to rebuild Jerusalem. What he sought and received from Artaxerxes was permission to make secure the community then living in Jerusalem, not to rebuild a completely desolate city.

Despite Nehemiah's gloomy description of Jerusalem, which he most likely had never visited, but had received reports of from others, there must have been a community living in Jerusalem at least in the form of an open village or town. Certainly it was not as in its former glory but nevertheless inhabited. We must conclude that the actual command to rebuild Jerusalem must be in accordance with the words of Isaiah, who said that this would be done by Cyrus: "He [Cyrus] shall rebuild My city" (see also Ezra 1:1–8, 6:1–5). Indeed, it was Cyrus who issued a proclamation (ca. 537 B.C.E.) for the return, and for the rebuilding to start, forty-nine years after the destruction of Jerusalem. Hence, the Scriptures teach that it was during the time of Cyrus that the rebuilding of the city began, symbolized, first of all, by the rebuilding of the Temple, which was completed ca. 516 B.C.E., seventy years after its destruction. It is with the completion of the Temple that the period of desolation officially terminates.

During the time of Nehemiah many of Jerusalem's inhabitants took part in the rebuilding of its walls (Nehemiah 3:1–32). Moreover, indications are given that there were many houses in Jerusalem at this time. Nehemiah 3:10 says that a man named Jedaiah, the son of Harumaph, repaired the wall adjoining his house; Azariah, the son of Maaseiah, the son of Ananiah, repaired the wall beside his own house (Nehemiah 3:23), and the priests repaired the wall next to their own houses (Nehemiah 3:28). Zadok, the son of Immer, repaired the wall next to his own house (Nehemiah 3:29), as did Meshullam, the son of Berechiah, next to his chamber (Nehemiah 3:30). Malchijah repaired the wall as far as the house of the Nethinim. If there were no houses in Jerusalem before Nehemiah began to rebuild the wall, these statements could not have been made. Consequently, what Nehemiah meant when he said that "the city was wide and large, but the people within it were few and no houses were built" (Nehemiah 7:4) was that the built-up area was not large and much of the city still lay in ruins. It is inconceivable that Jerusalem before Nehemiah consisted solely of the Temple. What Nehemiah was concerned with was the vulnerability of Jerusalem to attack because the walls were broken down (Nehemiah 2:3, 5). He could not mention this openly to Artaxerxes for fear that the Persian king might accuse him of wishing to fortify the city in order to lead a revolt against Persia. Clearly, the restoration of Jerusalem dates back to the decree of Cyrus, who God said will "rebuild My city." Such being the case, the seventy-week period cannot be dated back to Artaxerxes, as erroneously claimed by some Christian missionary exegetes.

The translation of the ninth chapter of Daniel as rendered by the Jehovah's Witnesses includes many of the errors that the other Christian translations contain. The Witnesses support much of their understanding of the text by recourse to the writings of certain Christian theologians. Therefore, a study of the Jehovah's Witnesses' reasons for translating as they do affords a cross-section of the Christian theological understanding of this chapter. The following is a critique of the Jehovah's Witnesses' translation as found in their Bible version, *The New*

World Translation of the Holy Scriptures, and as explained in their book, *Aid to Bible Understanding.*

1. The Jehovah's Witnesses also disregard the *ʾatnaḥ* giving the following reason:

> The Masoretic text, with its vowel pointings, was prepared in the latter half of the first millennium c.e. Evidently because of their rejection of Jesus Christ as the Messiah the Masoretes accented the Hebrew text at Daniel 9:25 with an *ʾAth·nahh'* or "stop" after "seven weeks," thereby dividing it off from the "sixty-two weeks"; in this way the sixty-two weeks of the prophecy, namely, 434 years, appear to apply to the time of rebuilding ancient Jerusalem.[2]

Answer:

    a. There is no proof that the Masoretes corrupted the text. Quite the contrary, the Masoretic text is the result of carefully handed down traditions. Only the written forms of the vowel signs and the accent marks were devised sometime during the seventh or eighth centuries c.e., but the oral tradition which these signs and marks represent goes back millennia.

    b. The Witnesses have not only disregarded the punctuation of the Hebrew text but have added their own. The Witnesses, thereby, create a sentence where none is indicated or intended in the original text. They render the crucial words of Daniel 9:25 as: "there will be seven weeks, also sixty-two weeks. She will return and be actually rebuilt." No justification for the formation of a new sentence can be given from the Hebrew text.

2. The Witnesses state further:

> Professor E. B. Pusey, in a footnote on one of his lectures delivered at the University of Oxford (published 1885), remarks on the Masoretic accenting: "The Jews put the main stop of the verse under שָׁבְעָה [seven], meaning to separate the two numbers, 7 and 62. This they must have done dishonestly, למען המינים as (Rashi [a prominent Jewish Rabbi of the twelfth century c.e.] says in rejecting literal expositions which

favored the Christians) 'on account of the heretics,' i.e. Christians. For the latter clause, so divided off, could only mean, 'and *during threescore and two weeks* street and wall shall be being restored and builded,' i.e. that Jerusalem should be 434 years in rebuilding, which would be senseless."[3]

Answer:

a. Because the Masoretic text with ʾ*atnah* shows that Jesus was not the Messiah, Professor Pusey accused the Jews of "dishonestly" changing the text. His accusation is based on the assumption that anything which shows that Jesus is not the Messiah must be a dishonest attempt by the Jews.

b. The Masoretic text does not say "that Jerusalem should be 434 years in rebuilding" but that it would be built up for this length of time. The verb *banah* ("to build") is sometimes used for "enlarging," as can be seen, for example, in the phrase: "from the day that they [the Israelites] built it [Jerusalem]" (Jeremiah 32:31). (In 1 Kings 12:25 the verb *banah* has the meaning of "fortify.") Since Jerusalem existed as a city long before its capture by David from the Jebusites, it is clear that what is meant by Jeremiah is the period when the city was enlarged by David and those who followed him. This, then, is also the meaning of the verb in Daniel. It is a reference to the period when the city was enlarged, as indeed it was during the second commonwealth.

3. The Witnesses state further:

> It may be noted, in this connection, that the *Septuagint* translation, made by Jewish scholars in the first three centuries B.C.E., reads, at verse 25, "from the going forth of the command for the answer and for the building of Jerusalem until Christ the prince *there shall be* seven weeks, and sixty-two weeks: and then *the time* shall return, and the street shall be built, and the wall, . . ." [Bagster] Thomson's *Septuagint* reads, in part: "seven weeks, and sixty-two weeks. They shall indeed return and a street shall be built and a wall, . . ."[4]

Answer:

a. Giving two English translations of the Greek Septuagint as proof is of no value, since these translations are influenced by the wording and the punctuation of the King James Version of the Bible. The fact that "Christ" is capitalized in one of the English translations proves its inaccuracy and tendentiousness since in the original Greek Septuagint there were no capitalizations, as all letters were written with capitals. Moreover, the ancient Greek Septuagint text did not have punctuation marks. Even the Jehovah's Witnesses' own *Aid to Bible Understanding* states, in the article entitled "Manuscripts of the Bible," under the subtitle "Styles of Writing":

> Biblical manuscripts written in Greek (whether translations of the Hebrew Scriptures, or copies of the Christian Greek Scriptures, or both) can be divided or classified as to writing style, which is also an aid in dating them. The older style (employed especially down to the ninth century c.e.) is the uncial manuscript, written in large, separate capital letters. In it there is generally no word separation, and punctuation and accent marks are lacking.[5]

Since ancient Greek, Latin, Syriac, etc., did not employ punctuation marks, they provide no proof of a divergent Masoretic text.

4. The Witnesses state further:

> Most English translations do not follow the Masoretic punctuation here, either having a comma after the expression "seven weeks," or in the wording indicating that the sixty-two weeks follow the seven as part of the seventy, and not denoting that the sixty-two weeks apply to the period of rebuilding Jerusalem. (Compare Daniel 9:25 in *AV, AT, Dy, NW, Ro, Yg.*) An editorial note by Professor James Strong in *A Commentary on the Holy Scriptures* (The Book of the Prophet Daniel, by Dr. Otto Zöckler), page 198, says: "The only justification of this

translation, which separates the two periods of seven weeks and sixty-two weeks, assigning the former as the *terminus ad quem* of the Anointed Prince, and the latter as the time of the rebuilding, lies in the Masoretic interpunction, which places the Athnac [stop] between them. . . . and the rendering in question involves a harsh construction of the second member, being without a preposition. It is better, therefore, and simpler, to adhere to the Authorized Version, which follows all the older translations."[6]

Answer:

    a. Strong is wrong in saying that "the rendering in question involves a harsh construction of the second member, being without a preposition." The Masoretic text is perfectly good and proper biblical Hebrew, and no comparison with English usage is of value since every language has its own grammatical and syntactic rules. In fact, whereas in English the preposition "for" is commonly used with time duration, in biblical Hebrew it is grammatically incorrect to include it (e.g., Genesis 5:6, 9, 12, etc., a.fr.). The King James Version usually follows the literal Hebrew and does not include the preposition "for." However, *The New World Translation of the Holy Scriptures*, the Jehovah's Witnesses' translation of the Bible, does add "for" in order to conform with the common English usage.

5. The Witnesses state further:

> The translation by Isaac Leeser reads: "Know therefore and comprehend, that from the going forth of the word to restore and to build Jerusalem unto the anointed the prince will be seven weeks: [the stop is represented here by a colon] and *during* sixty and two weeks will it be again built with streets and ditches (around it), even in the pressure of the times." The translation of the Jewish Publication Society of America reads similarly: "shall be seven weeks; and for threescore and two weeks, it shall be built again." In these two versions the words "during" and "for," respectively, appear in the English translation, evidently to support the translators' interpretation.[7]

Answer:
  a. As is well known, the Hebrew prefix *ve-* often is not only a conjunction, meaning "and," but serves as an adverb with a variety of meanings, such as "but," "however," "now," "then," "while," "or," "therefore," etc., according to the context, as can be seen from any modern English version of the Bible. Even the Witnesses' own Bible translation, *The New World Translation of the Holy Scriptures,* recognizes this: i.e., Genesis 7:23, "thus"; 1 Samuel 19:20, "at once"; 1 Samuel 19:21, "when"; 2 Kings 24:4, "so that"; Ezekiel 33:11, "for." Leeser and the Jewish Publication Society amplified the text for greater clarity. But these are additions within the context of the meaning represented by the prefix *ve-*. The lack of the preposition should not concern us (see answer 4), for we are dealing with Daniel's writing style and not with English grammar. The extreme versatility of the prefix *ve-* allows for the addition of the preposition "for" in translation.

If we merely use two of the most common translations for the Hebrew prefix *ve-*, that is, "and" and "then," we have the following: ". . . until an anointed one, a prince, shall be seven weeks; *and* sixty-two weeks it shall be built again" or ". . . until an anointed one, a prince, shall be seven weeks; *then* sixty-two weeks it shall be built again." The idea of two separate time periods, with Jerusalem to be rebuilt during the second time period, is clearly stated in either manner of translation. That the Jewish understanding of verse 25 is correct is corroborated by verse 26, which mentions the latter period of sixty-two weeks only: "And after *the* sixty-two weeks . . ." In verse 26, the definite article is placed before "sixty-two weeks" in order to emphasize that it is a separate time period. The verification of "the sixty-two weeks" as a separate time period, which we find in verse 26, is the key to the understanding that verse 25 speaks of two separate time periods. But, of course, most Christian Bible translations leave out the all-important definite article from verse 26 or do as the Witnesses do: simply ignore that it has any bearing on the meaning of Daniel's "seventy weeks."

6. The Witnesses state further:

Gabriel further said to Daniel: "After the sixty-two weeks Messiah will be cut off, with nothing for himself." (Vs. 26) It was sometime after the end of the "seven plus sixty-two weeks," actually about three and a half years afterward, that Christ was cut off in death on a torture stake, giving up all that he had as a ransom for mankind. (Isa. 53:8) Evidence indicates that the first half of the "week" was spent by Jesus in the ministry.[8]

Answer:

a. The word "after" in verse 26 is taken, by the Witnesses, to be three and one-half years later, spring 33 c.e., and the death of Jesus. Despite the Witnesses' preconceived notions, there is no reason for one not to expect that "sometime after the end of the 'seven plus sixty-two weeks'" means right after the sixty-nine weeks. If what the Witnesses say is correct, Gabriel would have said: "after sixty-nine and one-half weeks."

b. Concerning the Witnesses' contention that Jesus gave up "all that he had as a ransom for mankind," this is not the full story. The Witnesses say that Jesus was an angel before he came to earth. In assuming an earthly body, he knew exactly what God's purpose was for the future of mankind and what was expected of him in order to bring this about. Did Jesus have a free will to sin while on earth? The answer is obviously no, for had he not carried out God's expectations the whole timetable of God's purpose would have been eternally disrupted, and that is an impossibility. Had Jesus sinned he would not receive rewards on earth or in heaven. As a human being, Jesus certainly had very little. Yet because he allegedly stood in a special relationship to God he could expect, on reassuming his angelic state, great honors in heaven. Therefore, what did he give up in dying a human death? In sum, what they are really saying is that Jesus gave up a temporary earthly life for singular eternal honor. Clearly, it is unreasonable to say that this was "giving up all that he had as a ransom for mankind." By exchanging his transitory human life-span for eternal angelic honor, Jesus obviously made a manifold profit. To claim otherwise would be sheer distortion of what is alleged to be theological truth.

7. The Witnesses state further:

> God, through Christ, did extend the blessings of the *Abrahamic* covenant to the natural offspring of Abraham, excluding the Gentiles until the gospel was taken to them through Peter's preaching to the Italian Cornelius. (Acts 3:25, 26; 10:1–48) This conversion of Cornelius and his household occurred after the conversion of Saul of Tarsus, which is generally considered to have taken place in 34 or 35 C.E.; after this the congregation enjoyed a period of peace, being built up. (Acts 9:1–16, 31) It appears, then, that the bringing of Cornelius into the Christian congregation took place in the autumn of 36 C.E., which would be the end of the seventieth "week," 490 years from 455 B.C.E.[9]

Answer:
    a. It is necessary for the Witnesses to fit events into their chronology. Therefore, Saul's conversion, which they speculate to have taken place in 34 or 35 C.E., becomes hard fact in Witness chronology. But no substantiated proof is offered to support this conjecture.
    b. The Witnesses state: "It appears . . . that the bringing of Cornelius into the Christian congregation took place in the autumn of 36 C.E. This assumption ("it appears") becomes hard fact on which to base other assumptions, although there is absolutely no proof that Cornelius'

conversion took place in the autumn of 36 C.E. In sum, we are being offered an orchestration of assumptions to prove a presupposed contention.

c. Even the Witnesses' starting date of 455 B.C.E. is actually based on the process of working backward from the events they wish to prove. It is not Nehemiah, but Cyrus (Isaiah 45:13), who is given credit by God for the rebuilding of Jerusalem. Therefore, all the Witnesses' claims and calculations to the contrary are in vain.

1. Some Christian missionaries claim that there is something called a "prophetic year" of 360 days, thus shortening the interval between the beginning of the 483 years, which they claim began in 444 B.C.E., and the date of the crucifixion of Jesus. They do this in order to make the dates coincide, but the claim of a "prophetic year" is without any scriptural foundation.

2. *Aid to Bible Understanding* (New York: Watchtower Bible and Tract Society, 1971), p. 1475.

3. *Ibid.*

4. *Ibid.*

5. *Ibid.*, p. 1106.

6. *Ibid.*, pp. 1475–76.

7. *Ibid.*, p. 1475.

8. *Ibid.*, p. 1474.

9. *Ibid.*

BOOK II
The New Testament

27

A TRILOGY ON THE TRINITY

1. The Doctrine of the Trinity and the Hebrew Bible

It is a basic belief among most Christians that God is three beings in one: God the Father, God the Son, and God the Holy Spirit. This belief, called the Trinity, is not only diametrically opposed to Jewish belief, but is the very antithesis of the teaching of the Torah, the Prophets, and the Writings concerning the oneness of God.

Christianity has been misled into deifying Jesus because of its confusion concerning the meaning of the unity of God. This confusion is the result of the influence of the pagan religions on church doctrine and practice. In the Hellenized Egyptian cult of Isis, the goddess Isis, her consort Sarapis, and their child Horus formed a sacred trinity.[1] Roman emperors were usually deified during their lifetime.[2] The *post-mortem* deification of world rulers and their ascension to heaven, as well as salvation through identification with risen saviors, were established teachings among the pagan religions of the Roman Empire.[3] The title *Epiphanes* ("The God Made Manifest"), conferred on eastern kings, described their divine nature as manifestations of the glory of the pagan god. Thus, it was not difficult to advance the idea of a triune god in the early Christian church of the pagan world. The erroneous Christian interpretation of the nature of God as a triune being, with its roots lying deep in paganism, found its expression in the Nicene Creed, which became the foundation for both Catholic and later Protestant beliefs on the subject of the Trinity.

In the year 325, the Council of Nicaea was convened by the

emperor Constantine, who sought to secure through this body an authoritative declaration of Christian belief. It was to be the means of curbing the increasing violent dissension that prevailed in the Christian church concerning the nature of God and other theological subjects. The Council condemned some of the theories then current, including that of Arius, which asserted that the Son was created by the Father. Eventually, the Council promulgated a document that became known as the Nicene Creed.

Thus, by his political power, Constantine, a treacherous and unbaptized pagan, gave Christianity its doctrine concerning the nature of the deity it worshipped. This is the man who declared as indisputable law the false doctrine that became the basis for trinitarianism. The Nicene Creed asserts, in essence, that God is one, but within the *One* are three, equally sharing in His being and substance. The three sharing this godhead are designated a triune unity. The church, after many lengthy disputes, included the doctrine of the Trinity in its fundamental teachings. But this teaching, the result of theological and doctrinal speculation, is not even a pale reflection of what is taught in the Hebrew Bible. In their effort to shore up this claim, trinitarian missionary theologians were forced to distort the meaning of the Hebrew word ʾeḥad ("one") as applied to the absolute unity of God.

By careful examination of the use of ʾeḥad in the Hebrew Bible, we may ascertain its true meaning as it is applied to God in the Shema: "Hear, O Israel, the Lord our God, the Lord is One" (Deuteronomy 6:4). The occurrences of ʾeḥad are too numerous to be listed here in their entirety. It is true that in such verses as Genesis 1:5: "And there was evening and there was morning, one day," and Genesis 2:24: "Therefore shall a man leave his father and his mother and shall cleave to his wife, and they shall be one flesh," the term "one" refers to a compound united one. However, ʾeḥad often also means an absolute one. This is illustrated by such verses as 2 Samuel 13:30: "Absalom has slain all the king's sons, and there is not one of them left"; 2 Samuel 17:12: "And of all the men that are with him we will not leave so much as one"; Exodus 9:7: "There did not die of the cattle of

Israel even one"; 2 Samuel 17:22: "There lacked not one of them that was not gone over the Jordan." Of special interest is Ecclesiastes 4:8: "There is one [that is alone], and he has not a second; yea, he has neither son nor brother." Clearly, the word "one" used in these verses means an absolute one and is synonymous with the word *yaḥid,* "the only one," "alone." It is in this sense, with even greater refinement, that *ʾeḥad* is used in Deuteronomy 6:4: "Hear, O Israel, the Lord our God, the Lord is One." Here, *ʾeḥad* is used as a single, absolute, unqualified one.

ʾEḥad is used in Deuteronomy 6:4 to signify that the Lord is uniquely alone: "I am the first, and I am the last, and besides Me there is no God" (Isaiah 44:6). There is no mention here of a triune god unless one wants to claim that "I am the first" is God the Father, "I am the last" is the third person of the Trinity, the Holy Spirit, and "besides Me there is no God" designates the Son, Jesus, as "no God."[4] If the two names of God ("the Lord, the King of Israel, and his [Israel's] Redeemer the Lord of hosts"), used in the complete statement of Isaiah 44:6, are to be understood in a Christological sense, rather than as mere attributes of God, the whole verse would yield a dualistic concept, not a trinitarian one.

Missionary Christianity manipulates the Scriptures to establish the doctrine of the Trinity. If it had a quaternity to prove, this would be demonstrated just as easily from the biblical text. That this observation is not an exaggeration can be seen from the words *ruach ʾElohim* ("the spirit of God"), found in Genesis 1:2. According to trinitarian missionaries, the phrase "the spirit of God" represents one distinct entity of the triune god. Following this exegetical approach to its logical conclusion, we will obtain not a trinity but a quaternity. If the divine spirit is to be treated as an entity in itself, then the evil spirit should be granted similar status, for just as the "holy spirit" is referred to as a spirit of God, so is the "evil spirit." This is clearly found in the words of Saul's servants to him: "Behold now, an evil spirit of God is terrifying you" (1 Samuel 16:15), and the subsequent use of this term in verse 16: ". . . when the evil spirit of God comes upon you." Are we to surmise, then, that there really exists a divine quaternity—Father, Son, Spirit of God, and Evil Spirit of God (see also Judges 9:23, 1 Kings 22:21 ff.)? Evidently the terms "spirit of God" and "evil spirit of God" express certain aspects of God's will and action rather than His essence.

It has been maintained by Christian missionary theologians that the personification of "wisdom" found in Proverbs 8:22–23 refers to an actual person, i.e., Jesus: "The Lord created me as the beginning of His way, the first of His acts of old. I was set up ages ago, from the beginning, from the origin of the earth." Since it is clearly stated that God created "wisdom," it becomes self-evident that whoever or whatever is personified by "wisdom" cannot be God, for that which is created cannot be God. The verb *qanah* means "to create" (cf. Genesis 14:19, 22; Deuteronomy 32:6; Psalms 139:13). Although "wisdom" is figuratively given a personality of its own, it is a subservient creation of God. In fact, "wisdom" has neither a personal life of its own nor any ontological existence whatsoever.

A further indication of the futility of the Christian missionary viewpoint is found in Proverbs 3:19: "The Lord by wisdom founded the earth; by understanding He established the heavens." According to Christian missionary theology, "wisdom" is to be considered a real being, the second member of the Trinity, and the agent by which God created the world. But to follow this reasoning one may very well say that "understanding" also represents a real being and the agent by which God created the heavens. No doubt, if Christian missionary theologians needed to prove God a quaternity, they would claim that not only "wisdom" but also "understanding" is a distinct personality within the nature of God.

In their effort to substantiate the belief in a triune god, Christian missionary theologians have turned to the words of Jeremiah:

> Behold, the days are coming, says the Lord, that I will raise up for David a righteous branch, and he shall reign as king and prosper, and shall execute justice and righteousness in the land. In his days Judah will be saved, and Israel will dwell securely. And this is his name by which he will be called: "The Lord is our righteousness." (Jeremiah 23:5–6)

These theologians argue that only God could properly bear the name *'Ado-nai tsidkaynu*—"The Lord is our righteousness." However, names are often given to human beings, and even to inanimate objects, with the intention of expressing honor to God. It is not at all strange to find biblical names which incorporate the divine name within them (cf. Exodus 17:15). In this instance, the name is there to tell us why the Messiah's rule will be just and equal for all, since the source of the Messiah's righteousness is God. "The Lord is our righteousness" indicates that God will direct His Messiah's every step. By no means is there the slightest hint that the Messiah's being is of divine origin. Certainly, this name does not apply to Jesus, who was never known as "The Lord is our righteousness."

In Genesis 1:1, it is stated: "In the beginning God created the heavens and the earth." Here the word for God is *'Elohim*, having a plural form as though it meant "gods." This has been employed by Christian missionaries as proof that God is a plurality. However, a careful investigation of the actual use of this word in the Scriptures will unequivocally show that *'Elohim*, while plural in form, is singular in concept. In biblical Hebrew, many singular abstractions are expressed in the plural form, e.g., *raḥamim*, "compassion" (Genesis 43:14, Deuteronomy 13:18); *zequnim*, "old age" (Genesis 21:2, 37:3, 44:20); *nᶜurim*, "youth" (Isaiah 54:6, Psalms 127:4).

Scripture teaches us that *'Elohim*, which is the plural of majesty, is used not only in reference to God, but also for angels (divine beings) and human authorities of high stature in society. This can be clearly seen, for example, from the following usages. Manoah, the father of Samson (Judges 13:22), after seeing "an angel of the Lord," said: "We shall surely die for we have seen *'elohim*." Concerning human authority, we read in Exodus 22:8: "Both parties shall come before the *'elohim* ["judges"], and whom the *'elohim* ["judges"] shall condemn, he shall pay double to his neighbor."

It is, therefore, ludicrous to infer from *'Elohim*, in the first verse of Genesis, the existence of a plurality of persons in the Deity. Where is the plurality of persons in the angel, referred to as *'elohim*, that visited Manoah? How can missionaries explain the words of the woman to Saul when, upon seeing Samuel, she exclaimed: "I see *ʾelohim* coming up out of the earth" (1 Samuel 28:13)? Here, *ʾelohim* is followed by the verb in the plural. Yet only a single individual is referred to, as is clearly seen from verse 14: "And he said to her: 'What is his appearance?' And she said: 'An old man is coming up; and he is wrapped in a robe.' " Thus, even with a plural verb this noun may still refer to a single individual.

What also needs to be considered is the frequent use of the singular *ʾEloha*, as, for example: "Then he forsook God [*ʾEloha*] who made him" (Deuteronomy 32:15); "You that forget God [*ʾEloha*]" (Psalms 50:22); "At the presence of the God [*ʾEloha*] of Jacob" (Psalms 114:7). Following the view of *ʾElohim* as referring to a triune god, how can the advocates of the doctrine of the Trinity account for the alternative employment of *ʾElohim* and *ʾEloha*? In Isaiah 44:6 we read: "Thus says the Lord, the King of Israel, and his Redeemer the Lord of hosts: I am the first, and I am the last, and besides Me there is no God [*ʾElohim*]." This is followed in verse 8 by: "Is there a God [*ʾEloha*] besides Me?" If the truth of the doctrine of the Trinity depends in any measure on the plurality in form of the noun *ʾElohim*, the use of *ʾEloha*, the singular of the noun, most decidedly disproves it. The underlying reason for the grammatically plural form *ʾElohim* is to indicate the all-inclusiveness of God's authority as possessing every conceivable attribute of power. The use of the plural for such a purpose is not limited merely to *ʾElohim*, but also applies to other words of profound significance. For instance, Isaiah 19:4 uses *ʾadonim* ("lords") instead of *ʾadon* ("lord"): "Into the hand of a cruel lord" (literally "lords," even though referring to one person),[5] and Exodus 21:29: "Its owner [literally *beʿalav*, "its owners"] also shall be put to death."

ʾElohim means "gods" only when the Scriptures apply this plural word to the pagan deities. The pagan Philistines applied the title *ʾelohim* to their god Dagon (Judges 16:23–24, 1 Samuel 5:7). The Moabites, likewise, used the word *ʾelohim* to describe their god Chemosh (Judges 11:24). If the trinitarian missionaries are correct in their argument that the use of *ʾElohim* with a singular verb means there are three coeternal, coequal persons in one god, then the same thing must be true for the Philistine god Dagon and the Moabite god Chemosh. They must be respectively a plurality of persons in one god. How else could the missionaries explain the Philistines saying of Dagon: "Our god [*ʾelohaynu*] has delivered" (Judges 16:24)? Here, the verb is singular, yet the subject is, literally, "our gods" in the plural. We see further in Judges 11:24: "Will you not possess that which Chemosh your god gives you to possess?" Chemosh is in the singular number, and in apposition with it is *ʾelohecha* (literally "your gods"), which is in the plural number (see also Judges 6:31: "If he [Baal] is a god [*ʾelohim*]").

Some missionaries justify the use of the plural with Dagon and Chemosh on the basis of the assumption that they were not the name of one particular idol only, but were the names of innumerable idols throughout the respective kingdoms where they were worshipped. Hence, Dagon and Chemosh, though in the singular form, are collective nouns which embraced every idol of the realm. However, this interpretation is unattested and forced. It is nothing but a theory invented to support a theological need. That the plural form of *ʾElohim* does not at all imply the plurality of the divine essence is a fact that was already known in ancient times. This is reflected in the Septuagint version of the Scriptures, which renders *ʾElohim* with the singular title *ho Theos* ("the God").

As a further illustration of the attempt to justify the spurious belief in the Trinity, some Christian missionary theologians contend that two divine personalities appear in Hosea 1:7: "But I will have mercy upon the house of Judah, and will save them [Israel] by the Lord their God." The claim is made that if one should promise another that he will do a certain work by a third person, it would be quite evident that the one who promised the work is different from the one through whom he does it. Hence, the conclusion that the Lord who speaks is different from the Lord who actually delivers Israel. But this is an inconclusive argument, as it is not unusual for God to speak of Himself in the third person, e.g., Genesis 18:19; Exodus 3:12, 24:1; Numbers

19:1–2; Zechariah 1:12–17. If "the Lord their God" means, as Christian missionaries say, "the Lord their Gods," it would have to refer to all three members of the Trinity. Under the circumstances, then, which member of the Trinity made the promise? It must simply be God speaking about Himself in the third person. Furthermore, if we look carefully at the Hebrew text, we will discover that the particular names of God are used advisedly, as each carries a definite meaning bearing on the overall idea of the verse. Accordingly, it should be read: "But I will have mercy upon the house of Judah, and will save them by means of [Myself] the Lord of Mercy, their God of Justice." For the divine name "the Lord" (the Tetragrammaton)[6] represents God's quality of mercy, i.e., the God of Mercy, and *ʿElohim* represents God's quality of justice, i.e., the God of Justice.[7]

Not by weapons of war did God save Judah, but by using His own weapon, "an angel of the Lord,"[8] to inflict punishment on Judah's enemies. Christian missionary theologians claim that whenever the Scriptures mention "an angel of the Lord," the angel is Jesus. They translate all passages mentioning such an angel as "*the* Angel of the Lord," although the Hebrew may just as well mean "*an* angel of the Lord" (literally "a messenger of the Lord"; cf. Judges 2:1, 6:11–22). True, in the construct state, when the second noun has the definite article, the first noun is automatically definite without the need for the article. However, with proper nouns, which are automatically definite, only context will determine whether the first noun attached to it is to be taken as definite or indefinite. The context, in all the verses where *malach ʾAdon-ai* occurs, strongly indicates that it is not to be taken as definite.

Even when the noun "angel" (*malach*) appears with a definite article in a scriptural passage, it is not used in the sense of a definite personality, but only as a reference to the particular angel mentioned previously in the text. The angel is always an impersonal being whose name is not necessary, since he is simply a messenger (the Hebrew word *malach* means "messenger" as does the Greek *angelos*) to whom God, in whom all power resides, has entrusted a specific mission (1 Chronicles

21:16, 27; Zechariah 1:12–17). It is for this reason that the prophet Haggai, who conveyed God's message to Israel, is also called "a messenger of the Lord" (Haggai 1:13). The Hebrew term applied to Haggai, *malach 'Ado-nai,* is the same that is translated as "an angel of the Lord" and points to his prophetic role as an intermediary. Similarly, the priest is designated as "a messenger of the Lord of hosts" (Malachi 2:7). The angel who appears to Abraham does not swear by his own name but merely conveys God's message: " 'By Myself I have sworn,' says the Lord" (Genesis 22:16). God sends angels to act in His name, not in their own names. Therefore, to Jacob an angel says: "Why is it that you ask my name?" (Genesis 32:30), and to Manoah an angel says: "Why is it that you ask my name, seeing it is hidden?" (Judges 13:18).[9] There is no indication that these verses all refer to one specific angel. The angels that appeared to various biblical personalities were acting only as messengers bearing God's word. That the words of a messenger of God may be attributed directly to God is evident from Isaiah 7:10, which reads: "And the Lord spoke again to Ahaz." Ahaz, being unworthy of such a privilege, must have received this message through Isaiah, but it is nevertheless reported as if God Himself spoke directly to him because a messenger represents the one who sends him (see also 2 Chronicles 33:10). Therefore, an action of an angel may be credited directly to God, who gave him the message.

In describing the beginning of Moses' career as a prophet the Bible states:

And an angel of the Lord appeared to him [Moses] in a flame of fire out of the midst of a bush; and he looked, and, behold, the bush burned with fire, and the bush was not consumed. And Moses said: "I will turn aside now, and see this great sight, why the bush is not burnt." And when the Lord saw that he turned aside to see, God called to him out of the midst of the bush, and said: "Moses, Moses." And he said: "Here am I." Then He said: "Do not come near; put off your shoes from your feet, for the place on which you are standing is holy ground." And He said: "I am the God of your father, the God of Abraham, the God of Isaac, and the God of Jacob." And Moses hid his face; for he was afraid to look at God.

Then the Lord said: "I have surely seen the affliction of My people who are in Egypt and have heard their cry because of their taskmasters; for I know their pains; and I have come down to deliver them out of the hands of the Egyptians. . . . Come now, and I will send you to Pharaoh, that you may bring forth My people the children of Israel out of Egypt." But Moses said to God: "Who am I, that I should go to Pharaoh, and that I should bring forth the children of Israel out of Egypt?" And He said: "Certainly I will be with you; and this shall be the sign to you, that I have sent you: when you have brought forth the people out of Egypt, you shall serve God upon this mountain." Then Moses said to God: "Behold, when I come to the children of Israel, and shall say to them: The God of your fathers has sent me to you; and they shall say to me: 'What is His name?' what shall I say to them?" And God said to Moses: "I WILL BE WHAT I WILL BE"; and He said: "Thus you shall say to the children of Israel: I WILL BE has sent me to you." And God also said to Moses: "Thus shall you say to the children of Israel: The Lord, the God of your fathers, the God of Abraham, the God of Isaac, and the God of Jacob, has sent me to you; this is My name forever, and this is My memorial to all generations. Go, and gather the elders of Israel together, and say to them: The Lord, the God of your fathers, the God of Abraham, of Isaac, and of Jacob, has appeared to me. . . . And they shall hearken to your voice. And you shall come, you and the elders of Israel, to the king of Egypt, and you shall say to him: The Lord, the God of the Hebrews, has met with us. And now let us go, we pray you, three days' journey into the wilderness, that we may sacrifice to the Lord our God." (Exodus 3:2–8, 10–16, 18)

Trinitarian missionaries cite this passage as further evidence of their allegation that the term "angel of the Lord" refers to part of a triune deity. To them, the text seems to indicate that the angel who appears as a fiery manifestation to Moses is the same being as the God who afterwards speaks to him. However, on further examination, the textual evidence leans in favor of the view that this angel of the Lord functions here solely as a fiery manifestation which attracts Moses' attention, while it is the God of Israel who actually "appeared," that is, made Himself known and spoke to Moses. Yet the issue of whether God Himself or an angel speaks to Moses cannot be conclusively decided one way or the other.

For our discussion, a final decision as to whether God speaks directly to Moses or through the medium of an angel is not crucial. Even if one believes that the angel, rather than God, speaks to Moses, it should be remembered that when, as God's representative, an angel appears before a person, it is considered as if God Himself has appeared, for, as stated above, an angel repeats the exact message given to him by God. If, in verse 14, it is actually an angel that speaks directly to Moses, then he is merely conveying the Lord's message concerning His name. That the message in this verse, even if delivered through an intermediary, is actually from the Lord is indicated by the fact that whenever an angel of the Lord is asked in the Scriptures for his name, he always refuses to give it. This is understandable, since he is only a messenger, with his own personal identity being of no importance. As a result, he is identified with the sender of the message. Yet in verse 14, the God of Abraham, Isaac, and Jacob does give His name. In so doing, He indicates that He is not synonymous with what the Scriptures call "an angel of the Lord." All in all, "an angel of the Lord" can in no way be identified as part of the divine essence.

Trinitarian missionaries make use of *ʾEl, ʾElohim,* and *ʾAdo-nai* (the Tetragrammaton), employed in Joshua 22:22 and Psalm 50:1, as proof of their doctrine. In actuality, these three distinct appellations are juxtaposed for the express purpose of heightening the effect, and they do not at all imply that God is a triune personality. The effect is heightened by using the names in ascending order. The first of these, *ʾEl,* is the most general, the second, *ʾElohim,* the ordinary name, and the third, *ʾAdo-nai,* the most specific name for God used in the Scriptures. As a rule, these names are used with the following connotations: *ʾEl,* the Mighty One; *ʾElohim,* the Judge; *ʾAdo-nai,* the Merciful One. Their use certainly does not imply any division in the absolute unity of God's essence. In 2 Samuel 22:32, David uses these three words: "For who is God [*ʾEl*] but the Lord [*ʾAdo-nai*]? And who is a rock except our God [*ʾElohaynu*]?" Obviously, no division in the absolute unity of God is intended in this verse, since its entire thrust is to impress us with the oneness of God.

Some Christian missionaries believe that the idea of the

existence of three divine personalities active in man's salvation is to be found in Isaiah 63:7–10.

> I will make mention of the mercies of the Lord, and the praises of the Lord, according to all that the Lord has bestowed on us; and the great goodness toward the house of Israel, which He has bestowed on them according to His compassions, and according to the multitude of His mercies. For He said: "Surely, they are My people, children that will not deal falsely", so He was their savior. In all their affliction He was afflicted, and the angel of His presence saved them; in His love and in His pity He redeemed them; and He bore them, and carried them all the days of old. But they rebelled, and grieved His holy spirit; therefore He turned to be their enemy, and Himself fought against them.

An examination of this passage will show that it merely describes God's special relationship with Israel, acting as Israel's savior and redeemer in times of affliction. It does not at all contain any reference or implication concerning a division in His unity. The phrase "angel of His presence" refers to the angel which God chooses in any given incident to do His bidding.

Basing themselves on the Hebrew, which literally translated reads "angel of His face," certain Christian missionaries argue that this proves that the angel is a being in God's likeness. They then infer that this angel is synonymous with the "angel of the Lord," who, they claim, is the second member of the Trinity. To say that the angel is a being in God's likeness is an obvious distortion of the phrase, because "of His face" is used in a possessive and not a qualitative sense. Furthermore, the term "face" (*panim*) is never used for "likeness" or "image." *Panim* is used here to mean "presence" (cf. Genesis 4:16; Isaiah 59:2, Jonah 1:3, 10). In this passage, "angel of His presence" is simply the angel whom God appoints as His emissary to act as the representative of His presence in the cause of Israel.

Continuing our study of this passage, we see in verse 11 that it is God who "put His holy spirit in the midst of them: "Then His people remembered the days of old, the days of Moses: 'Where is He that brought them up out of the sea with the shepherds of His flock? Where is He that put His holy spirit in the midst of them?' " The holy spirit is thus subordinate to God since God may dispense it to His chosen ones. If the holy spirit is one part of a coequal triune god, how can David petition one part of this triune god: "Cast me not away from Your presence" about matters pertaining to another part of this triune god: "And take not Your holy spirit from me" (Psalms 51:13). That God constitutes an absolute unity is seen in Isaiah 63:16: "For You are our Father. . . . You, O Lord, are our Father, our Redeemer from everlasting is Your name."

Due to a faulty understanding of Isaiah 48:16, those who are bent on finding trinitarian allusions in the Bible translate part of this verse as: "The Lord God and His Spirit have sent me." However, a proper rendering of the verse reads: "And now the Lord God has sent me, and His spirit." The last two Hebrew words in this verse are *shelaḥani ve-ruḥo* ("He has sent me, and His spirit"), with "me, and His spirit" being the direct objects of "sent." Even though a definite direct object is usually preceded by the participle ʾ*et*, this grammatical rule is frequently not observed in the Bible, e.g., Exodus 15:9; Judges 5:12, Psalms 9:5, 20:3–4, 45:4. In fact, ʾ*et* rarely occurs in the poetic parts of the Bible. Thus, the meaning of the verse is that God has sent Isaiah accompanied by His prophetic spirit. There is no mention of the third member of the Trinity doctrine. Instead, Isaiah affirms that he was sent by God, who has placed within him the power of prophecy. The spirit is always at the disposal of God to bestow upon whomever He chooses, as stated in Numbers 11:17, 25, 29; Isaiah 42:1, 44:3; Joel 3:1. If this spirit referred to the third member of a coequal triune god, how could it be ordered about at the discretion of the other members of this group?

> And I will take of the spirit which is upon you, and I will put it upon them. . . . And He took of the spirit which was upon him, and he put it upon the seventy men, the elders, and it came to pass, when the spirit rested upon them, that they prophesied. . . . And Moses said . . . "would that all the Lord's people were prophets, that the Lord would put His spirit upon them." (Numbers 11:17, 25, 29)

Such a condition makes it obviously impossible to consider the spirit as being an associate of God, let alone coequal with Him.

Christian missionaries take Genesis 18 and 19 as proof for their trinitarian views. In their search for evidence in support of the doctrine of the Trinity, the missionaries claim that the three angels who appeared to Abraham as he sat in his tent door under the oaks of Mamre were actually the first, second, and third persons of the Trinity. Although the complexity of the context may lend itself to several interpretations, the Christian missionary understanding of these chapters as referring to a triune god is totally unacceptable on scriptural grounds alone.

Genesis 18:1 may be interpreted as the Lord speaking to Abraham prior to the arrival of the three men mentioned in verse 2. Most probably, however, verse 1 acts as an introductory remark informing the reader that the Lord spoke to Abraham, with the following verses being the details of how that encounter was accomplished. The text of Genesis 18 and 19 is not clear as to whether the Lord spoke, at any time, directly to Abraham or solely through an angel, in the guise of a man, who acted as an intermediary. But these are minor problems compared to the problems involved in the Christian missionary interpretation. The latter are of a nature which reveals the shallowness of the theological assertions of Christian missionaries concerning these two chapters.

As already mentioned, Christian missionaries believe that the three men who visited Abraham are the three personalities of the alleged Trinity. But, then, which part of God would they say is the Lord who speaks to Abraham after two of the men depart (Genesis 18:22)? If the three angels are the three persons of the Trinity, then how could the Lord say: "You cannot see My face, for man shall not see Me and live" (Exodus 33:20)? Abraham and Sarah would have certainly died had they gazed upon the supposed Father, Son, and Holy Spirit, unless what they saw was not God but three angelic beings manifested in human form for the several purposes assigned to them. Even John exposes the error when he declares that "no man has seen God at any time" (John 1:18, 1 John 4:12). Since a number of people saw the faces of the three angels and still lived, we must presume that they were not God.

Of the three visitors, one is specifically sent as a messenger from the Lord to Abraham. Through him, the Lord speaks, in Genesis 18, to Abraham. He is the one who delivers God's message concerning the birth of Isaac, and it is through him that the Lord speaks to Abraham concerning the possibility of saving the two cities. Thus, for example, in verse 22: "And the men turned from there, and went toward Sodom; but Abraham stood yet before the Lord," and in verse 33 it says: "And the Lord went His way, as soon as He had left off speaking to Abraham." As the Lord's agent the messenger speaks as the Lord and is referred to accordingly. The authority which he expresses is not his own but God's. It is God who oversees all events, and that is why, even though the Scriptures describe the angels as going to Sodom, the Lord states, in verse 21: "I will go down now, and see whether they have done altogether according to the cry of it, which has come to Me; and if not, I will know."

In Genesis 19:1, two of the men are now referred to as angels, literally, "messengers," while the third, having accomplished his mission of speaking to Abraham, is no longer involved in the narrative. That is why only two of the visitors are mentioned as arriving at their destination. The text indicates that the function of these two men is to bring about the destruction of Sodom by exposing, through their mere presence, all the evil that resides in the hearts of the inhabitants. The two angels are never referred to as God, as should be expected if the Christian missionary position is correct. They are portrayed as God's agents carrying out His commands. Simply stated, they cannot be God if they are sent by Him to do His bidding. At no time do the two angels take the initiative in making critical decisions concerning Sodom. Hence, they exclaim: ". . . we will destroy this place, because their cry has become great before the Lord; and the Lord has sent us to destroy it" (Genesis 19:13).

It is obvious that it is not the angels who decide to destroy Sodom and Gomorrah; they only act as agents for the Lord. He made the decision and sends them to carry it out. At no time do the Scriptures say that the angels declare "we heard their cry" or "we have come on our own initiative." The angels only speak in terms of what they are commanded to do. In contrast, the Lord, apparently through the medium of the third man, speaks with authority throughout the narrative. However, this man is not God in human form, as Christian missionaries argue, but an angel in the guise of a human being. In the end, it is God, and not the angels, who causes the destruction of the wicked cities, as is clearly stated in Genesis 19:24: "Then the Lord caused to rain upon Sodom and Gomorrah brimstone and fire from the Lord out of heaven." Christian missionary theologians infer that there were two divine personalities, one on earth, conversing with Abraham, and the other in heaven. The one on earth rained down fire upon the two cities from the one in heaven. There is, however, no grammatical basis for such an inference. Actually, in accordance with the construction of the Hebrew language, we find that in the first half of the verse, the reader is informed who caused the brimstone and fire to fall upon the two cities, and in the second half of the verse he is told for emphasis, not only from whom it came but also from where. The verse emphasizes that it is "from the Lord," in order to leave no doubt as to who is in command of events. Furthermore, the technique of speaking in the third person about Himself is used by God in other scriptural contexts (see above, p. 131–132). It is a common feature of the Scriptures to repeat the noun rather than make use of a pronoun. In addition, an individual will frequently speak of himself in the third person instead of using the first person. Examples of this may be seen in the following: Lamech said, "Hear my voice you wives of Lamech" (Genesis 4:23), not "my wives"; similarly David said, "Take with you the servants of your lord" (1 Kings 1:33), and not "my servants"; and Ahasuerus said, ". . . in the name of the king" (Esther 8:8), not "in my name." In the same way, the use of "from the Lord" rather than "from Him," in the verse under discussion, conforms with the biblical usage.

These very verses, by which trinitarian missionaries attempt to prove their claims, demolish, in effect, the theory of a coequal triune partnership. If the destruction of Sodom and Gomorrah is the act of a triune god, in which all three divine personalities take part, it would show them to be unequal partners. It is stated in Genesis 19:13: ". . . we will destroy this place, because their cry has become great before the Lord, and *the Lord has sent us* to destroy it," implying that two of the divine personalities are inferior in position since they do the bidding of the third. The claim that any, or all, of these three angels was God is a contradiction of the biblical text of Genesis 18 and 19.

Certain Christian missionary theologians entertain the idea that the name of God, translated as "the Lord" in English, refers to God the Father, while others believe it refers to God the Son. Yet they believe that the word *ʾElohaynu* ("our God"), which appears in the Shema (Deuteronomy 6:4), is plural and should be understood in its literal sense as "our Gods." For this reason, they interpret Deuteronomy 6:4 as: "Hear, O Israel, the Lord our *Gods, the Lord is a unity.*" If their supposition is correct, the divine name "the Lord" could not refer to either God the Father or God the Son alone, but must refer to all three members of the Trinity as a whole. This being the case, how is it possible for Christian missionaries to maintain that the phrase "to my lord" in the verse: "The Lord [the Tetragrammaton] says to my lord [*ʾadoni*]: 'Sit at My right hand. . .' " (Psalms 110:1) refers to Jesus? If "my lord" refers to the second member of the Trinity, Jesus, then who is the first "Lord" mentioned in this verse? According to the way trinitarian missionaries explain the term "the Lord" (the Tetragrammaton) in the Shema as referring to three gods being united in the divine name, i.e., "the Lord is our Gods," the first "Lord" in Psalm 110:1 must refer to the united Trinity. If this is so, then the phrase "to my lord" automatically excludes Jesus, who is already included in the first part of the verse, "the Lord." Furthermore, if the second "lord," Jesus, is sitting next to the first "Lord," the triune godhead or two-thirds of it, or any aggregate of it, he cannot be part of it. That which exists outside of God cannot be God.

Christian missionary theologians use the biblical story of Jacob's wrestling with an angel as a proof of their belief in a triune deity. As with Genesis 18 and 19, they claim that this narrative proves God manifested Himself in human form.

> And Jacob was left alone; and a man wrestled with him until the breaking of the day. And when he saw that he did not prevail against him, he touched the hollow of his thigh; and the hollow of Jacob's thigh was strained, as he wrestled with him. Then he said: "Let me go, for the day is breaking." But he said: "I will not let you go, unless you bless me." And he said to him: "What is your name?" And he said: "Jacob." Then he said: "Your name shall no more be called Jacob, but Israel; for you have striven with a divine being and with men, and have prevailed." And Jacob asked him, and said: "Tell me, I pray, your name." But he said: "Why is it that you ask my name?" And he blessed him there. And Jacob called the name of the place Peniel: "For I have seen a divine being face to face, and my life is preserved." (Genesis 32:25–31)

As already demonstrated (above, p. 129), the word *'elohim* may mean an angel (divine being), and this indeed is its meaning in this verse: "I have seen an angel [or "a divine being"] face to face." Further confirmation for this rendering is found in Hosea 12:4–5: "And by his strength he strove with a divine being [ʾ*elohim*]; so he strove with an angel [*malach*], and prevailed."

Jacob calls the place *Peniʾel*—"The face of God." The name *Peniʾel* is the most natural and proper commemoration of the incident that Jacob could give, since it honors God, who sent the angel. The importance of only honoring God is highlighted by the angel's refusal to divulge his name to Jacob when the latter requests it. The angel is aware that the knowledge of his name would not be of any benefit to Jacob, for all the power he possesses is directly from God. Therefore, in striving with the angel, Jacob is, in effect, striving with God.

Only God must be honored, not his messenger. The messenger only represents the one who sends him and in whose name he repeats the message exactly as given to him. To see the messenger is equivalent to seeing the sender. As a result, *Peniʾel* ("The face of God") is the only appropriate name Jacob could give to honor the sender rather than the messenger.

Any interpretation which would have Jacob seeing God is in direct contradiction to the teaching of the Hebrew Bible, in which God says: "You cannot see My face, for man shall not see Me and live" (Exodus 33:20). The fact that Jacob sees *"'elohim* face to face" only goes to prove that the divine being that Jacob wrestles with is not God. But, since the angel represents God, Jacob views the messenger as if it is God Himself. It is quite clear that this angel is not God manifested on earth as a human being. At no time does the Hebrew Bible teach this belief.

Biblical passages in which anthropomorphic terms are used in describing the experience of apprehending God do not in the least imply that God actually appeared on earth clothed in a human body. They are, at times, mere mental representations, and at other times, external manifestations, of the divine glory. These experiences are essentially undefinable, but in order to give the reader or listener an appreciation of the experience, the prophet must resort to metaphors borrowed from the physical world.

As already stated, even John the evangelist agrees that God does not manifest Himself in a human form. He emphatically declares the impossibility of seeing God at any time (John 1:18, 1 John 4:12). Of Jesus, who trinitarian missionaries assert is God incarnate, that is, God in the flesh, John says he is "the only begotten god [alternately 'son']" whose function is to explain God (John 1:18). He does not consider Jesus to be the Lord God of Israel, only an angelic being who bridges the gulf between God and man. (For further information on how John views Jesus, see Part 3 of this chapter.) There is no legitimate reason to believe that Jacob's encounter with an angel testifies in any way to a claim that God has ever appeared in human form or to a belief in a triune deity.

Another proof for the Trinity is deduced, by some Christian missionary theologians, from the use of the plural in the verse: "Let us make man in our image . . ." (Genesis 1:26). Such an inference, however, is refuted by the subsequent verse, which relates the creation of man to a singular God: "And God created man in His image" (Genesis 1:27). In this verse the Hebrew verb "created" appears in the singular form. If "let us make man" indicates a numerical plurality, it would be followed in the next verse by: "And *they* created man in *their* image." Obviously, the plural form is used in the same way as in the divine appellation ʾ*Elohim*, to indicate the all-inclusiveness of God's attributes of authority and power, the plurality of majesty. It is customary for one in authority to speak of himself as if he were a plurality. Hence, Absalom said to Ahithophel, "Give your counsel what we shall do" (2 Samuel 16:20). The context shows that he was seeking advice for himself, yet he refers to himself as "we" (see also Ezra 4:16–19).

There is another possible reason for the use of the plural on the part of God, and that is to manifest His humility. God addresses Himself to the angels and says to them: "Let us make man in our image." It is not that He invites their help, but as a matter of modesty and courtesy, God associates them with the creation of man. This teaches us that a great man should act humbly and consult with those lower than him. It is not unusual for God to refer to His heavenly court (angels) as "us," as we see in Isaiah 6:8: "And I heard the voice of the Lord, saying: 'Whom shall I send, and who will go for us?' " Although God often acts without assistance, He makes His intentions known to His servants. Thus, we find: "Shall I conceal from Abraham that which I am doing" (Genesis 18:17); "He made known His ways to Moses, His doings to the children of Israel" (Psalms 103:7); "For the Lord God will do nothing without revealing His counsel to His servants the prophets" (Amos 3:7).

A misconception similar to that concerning Genesis 1:27 is held by certain Christian missionary theologians with reference to the verse, "Come, let us go down, and there confound their language" (Genesis 11:7). Here, too, the confounding of the language is related in verse 9 to God alone: ". . . because the Lord did there confound the language of all the earth." In this verse the Hebrew verb "did" appears in the singular form. Also, the descent is credited in verse 5 to the Lord alone: "And the Lord came down to see the city and the tower." In this verse the Hebrew verb "came down" appears in the singular form. If a doctrine of plurality of persons is to be based on the grammatical form of words, the frequent interchanging of the singular and the plural should vitiate such an attempt as being without foundation or merit. We may safely conclude that the Bible refutes most emphatically every opinion which deviates from the concept of an indivisible unity of God.

Chapter 45 of Isaiah, using the Tetragrammation, unequivocally asserts that the Lord alone is the creator and ruler of all things in the universe. The six uses of *ʾElohim* in this chapter (verses 3, 5, 14, 15, 18, 21) show that the term *ʾElohim* is synonymous with the Tetragrammaton, and that both epithets refer to the absolute one-and-only God. The singularity of God, expressed in the first-person singular in verse 12, clearly shows who is meant by the phrase, "Let us create man in our image": "I, even I, have made the earth, and created man upon it; I, even My hands, have stretched out of the heavens, and all their host have I commanded." As for the Messiah, of him God says: "And I will set up one shepherd over them, and he shall feed them, even My servant David; he shall feed them, and he shall be their shepherd. And I the Lord will be their God, and My servant David prince among them; I the Lord have spoken" (Ezekiel 34:23–24). The Lord alone will be worshipped as God, while the Messiah, as the servant of God, lives with the people. God and the Messiah are not and cannot be equals, for it is God alone who gives the Messiah power to rule in the capacity of His appointed servant.

2. *The Influence of Philo on the Doctrine of the Trinity*

The Christian doctrine of the Logos, "Word," has its origins in the writings of Philo. The Philonic Logos is the result of an attempt to harmonize the Greek Logos and certain Jewish ideas concerning the nature and role of God in the universe. This was to deeply influence early Christian theologians, who paganized and distorted the meaning of the Logos in Philo's writings. The metaphorical phrases employed by Philo to explain his concept of the Logos were taken literally by the early Christian church, still under pagan influence. The misconstruing of Philo's view led early Christian theologians to make God into a triune being, a belief that Philo would have unquestionably rejected out of hand.

God, according to Philo, is an incorporeal, indefinable, absolute Being without any knowable attributes and qualities. God, being so removed from the world, does not have direct relations with it.[10] As a result, Philo introduces an intermediary existence between God and the world. This is the medium of God's "words."[11] The "words" are identified with the angels in the Scriptures. These powers are also conceived of as a single independent being called *Logos*, a term which Philo borrowed from Greek philosophy. The Logos becomes the intermediary between the transcendent, absolute spiritual God, and the material creation, the only form in which God reveals Himself to mankind. The Philonic conception has its roots in the Platonic and Stoic speculations concerning the relationship of the First Divinity (God) to the world. Philo's system follows that of the Greeks in that it is irreconcilably dualistic, with spirit and matter constituting a polarity. God and the world stand at opposite ends. By means of the Logos, Philo seeks to solve the problem as to how an absolutely transcendent God may be intimately concerned with the world He created. Philo portrays the Logos as the instrument of God's creation and revelation, and of His activity in the universe. This conception of the Logos is derived not from the biblical text, but from Hellenistic sources. It is primarily from the latter sources that Philo developed the concept of the Logos as mediator between God and the world in the ordering of creation. Philo judaizes his idea by identifying the Reason of the Greek philosophers (*Logos* in Greek means both "word" and "reason") with the Aramaic term *memra*ʾ ("the Word").

Examining the Jewish sources, we find, for example, in the Mishnah: "By ten sayings [*maʾamorot*] was the world created" (Avot 5:1). More extensive use of the term is found in the *targumim*, the ancient Aramaic translations of the Bible, where "the Word [*memra*ʾ] of God" is used in various instances. The *memra*ʾ is the manifestation of God's power in creating the world and acts as a vehicle for His activities in the world, but more often it is used in the *targumim* as a circumlocution for God with no special philosophical or mystical implications. In their effort to avoid all anthropomorphisms, the *targumim* employ the term *memra*ᵓ ("the Word") as a substitution for the name of God in every instance where otherwise what is being said about God might sound harsh or offensive. By the use of this substitute, many of the human qualities or emotions attributed to God in the Bible are moderated or removed, thus preserving the pure spiritual conception of God.

There are biblical passages in which the divine word is portrayed figuratively as a personified entity (Isaiah 55:11; Psalms 119:89, 147:15), similar to the personification of *ḥochmah* ("wisdom") in the wisdom literature (Proverbs 8:1 ff., 9:1–6; Job 28:12, 28). However, throughout the Bible, the figurative character of the personification is never in doubt to the discerning reader.

As for Philo, while personifying the Logos to a significant extent, he does not do so in an absolute sense. For him, the Logos is the representative of God and the mediator for man before God. The Logos is the "High Priest His firstborn, the divine Word."[12] The Logos announces God's intentions to man, acting, in this respect, as prophet and priest. It is through the Logos that man knows of God and raises himself toward Him. The Logos is definitely inferior to God. It stands midway between the unbegotten God and begotten mankind. He is neither unbegotten nor begotten.

To His Word, His chief messenger, highest in age and honor, the Father of all has given the special prerogative, to stand on the border and separate the creature from the Creator. This same Word both pleads with the immortal as suppliant for afflicted mortality and acts as ambassador of the ruler to the subject. He glories in this prerogative and proudly describes it in these words "and I stood between the Lord and you" (Deut. 5:5), that is neither uncreated as God, nor created as you, but midway between the two extremes, a surety to both sides.[13]

As a result of his philosophic speculations, Philo deviates from the purity of the biblical teachings to the point of treating the Logos as a godlike personality higher than any of the ordinary angels. He describes it as a "god" (a "god," without a definite article, in distinction from "the God").[14] Philo states that while some mistakenly "regard the image of God, His angel the Word, as His very self,"[15] it is his opinion that God only "stamped the entire universe with His image and ideal form, even His own Word."[16] The Logos is the instrument by which God created the world.

> For that man is the eldest son, whom the Father of all raised up, and elsewhere calls him His firstborn, and indeed the Son thus begotten followed the ways of his Father, and shaped the different kinds, looking to the archetypal patterns which that Father supplied.[17]

> But if there be any as yet unfit to be called a Son of God, let him press to take his place under God's firstborn, the Word, who holds the eldership among the angels, their ruler as it were. And many names are his, for he is called, "the Beginning" [*arche*], and the Name of God, and His Word, and the Man after His image, and "he that sees," that is Israel. . . . For if we have not yet become fit to be thought sons of God yet we may be sons of His invisible image, the most holy Word. For the Word is the eldest-born image of God.[18]

Analagous ideas recur in the Christological thought of Paul and his followers (e.g., Colossians 1:15, Hebrews 1:3–4), and the metaphorical usages employed by Philo foreshadowed those used by pagan-influenced Christian theologians in their attempts to define the relationship between the nature of the Father and the Son. Much of the terminology characteristic of fourth-century trinitarian polemics is already in use here, e.g., the Logos is the firstborn Son of God, His image, His impress, His likeness, a second God. However, while Philo employs these terms in a metaphorical sense, the early Christian theologians construed them in a literal sense. Despite Philo's exaggerated personification of the Logos, he believes it to be nothing more than the messenger and minister of God, like the ministering angels.

Yet Philo's Logos is nevertheless alien to Judaism. Under strong philosophical influence, Philo emphasizes mediation by the Logos in his conception of the relationship between God and man. But according to the teachings that predominate in the Bible, God is directly active in the world. The God of the Bible is a living and concerned God, not the detached being of Greek metaphysics. He does employ intermediaries to do His bidding, but He maintains His control throughout. To be sure, the priests, the prophets, and the angels often act as messengers between God and man. Even the Torah was received through an intermediary (Moses); the Scriptures teach us, however, that at no time is God inaccessible to direct contact. The biblical record teaches that there is never a gap between God and man: "The Lord is near to all who call upon Him, to all who call upon Him in truth" (Psalms 145:18). The God of Philo is heavily overlaid with Platonic ideas. It is a God who does not act directly upon the world once He set it going. Philo's view, like that of the Stoics, is incompatible with Judaism. The conception of the Logos as a second god, a divine being higher than the ordinary angels, runs counter to the absolute monotheism of the biblically based Jewish religion. Many of Philo's concepts and conclusions have no roots in Judaism, as they contain many alien admixtures.

This accounts for the small influence Philo exerted on Jewish thought. Philo paved the way for later Christian theology, which borrowed much from him. Philonic influence is to be found in the literature of the church fathers, where Philo is highly esteemed because of his Logos doctrine. His works were studied diligently by the church fathers, who adopted much of the material found in them for their explanation of the Christian Logos. The influence of Philo's Logos on Christianity is often denied because of its implications. The truth is that while the exact degree of independence enjoyed by the Logos as conceived by Philo must remain doubtful because he is often vague about it, there is no doubt that in the hands of Paul, the author of the Gospel of John, and early Christianity in general, the

Philonic Logos is raised to the status of a divine being who appeared on earth in a bodily form. Christianity depended on Philo's Logos for the development of its own Logos, which subsequently culminated in the development of the doctrine of the Trinity. This relationship, however, has been denied by Christian theologians because it is the antithesis of their belief that this doctrine is of divine origin.

3. *The Doctrine of the Trinity and the New Testament*

The doctrine of the Trinity is nowhere indicated in the Hebrew Bible; neither Jesus nor his early followers claimed its existence. An examination of the purported words of Jesus clearly shows that he never said he was God or a part of God. Jesus spoke of his Father in heaven as his God (John 20:17), to whom he attributed superior authority, knowledge, and greatness (Matthew 20:23, Mark 13:32, John 14:28).

Jesus certainly was not equal to God, for he admitted freely that there were things that neither he nor the angels knew, but only God knew: "But of that day or the hour no one knows, neither the angels in heaven, nor the Son, but the Father" (Mark 13:32). Furthermore, when experiencing difficulty, he displayed submission to God and prayed for help: "Father, if you are willing, remove this cup from me; yet not my will, but Yours be done" (Luke 22:42). Are these quotations from the New Testament consistent with the claim that Jesus is in fact one in substance and power with God?

Lest the reader think these are random samplings not really representative of the Gospels' teaching concerning the Trinity, let us look at other New Testament verses which are purported to be the words of Jesus.

In Matthew 12:31–32 it is stated:

Therefore I say to you, every sin and blasphemy shall be forgiven men, but blasphemy against the Spirit will not be forgiven. And whoever speaks a word against the Son of Man, it shall be forgiven him; but whoever speaks against the Holy Spirit, it shall not be forgiven him, neither in this age nor in that to come.

Hence, we may reasonably presume that Jesus, if he is to be equated with the "Son of Man" (John 8:28), is not of equal status with the "Holy Spirit."

In Matthew 20:20–23, the mother of the sons of Zebedee requests of Jesus that her sons be given prominent positions to the right and left of him in his kingdom. Jesus explains to her that such decisions are not made by him, but by the Father: ". . . this is not mine to give, but it is for those for whom it has been prepared by my Father." Does this statement illustrate equality within the Trinity?

In Matthew 24:35–36 (see also Mark 13:32) it is declared: "Heaven and earth will pass away, but my words will not pass away. But of that day and hour no one knows, neither the angels of the heavens nor the Son, but only the Father." Do the various parts of the Trinity keep secrets from each other? How can the Father and Son be of one essence if the Father knows things of which the Son is ignorant?

Similarly, when asked if he would "at this time" restore the kingdom of Israel (Acts 1:6) Jesus replied: "It is not for you to know times or seasons which the Father has placed in His own jurisdiction" (Acts 1:7). Are we to conclude that the "equal" partners of the triune godhead have powers and knowledge which they do not share with each other?

Luke 2:52 says: "And Jesus kept increasing in wisdom and in physical growth, and in favor with God and men." Do the members of the Trinity have likes and dislikes about each other? Did Jesus, the perfect god-man, need to increase in favor with God, or shall we say two-thirds of God?

In John 5:30 (see also John 6:38) Jesus acknowledges: "I can do nothing on my own initiative. As I hear, I judge; and my judgment is just, because I do not seek my own will, but the will of Him who sent me." Are some members of the coequal Trinity subservient, and less than equal, to other members? Even though they have different wills ("I do not seek my own will"), do they obey without question the others' commands ("the will of Him who sent me")? John's Jesus admits to subordinating his own distinct will, yet according to the trinitarian doctrine they should all have the same will. Should one of the triune partners have to forgo his own will in favor of the will of another member of the Trinity? Should not they all have the exact same will?

In John 8:28–29 Jesus says:

> When you lift up the Son of Man, then you will know that I am he, and that I do nothing on my own initiative, but I speak these things as the Father taught me. And He who sent me is with me; He has not left me alone, because I always do the things that are pleasing to Him.

Do the members of the Trinity have varying knowledge, which they dispense to their other parts when the latter behave properly?

John 14:28 quotes Jesus as saying: ". . . I am going to the Father, because the Father is greater than I am." Is this coequality within the Trinity?

In John 14:31 Jesus says: "As the Father gave me command, even so I do." Are we to presume that the Son has no authority without the consent of the Father?

In John 20:17, John's Jesus recognizes that he is not the equal second partner of a triune god when he says to Mary Magdalene: "I am ascending to my Father and your Father, and my God and your God."

According to Hebrews 5:8, the perfect god-man "learned obedience from the things which he suffered." Why did Jesus have to learn to be obedient if he is God? Whom does he have to obey? Do the equal members of the Trinity exercise authority, one over another?

Even Paul states: "Christ is the head of every man, and the man is the head of a woman, and *God is the head of Christ*" (1 Corinthians 11:3). "You belong to Christ," Paul claims, but he goes on to say that "Christ belongs to God" (1 Corinthians 3:23). As man is subservient to Christ, and woman to man, so Christ is subservient to God. In Philippians 2:5–11, we have another Pauline statement of Jesus' subservient position to God.

> The attitude you should have is the one Christ had: Although he existed in the form of God he did not think that by force he should try

to become equal with God. Instead, he emptied himself and took the form of a slave and came to be in the likeness of men. And being found in appearance as a man, he humbled himself and became obedient until death, even on a cross. For this reason God highly exalted him and gave him the name that is above every name. And so, in the name of Jesus every knee should bend of those in heaven and of those on earth and of those underground. And every tongue should confess that Jesus Christ is Lord, to the glory of God the Father.

The statement that Jesus had the "form of God" could not mean that he was God or even one-third of God. Paul's Jesus is not equal to God but is considered to have been raised to an exalted position by God. That which is not equal to God cannot be God. Furthermore, Jesus is proclaimed Lord, but Paul does not use "Lord" and "God" here as synonymous terms.

In Revelation, written toward the end of the first century, we have the statement: "The kingdom of the world has become the kingdom of our Lord and of His Christ" (Revelation 11:15). Significantly, "our Lord" here is not Jesus but God Himself, and Jesus is clearly distinguished from God as "His Christ." While the term "Lord" is often used in the New Testament to refer to either God or Jesus, there is always a distinction made between the two. God and Jesus are never used synonymously.

John has Jesus saying: "I and the Father are one [*hen*]" (John 10:30). But this statement does not suggest a triune deity. What John's Jesus meant by the word *hen* ("one") becomes clear from his prayer concerning the apostles: "That they may be one [*hen*], just as we are one [*hen*]" (John 17:22), which means that they should be united in agreement with one another as he (Jesus) is always united in agreement with God, as stated: "I [Jesus] always do the things that are pleasing to Him [God]" (John 8:29). There is thus no implication that Jesus and God, or the twelve apostles, are to be considered as of one essence.

The author of the Gospel of John claims that on hearing Jesus say: "I and the Father are one," the Jews accused him of making himself out to be a god: "For good works we do not stone you but for blasphemy, and because you, being a man, made yourself a god" (John 10:33). According to John, the Jews understood Jesus' words as an assertion, on his part, that he is an angelic being (ʾelohim, i.e., a god). In answering the Jews, John's Jesus does not explain directly how he and the Father are one but explains rather that the concept of his being "a god" is not a farfetched idea. John has Jesus reply: "Has it not been written in your Law, 'I said you are gods'?" (John 10:34). This is taken from Psalm 82:6, which reads: "I said: You are godlike beings [ʾelohim], and all of you sons of the Most High." By this explanation, John's Jesus wishes to show that there is nothing wrong, according to scriptural usage, in his claiming to be "a son of God" (John 10:36), for God declares this to be true of all the children of Israel. However, John's Jesus thinks himself to be in a closer relationship with God than any of the other "sons of the Most High."

Continuing his response to their accusation, John's Jesus explains that he is a messenger of God sent to do His bidding. John's Jesus endeavors to convince the Jews that they misunderstand him, "whom the Father sanctified and sent into the world" (John 10:36). It is only because he is God's consecrated messenger, doing the works of his Father, that he believes himself to be "one" with God, strictly obedient to His every command (John 10:37–38). John's Jesus is so exact in his obedience to God's every desire that he claims "the Father is in me and I am in the Father" (John 10:38). At no time does he claim to be one in essence with God. Although he presents himself to be at one with God in will and purpose, John's Jesus never claims a unity of person or equality in substance with the Almighty. In the final analysis, if Jesus is truly God Himself, there would be no need for him to be "sanctified" nor "sent" by anyone or anything.

Revelation 1:17–18 says: ". . . I am the first and the last, and the living one; and I was dead, and behold, I am alive forevermore, and I have the keys of death and of Hades." By connecting this verse with Isaiah 44:6, ". . . I am the first, and I am the last . . . ," certain Christian missionary theologians claim to have proved that Jesus is God. In actuality, the author of

Revelation is not making a comparison with Isaiah's words. He is expressing his belief that Jesus is the first and the last, not in terms of everlasting existence, but with regard to the manner of his resurrection. For this reason, the author calls Jesus "the firstborn of the dead" (Revelation 1:5). According to him, Jesus was the first one God raised from the dead to be "alive forevermore." He is also the last one whom God will raise directly in this manner, for now God has given the power to resurrect the dead, the "keys of death and Hades," exclusively to Jesus (see also John 5:21). Disregarding the question of veracity, these verses do not at all provide any ground for proclaiming Jesus as part of a triune god.

John 14:9 states: "Jesus said to him: 'Have I been so long with you, and yet you have not come to know me, Philip? He who has seen me has seen the Father; how do you say, "Show us the Father"?' " If Jesus is actually God, this statement would contradict the assertion that "no man has seen God at any time" (John 1:18, 1 John 4:12). Actually, John is applying Philo's teaching that the Logos is the only mediator between God and the world. Therefore, he has Jesus say: "And the Father who sent me, He has borne witness of me. You have neither heard His voice at any time, nor seen His form. And you do not have His word abiding in you, for you do not believe him whom He sent" (John 5:37–38). Obviously, when John's Jesus says: "He who has seen me has seen the Father," it is not to be understood literally as actually seeing God in a physical sense. What John's Jesus meant is that by representing God to mankind (John 1:18), he produces, by his actions, an effect which comes closest to seeing God.

In sum, John does not consider Jesus to be a mere mortal, but neither does he believe that he is God. He considers Jesus to be God's most intimate messenger, the Logos, who, as Philo states, is made in the most exact image of God, but is not God Himself.

In Part 1 of this chapter, the word ʾeḥad was shown to mean an absolute one, synonymous with the word yaḥid, "the only one," "alone," when it applies to God in the Shema. This is contrary to the Christian missionary claim that ʾeḥad refers to a compound unity. But, how did Jesus view the possibility of a division in the divine essence? Chapter 17 of the Gospel of John records a prayer which its author attributes to Jesus. In verse 2 of this prayer, Jesus views himself as being sent by God, his Father, who "gave him authority over all mankind." But of his Father he is quoted, in verse 3, as saying that he is "the only true God." Jesus does not say, "we are the only true God," or even, "You, Father, and the Holy Spirit are the only true God," but refers his remarks solely to the God whom he depicts as "Father." Even assuming Jesus to have been God manifested in a human form, he still would be God, and as such, he could not possibly have made this statement. Thus, by calling his Father not just the "true God" but "the only true God," he avows that he himself cannot be part of God. Jesus may claim to be united in oneness with God in doing only what the Almighty wishes, but he never asserts that he is part of the essence of God. If Jesus is of one substance with the Father, he could not say that the Father (verse 1), as differentiated from "Jesus Christ" (verse 3), is "the only true God." By definition, "only" must imply the singularity of God to the exclusion of all, including Jesus. Thus, it is clear that Jesus himself confirms that the Father, not the Son or the Holy Spirit, is "the only true God."

In Acts 2:36, Luke, the friend and companion of Paul, reports that Peter said that God has made Jesus "both Lord and Christ." If Jesus is the one-and-only God, he would not need God to exalt him. Obviously, "Lord" is not used here in the sense of God; rather, it must refer to someone who has only attained a high station through the grace of God. Such a one could not be God.

Many Christian translations render certain New Testament verses as referring to Jesus as both "God and Savior." While such renderings would conform with John 1:1, 18, "and the Word was a god," and, "the only begotten god,"[19] they still would not refer to Jesus as the Eternal God. Some historians see in the phrase "God and Savior" a Christian usage borrowed from the pagan formula used in deifying rulers. However, the New Testament writers do make a definite distinction between the one-and-only God and Jesus, never considering them one and the same. For instance, in 2 Peter 1:2, we find this distinction expressed in the statement: "Kindness and peace be multiplied to you in the knowledge of God and of Jesus our Lord." This clarifies the meaning of the preceding verse, which reads, in part, "by the righteousness of our God and of [the] Savior Jesus Christ" (2 Peter 1:1). The author of these two verses indicates that he considers God and Jesus to be two distinct beings. On occasion, the New Testament writers alternate their use of the term "savior," applying it to both God and Jesus. Thus, Paul, in Titus 1:3, calls God, "our Savior," and then in verse 4, differentiates between "God [the] Father and Christ Jesus our Savior." This does not show that God and Jesus are of one essence, but illustrates the function which the New Testament writers believe Jesus has in God's relationship with humanity. This function can be seen from the following discussion of what some of the New Testament writers have to say about Jesus as savior.

Paul writes in Titus 2:13: "Awaiting the blessed hope and manifestation of the glory of the great God and of our Savior Christ Jesus." Paul designates Jesus as "our Savior," but not as God Himself. Yet even Paul could not deny that ultimately God is the true savior (Isaiah 43:11, 45:21; Hosea 13:4), which leads him to argue that God works through Jesus, as He worked, in former times, through others who were raised up as saviors (Judges 2:16; 3:9, 15; Nehemiah 9:27). Thus, God is still considered the only source of salvation. However, salvation is now executed through Jesus. Accordingly, in Paul's epistles we find the Father and the Son spoken of together in connection with salvation (1 Timothy 1:1; 2 Timothy 1:8–10; Titus 1:3–4, 2:10–13, 3:4–6). The author of Acts, who was greatly influenced by Paul, attributes to Peter a statement which indicates Jesus' position as a savior: "He is the one whom God exalted to His right hand as a leader and a savior. . ." (Acts 5:31). This is expressed in 1 John 4:14 with the words: ". . . the Father has sent the Son to be Savior of the world." Curiously enough, even though Jesus is described as man's savior, God is described as Jesus' savior in Hebrews 5:7: "In the days of his flesh, he offered up both prayers and supplications with loud crying and tears to the one able to save him from death, and he was heard because of his piety." While Jesus is, for Paul and the other New Testament writers, the sole agent through which God deals with mankind, i.e., man's Lord and Savior, he is not at all God.

John 8:56–58 states: " 'Abraham your father rejoiced to see my day; and he saw it, and was glad.' The Jews therefore said to him: 'You are not yet fifty years old, and have you seen Abraham?' Jesus said to them: 'Truly, truly, I say to you, before Abraham came into being, I am.' "

Trinitarians argue that the Greek words *ego eimi* ("I am"), allegedly spoken by Jesus (John 8:58), indicate that Jesus is God (see also John 8:24, 28). They arrive at their contention by connecting the phrase "I am" with the words spoken by God in Exodus 3:14 and often translated: "I AM THAT I AM. . . . Thus you shall say to the children of Israel: I AM has sent me to you." However, the literal and proper translation of this verse is: "I WILL BE WHAT I WILL BE. . . . Thus you shall say to the children of Israel: I WILL BE has sent me to you."

Since the author of the Gospel of John utilized the Greek Septuagint translation of the Bible in his writings, it cannot be assumed that John's Jesus is referring to the words in Exodus 3:14. Although Jesus actually spoke in Hebrew or Aramaic, not Greek, John recorded Jesus' alleged words in Greek. *Ego eimi* ("I am"), used by John's Jesus, is not the same as *ho on* ("The Being, The One Who Is"), which is used in the Septuagint's rendering of Exodus 3:14: "And God spoke to Moses, saying, I am THE BEING; and He said, Thus you shall say to the children of Israel: THE BEING has sent me to you." Even though *ho on* appears in the Gospel of John, it is never used as a title or name or exclusively as a reference to Jesus. In the Book of Revelation, also credited to John by missionaries, *ho on* appears five times (Revelation 1:4, 8; 4:8; 11:17; 16:5). Significantly, in each instance, it is used as a title or designation applied to God, not Jesus. Thus: "John to the seven churches that are in Asia: Grace to you and peace, from Him who is [*ho on*] and who was and who is to come; and from the seven spirits who are before His throne" (Revelation 1:4). That this verse refers to God and not Jesus is seen from the following verse, which continues the greeting by now including Jesus as one of those sending greetings. Hence, John says, in verses 4 and 5, that greetings are sent by God, the seven spirits, and Jesus.

In verse 8 John writes: " 'I am the Alpha and the Omega,' says the Lord God, 'who is [*ho on*] and who was and who is to come, the Almighty' " (Revelation 1:8). This verse also speaks of God, not Jesus. In Revelation 4:8, *ho on* is applied to "the Lord God, the Almighty," not Jesus, who, as the "Lamb" referred to in Revelation 5:6–7, comes to God, who is sitting on His throne. That they are two separate entities is seen from Revelation 5:13: "To the one sitting on the throne, and to the Lamb, be blessing and honor and glory and dominion forever and ever." In addition, *ho on* is applied to the "Lord God, the Almighty," not Jesus, in Revelation 11:17 and Revelation 16:5. That *ho on* in Revelation 16:5 refers to God and not Jesus can be seen from verse 7, which, referring to the subject of verses 5 and 6, states: "And I heard the altar saying: "Yes, Lord God, the Almighty, true and righteous are Your judgments." These are further indications that *ho on* and *ego eimi* are not used as synonymous terms by John.

In John 8:56–58, John is expounding his belief that Jesus had a prehuman existence as an angelic being in heaven. John's Jesus is proclaiming here that this prehuman existence began before Abraham was born: "Before Abraham came into being, I am." The fact of the matter is that the text does not at all indicate how long Jesus supposedly lived before Abraham. In no honest way can John's statement be taken to identify Jesus as God.

Matthew 28:19 states: "Go therefore, and teach all nations, baptizing in the name of the Father, and the Son, and the Holy Spirit." Although the Father, the Son, and the Holy Spirit are grouped together, this verse does not prove the existence of a triune deity. The verse merely indicates the author's belief that they are to be mentioned together during baptism. Each is thought to have a function in the initiation of the believer during the baptism ritual. Yet no doctrine of coequality among them is promulgated in this verse.

One of the better proofs for the doctrine of a triune god is adduced from 1 John 5:7–8. As rendered in the King James Version of the Bible, it reads: "For there are three that bear record in heaven, the Father, the Word, and the Holy Ghost: and these three are one. And there are three that bear witness in earth, the spirit, and the water, and the blood: and these three agree in one." However, these verses do not occur in any reliable Greek manuscript. There is an interesting footnote to the above to be found in the Catholic Jerusalem Bible (1966), which does not have the added words in the main text. It states:

> Vulg[ate] vv. 7–8 read as follows "There are three witnesses in heaven: *the Father the Word and the Spirit, and these three are one; there are three witnesses on earth*: the Spirit the water and the blood." The words in italics (not in any of the early Greek MSS, or any of the early translations, or in the best MSS of the Vulg. itself) are probably a gloss that has crept into the text.

These spurious words may have been the work of an overzealous copyist, who inserted this statement so as to lend credence to the doctrine of the Trinity.

Even the authors of John, Colossians, and Hebrews, who elevate Jesus to a point where he is viewed as the medium *through* whom things are done, do not claim that he is the Creator or part of a triune god. They consider him to be the instrument through which the Creator works:

> All things came into being through him, and apart from him not even one thing came into being. (John 1:3)

> For in him all things were created in the heavens and upon earth, visible and invisible, whether lordships or governments or authorities. All things have been created through him and for him. (Colossians 1:16)

> In these last days He has spoken to us by a Son, whom He appointed heir of all things, through whom also He made the ages. (Hebrews 1:2)

Do the preceding quotations from the Christian Bible show

oneness of substance and coequality within the Christological concept of a triune god? On the contrary, they show that the various members of the so-called Trinity could not be considered one or coequal. Those Jews who believe in a triune god should realize that the New Testament declares most emphatically that Jesus did not view himself as equal to God. To believe in the Trinity, one must assume the existence of three separate gods of unequal status, which would nullify any Christian missionary claim to a belief in monotheism.

The Hebrew Scriptures inform us that only God, who is "from everlasting to everlasting," is eternal, and has no beginning (Psalms 90:2). In contrast, the New Testament refers to Jesus as, "the beginning [*arche*] of the creation of God" (Revelation 3:14). Revelation's author does not imply that Jesus always existed. The word "beginning" expresses the idea of a starting point in time. This clarifies John 1:1, "In the beginning was the Word," referring to the beginning of creation. John does not state that Jesus was eternally with God, only that he existed for an unspecified time before being used as the means through which God's creative works were accomplished. It is only after creation began that John's Jesus became God's spokesman, the Word. The suggestion that Jesus is the author of the creation, and in that sense the beginning, does not accord with the meaning of the word *arche*. The claim that *arche* means the originating source of creation has no New Testament support. New Testament usage demonstrates that *arche* is not used in Revelation 3:14 in the sense of causing anything to come into being, but rather as a reference to the first thing created by God.

Albert Barnes writes, concerning the Greek word *arche*, "beginning" or "origin":

> The word properly refers to the *commencement* of a thing, not its *authorship*, and denotes properly primacy in time, and primacy in rank, but not primacy in the sense of causing anything to exist. . . . The word is not, therefore, found in the sense of *authorship*, as denoting that one is the *beginning* of anything in the sense that he caused it to have an existence.[20]

Nevertheless, Barnes believes that Jesus is himself the uncreated and eternal Creator. However, he does not base his belief on Revelation 3:14. Of this verse he says:

> If it *were* demonstrated from other sources that Christ was, in fact, a created being, and the first that God had made, it cannot be denied that this language would appropriately *express* that fact. But it cannot be made out from the mere use of the language here; and as the language is susceptible of other interpretations, it cannot be employed to prove that Christ is a created being.[21]

While it is true that on the basis of language usage alone, this verse may not prove that its author considered Jesus a created being, it can be shown that the authors of the New Testament considered Jesus a created being, the first so made by God: "And he is the image of the invisible God, the firstborn of all creation. . . . And he is before all things . . ." (Colossians 1:15–17). Barnes disregards this evidence, which depicts Jesus as a created being. He is of the opinion that Revelation 3:14 teaches solely that Jesus "holds the primacy over all, and is at the head of the universe." He maintains that this verse refers to Jesus as ruler of the world, not as the creator of the world or as the first thing created. Accordingly, Jesus "is 'the beginning of the creation of God,' in the sense that he is the head or prince of the creation; that is, that he presides over it so far as the purposes of the redemption are to be accomplished, and so far as is necessary for those purposes."[22] However, the validity of this explanation is open to question. Barnes' statement that this verse refers to Jesus as ruler of the world seems more the result of his desire to propose an explanation that will be acceptable to trinitarians than to determine the original intention of its author. There is no question that the authors of the New Testament regarded Jesus as the one through whom God rules the universe. They also attributed to Jesus the attaining of his exalted position only at the behest of God (Philippians 2:9). But what we are mainly concerned with here is that the wording of Revelation 3:14 does not at all establish Jesus as being the eternal Creator of the universe. It does not show Jesus to be the *author* or origin of creation. As we have seen, Barnes agrees with this. Furthermore, when he refers to Jesus as ruler, it should be understood that there is a difference in meaning between saying one is the "head," "chief," "prince," or "ruler" of creation, and saying he is the "beginning" of creation. To be the "beginning" of something does not imply leadership. Primacy in creation, as the first being created by God, and primacy over creation, as the one through whom God rules the creation, are two distinct attributes that the authors of the New Testament applied to Jesus. One does not naturally follow from the other.

In Revelation 3:14 *arche* is properly translated "beginning" to indicate that Jesus was the first being created. A futher example of this usage may be found in Colossians 1:18. There, Jesus is called "the beginning [*arche*], the first born from the dead," indicating Paul's belief that Jesus is the first one of those who will be resurrected from the dead, "in order that he might come to have first place in everything." As we have seen, Jesus, "the beginning of the creation of God," is thought by the authors of the New Testament to be the first thing created by God, "the firstborn of all creation" (Colossians 1:15) through whom everything else was created. The very fact that Jesus' existence is connected with the beginning of creation nullifies the claim that Jesus is God. What is begotten cannot be eternal, and what is not eternal cannot be equal to God; moreover, that which is created by God cannot be God.

John expounds the belief that Jesus had a prehuman existence as the Word who was "in the beginning with God" and through whom "all things came into being." John emphasizes this belief throughout his entire Gospel (John 1:1–3, 17:5, 24). He describes Jesus as "an only begotten from a father" (John 1:14) and "the only begotten Son of God" (John 3:18; see also John 3:16, 1 John 4:9). John's belief in Jesus as "the only begotten Son of God" rests, as with Paul's belief, on the contention that Jesus is the only being created directly by God. All other creatures were created through Jesus. He is the image of the invisible God, the firstborn, and chief among all creation (Colossians 1:15–17). He is even higher than the ordinary angels (Hebrews 1:3–13). Yet despite the exalted position to which John raised Jesus, he, like Paul, did not consider him to be the one-and-only God.

The Jesus of the New Testament never asked to be recognized as God, only as the "Son of God," that is, one who is in a close relationship with God. In fact, even after his alleged resurrection, he is still referred to by the term "Son of God" (Revelation 2:18), nothing more. This is not surprising, since in the New Testament Jesus always speaks of himself, and is spoken of by others, as separate and distinct from God. Nowhere in the New Testament, including the Gospel of John, where it specifically mentions the Word becoming flesh, is the claim made that Jesus is God incarnate, a combination of God and man. Some Christian missionary theologians, believing Jesus to be God incarnate, see an important significance in John's use of the Greek verb *eskenosen*, translated "dwelt," in John 1:14: "And the Word became flesh, and dwelt among us." This verb has its root in the noun meaning "dwelling," "tent," "booth," "tabernacle." These missionaries interpret this word to indicate that Jesus was God in spirit while tabernacling, that is, dwelling in, a human body; hence, his incarnation as a god-man. However, John's usage of this verb does not imply that Jesus is the incarnation of God. The author of the Second Epistle of Peter uses the same manner of expression: "And I consider it right, as long as I am in this dwelling [*skenomati*], to stir you up by way of reminder, knowing that the laying aside of my dwelling [*skenomatos*] is imminent, as also our Lord Jesus Christ has made clear to me" (2 Peter 1:13–14). Does the author of this epistle mean, by the use of the Greek noun *skenoma*, "dwelling," "tabernacle," that Peter also is an incarnation, a god-man? The Christian missionaries' answer must be that the author most certainly does not intend to express such an opinion. What the author wishes to express is that Peter would remain alive for a short time longer in his human body, and that is all. Therefore, word usage indicates that John 1:14 does not support the incarnation doctrine.

Christianity is the development of Paul and his theological descendants, who presented the pagans with a diluted form of Judaism in Hellenized garb. It is true that the Hellenistic Jewish philosophy of Philo paved the way to such a syncretism, but Philo certainly would have been shocked at the resulting distortion which followed in Paul's wake. Philo expected the Messiah, but he never identified the Messiah with the Logos, as was done by later Christian theology. For Paul, under the influence of a Hellenized Philonic philosophy, the Christ is:

> the image of the invisible God, the firstborn of all creation. For in him all things were created, in the heavens and upon earth, visible and invisible, whether lordships or governments or authorities. All things have been created through him and for him. And he is before all things, and in him all things hold together. . . . For it was [God's] good pleasure for all the fullness to dwell in him, and through him to reconcile all things to Himself. . . . He [Jesus] has now reconciled you in his fleshly body through death, in order to present you before Him [God] holy and blameless and beyond reproach. (Colossians 1:15–22)

Paul's view is that Jesus is not God. He is God's first creation and the means by which God acts in the universe. He sees Jesus as the temporary incarnation of a preexistent heavenly being. Paul's Jesus is patterned after Philo's Logos. Jesus is in the image of God. He is the link between God and man and the agent for man's redemption. He intercedes with God on man's behalf and, as heavenly advocate, pleads man's cause before God (Romans 8:34; Hebrews 7:25, 9:24; 1 John 2:1). He is the mediator between man and God: "For there is one God, and also one mediator between God and men, a man Christ Jesus" (1 Timothy 2:5). Paul further states: "But for us there is but one God, the Father, from whom are all things, and we exist for Him; and one Lord, Jesus Christ, through whom are all things, and we exist through him" (1 Corinthians 8:6). Christian theology misunderstood Paul's Father-Son relationship. Paul says that the Father is "the God of our Lord Jesus Christ." He is the God and Father of Jesus, not his equal (Ephesians 1:3, 17).

In all of his writings, Paul does not identify Jesus with God or portray him as equal to God: "And when all things are subjected to him, then the Son himself will also be subjected to the

One who subjected all things to him, that God may be all in all" (1 Corinthians 15:28). In Philippians 2:9, Paul writes of Jesus that it is God who "highly exalted him," which means that God did not make him His equal. Even after his exaltation, Jesus still remains subject to God. It is obvious that if Jesus is "highly exalted" by God, he must have first occupied an inferior position in relation to God. Since his prior position was lower than God's, and at best he will attain a level where he will still be "subject to the One who subjected all things to him," he could not be part of that "One."

Wherever the relationship of Jesus to God is treated in the New Testament, Jesus is always represented in a subordinate position. This subordinate role can be seen in the fact that Jesus views himself as a messenger: "He who receives you receives me, and he who receives me receives Him who sent me" (Matthew 10:40; see also John 5:36). Jesus acknowledges his subordination and subjection to God when he declares that God is greater than he is (John 14:28), that he does nothing on his own initiative, speaking and doing only what God has taught him (John 8:28–29), and seeking not his own will, but the will of God who sent him (John 5:30, 6:38).

Obviously, John's Jesus is not God, whose will is to be done, but is lower than God, doing God's will in accordance with Philo's conception of the Logos as a heavenly being distinct from God. In accordance with Philo's concept of the Logos as the mediator between God and mankind, John's Jesus said: "You are seeking to kill me, a man who has told you the truth, which I heard from God" (John 8:40). To the apostles he reveals the source of his alleged knowledge: "I have called you friends, because all the things which I have heard from my Father I have made known to you" (John 15:15). John's Jesus repeatedly speaks of himself as being sent by God.

> But Jesus cried out and said: "He who believes in me does not believe in me, but in Him who sent me. And he who beholds me beholds the One who sent me. . . . For I did not speak on my own initiative, but the Father Himself who sent me has given me commandment as to

what I should say and what I should speak. And I know that His commandment is life everlasting. Therefore the things I speak are just as the Father has spoken to me, thus I speak." (John 12:44–50)

John's Jesus acknowledges: "A slave is not greater than his master, neither one who is sent greater than the one who sent him" (John 13:16). As God is greater than Jesus in sending him, so Jesus is greater than his disciples in sending them: "As the Father has sent me, I also send you" (John 20:21). The one who has greater authority sends the one who has less authority. John's Jesus himself disavows any triune coequality with God. In John 17:3, it is stated: "This is everlasting life, that they may know You, the only true God, and Jesus Christ whom You have sent." The true God is superior to, separate, and distinct from Jesus.

Despite the distinctiveness with which God and Jesus are regarded in the New Testament, Christian missionaries are under the misconception that God and Jesus form two-thirds of a triune deity. Partial responsibility for this error is due to the New Testament writers, who use a number of designations for Jesus which are the same as those given to God in the Hebrew Bible and in the New Testament. The resulting confusion as to whether certain New Testament passages refer to God or to Jesus helped to produce the belief in a triune god. That Jesus, who is considered by the New Testament writers to be the link between God and creation, is called by some of the same designations that are applied to God is understandable. After all, the New Testament writers believed that God had conferred a tremendous amount of power upon this angelic being, so why not, as well, some of His names, which express certain facets of His being? But it is nevertheless clear that although the God of the New Testament interacts with the world He created solely through His "firstborn," the latter is still subservient to God. Because of the exalted yet subservient position in which they envision Jesus, the New Testament writers do not believe it compromises God's status to apply some of His names to Jesus (cf. Ephesians 1:21, Philippians 2:9, Hebrews 1:4). The use of common names is not intended to indicate that Jesus is of one substance with God. The claim that the use of these names bears significance is of uncertain value since the texts are often unclear as to whether the reference is to God or to Jesus. For example, while such terms as "Lord" and "Savior" are sometimes applied to both, other terms, like "King of Kings and Lord of Lords" (Revelation 19:16) and "Alpha and Omega" (Revelation 22:13), may not refer to Jesus at all and, in any case, provide no proof of equality of substance. What is significant is not so much the use of these names as the fact that wherever the relationship between God and Jesus is treated, the New Testament writers always describe God as superior to Jesus. As God's spokesman, Jesus is subservient to Him. This fact cannot be overriden.

It is only through a cumulative study of how the relationship of Jesus to God is treated in the entire New Testament that we can determine the nature and role of the Logos as visualized by the early Christians. There is no doubt that the New Testament is greatly indebted to Philo. It is from him that the New Testament writers borrowed the concept of the Logos. Parallels to Philo's teachings on the Logos abound in the New Testament to the extent where they could not be coincidental. In essence, Philo's Logos, the most perfect image of God, is the elder among the angels, and acts as the creative mediator between the all-perfect, all-good God and the inherently evil world of matter. In the New Testament, we find references to such Philonic concepts as the "firstborn Son of God," the "image of God," and the "mediating high priest," but the fullness of Philo's doctrine of the Logos finds its culmination in the Gospel of John. This book was written by a man deeply influenced by Philonic thought. This influence is most evident from a study of the Logos doctrine as set forth in the first chapter of that gospel. Modifying Philo's description of the Logos as a god, John describes the Logos as a separate divine entity who "became flesh," and identifies it with Jesus. The task John sets for himself is to proclaim to the Greeks that the Messiah, the Christ, the "only begotten Son of God," has existed from the beginning of creation as a mediator, and that this divine Logos has become flesh in Jesus.

It is in John 1:1 that the nature of the Logos (the Word) is explicitly stated. The first verse of John, as translated in the King James Version, reads: "In the beginning was the Word [*ho logos*], and the Word was with God [*ton theon*, accusative case of *ho theos*], and the Word was God [*theos*]" (John 1:1). In the Greek this is: *En arche en ho logos, kai ho logos en pros ton theon, kai theos en ho logos.* The Greek sentence ends with the crucial words: *kai theos en ho logos* ("and god was the Word"). We are concerned here with the Greek noun *theos* ("god") written without the definite article. This is in contrast to the first mention of this noun expressed by *ton theon*, the accusative case of *ho theos* ("the God"), i.e., the noun *theos* preceded by the definite article *ho*.

In this verse, reference is made to God and the Logos, not to three beings. When John 1:1 refers to the Word as "god," there really is no basis for concluding that he is the second person of a triune god. This is evident from the Greek text, where, as we have just seen, the definite article *ho* appears before the first mention of God in the sentence, but is omitted before the second. The presence of the definite article before the noun suggests an identity, a personality, whereas its absence suggests a quality about someone. In the New Testament, the definite article usually precedes the noun *theos* when it denotes the one-and-only God. Since there is an omission of the Greek definite article before the second mention of *theos*, no proof for the existence of a triune god can be accurately adduced from this verse. The omission of the definite article before the second mention of *theos* causes the word *theos* to act as an adjective that describes the nature of the Word. It thus serves as a predicate adjective rather than as a predicate noun.[23] For this reason, some translators render John 1:1 as "the word was deity" or "was divine." This is quite different from the trinitarian missionary statement that the Word was God and was identical with God. If the Word was toward God, or with God, or for God, it is impossible to say that it was God. If it was God, it could stand in no relationship to God.

The author of John is expressing his belief that Jesus, the Word, was not "the God" but "a god." It should not be considered unusual that a New Testament writer refers to Jesus as "a god" since he is considered to be an angelic being who is the decisive link between God and His creation. The term "god" is applied even to the evil angel Satan, "the god of this world" (2 Corinthians 4:4). Indeed, Paul says: ". . . there are many gods and many lords but for us there is but one God, the Father, . . . and one Lord, Jesus Christ . . ." (1 Corinthians 8:5–6). Since referring to Jesus as a god would not make him, in any way, part of the one-and-only God, the proper translation of John 1:1 should be: "In the beginning was the Word, and the Word was with [literally 'toward'] God, and the Word was a god." There is no reason to assume that the need for a definite article is understood from the context in order to be able to translate the end of the verse as, "and the Word was God." John's meaning is that the god mentioned here was not the only god, i.e., divine being or angel.

E. C. Colwell offers a grammatical rule explaining the use of the article with a predicate nominative in the Greek New Testament.[24] This rule seems to justify the trinitarian translation of John 1:1. Colwell says:

> A definite predicate nominative has the article when it follows the verb; it does not have the article when it precedes the verb. Of course, this can be claimed as a rule only after it has been shown to describe the usage of the Greek New Testament as a whole or in large part. . . . The opening verse of John's Gospel contains one of the many passages where this rule suggests the translation of a predicate as a definite noun. *Kai Theos en ho logos* looks much more like "And the Word was God" than "And the Word was divine" when viewed with reference to this rule. The absence of the article does *not* make the predicate indefinite or qualitative when it precedes the verb; it is indefinite in this position only when the context demands it. The context makes no such demand in the Gospel of John, for this statement cannot be regarded as strange in the prologue of the gospel which reaches its climax in the confession of Thomas. (pp.13,21)

On closer examination, one finds that rather than supporting the trinitarian view, Colwell's evidence and conclusions disprove the belief that John teaches the doctrine of a triune godhead. Colwell's evidence indicates that this is not an absolute rule but one which has a number of exceptions (pp. 16–18). In addition, citing John 1:1 as an example, he states that context is important in determining whether a predicate nominative before a verb is indefinite. However, in support of his position that context demands that the predicate be definite in this verse, he states that this Gospel "reaches its climax in the confession of Thomas" (John 20:28) in which Thomas refers to Jesus as "my Lord and my God."[25] At the heart of Colwell's statement is a theological bias on his part, not a judicious opinion based on either grammar or context. Colwell says: "The absence of the article does *not* make the predicate indefinite or qualitative when it precedes the verb; it is indefinite in this position only when context demands it." According to his explanation, a predicate noun, e.g., "god," in the predicate nominative "and god was the Word," is indefinite before the verb only when the context demands it. He then asserts that "the context makes no such demand in the Gospel of John." Actually, the very opposite is true. In John 1:1, context does demand that the second "god" mentioned in this verse be indefinite. In fact, the context of the entire New Testament indicates that Colwell's rule is not applicable to John 1:1. Actually, John 1:1 is the most notable exception to his rule. As a result, no definite article should be understood as being implied before the second mention of "god" in John 1:1. To translate the word *theos* as "divine" or "a god" in order to express the nature of the Word, rather than to identify his person, is consistent with John's use of Philo's teachings and terminologies to explain his own Logos doctrine. The lack of the definite article before the word "god" most certainly represents John's theological intention.

In a study made by Philip B. Harner, an examination was conducted of clauses in which an anarthrous predicate noun precedes the copulative verb. Harner states that:

> . . . E. C. Colwell examined this type of word-order and reached the tentative conclusion that "definite predicate nouns which

precede the verb usually lack the article." In accordance with this rule he regarded it as probable that the predicate noun in both Mark 15:39 and John 1:1 should be interpreted as definite. Colwell was almost entirely concerned with the question whether anarthrous predicate nouns were definite or indefinite, and he did not discuss at any length the problem of their qualitative significance. This problem, needs to be examined as a distinct issue.[26]

Harner's findings "suggest that anarthrous predicate nouns preceding the verb may function primarily to express the nature or character of the subject, and this qualitative significance may be more important than the question whether the predicate noun itself should be regarded as definite or indefinite."[27]

According to Harner, the Gospel of John has fifty-three anarthrous predicates before the verb and the Gospel of Mark has eight. Examining Mark's usage of this grammatical form, he concludes that it "gives little if any support to the idea that an anarthrous predicate noun preceding the verb is necessarily definite."[28] In examining John's fifty-three examples of an anarthrous predicate preceding the verb, he finds that there is reason to expect "some qualitative significance in the predicate noun, and we cannot assume that the predicate is necessarily definite."[29] Harner cites John 6:51 and 15:1 as two examples of the type of clause in which an arthrous predicate precedes the verb. "The fact that John sometimes uses this type of clause supports the view that he did not necessarily regard an anarthrous predicate as definite simply because it precedes the verb."[30] He does not rule out the possibility that "an anarthrous predicate preceding the verb . . . may be definite if there is some specific reason for regarding it as definite."[31] But this type of anarthrous predicate, he emphasizes, would be an exceptional case. Harner maintains that the majority of anarthrous predicates in the Fourth Gospel are of the type for which "there is no basis for regarding such predicates as definite, and it would be incorrect to translate them as definite."[32]

In his detailed examination of John 1:1 Harner states that "our study so far suggests that the anarthrous predicate in this verse has primarily a qualitative significance and that it would be definite only if there is some specific indication of the definiteness in the meaning or context."[33] However, Harner writes that the clause *ho logos en pros ton theon*, "the Word was with God" "suggests relationship, and thus some form of 'personal' differentiation, between the two."[34] As such, *theos en ho logos* "means that the *logos* has the nature of *theos* (rather than something else)" and that "the word *theos* is placed at the beginning for emphasis."[35] Therefore, he concludes that:

> Perhaps the clause could be translated, "the Word had the same nature as God." This would be one way of representing John's thought, which is, as I understand it, that *ho logos*, no less than *ho theos*, had the nature of *theos*.[36]

Harner, like Colwell, is a trinitarian, yet his study does not enhance the trinitarian contention that John 1:1 speaks of God and the Logos as being of one essence. Furthermore, his analysis makes Colwell's "definite rule" even less definite than ever. At the end of his study Harner reminds the reader that:

> At a number of points in this study we have seen that anarthrous predicate nouns preceding the verb may be primarily qualitative in force yet may also have some connotation of definiteness. The categories of qualitativeness and definiteness, that is, are not mutually exclusive, and frequently it is a delicate exegetical issue for the interpreter to decide which emphasis a Greek writer had in mind. As Colwell called attention to the possibility that such nouns may be definite, the present study has focused on their qualitative force. . . . In John 1:1 I think that the qualitative force of the predicate is so prominent that the noun cannot be regarded as definite.[37]

It follows that it should be quite acceptable to render *theos en ho logos* as "the Word was a god" for here John is expressing his belief about the quality or nature of the Word. He is not identifying the essence of the Word as being one with God. For the writer of the Gospel of John *ho theos* and *ho logos* are not interchangeable terms. If they were he could not say "the

Word was *with* God." John's Word is a divine being but he is not the Divinity.

The trinitarian missionary argument that the second *theos* in John 1:1 does not require the article can only be motivated by theological considerations, whereas to translate the word *theos* as "a god" is consistent not only with John's use of the Philonic Logos, but with the New Testament's general explanation of Jesus' relationship to God. There is no reason to assume that the absence of a definite article is implied or understood. The absence of the article is intentional and essential to express John's belief. Similarly, in Revelation 19:13, attributed to John, Jesus is called "the Word of God" (literally "the Word of the God," *ho Logos tou Theou*), not "God the Word." Under the influence of Philo's teachings, John did not promulgate the idea that the Word was "the God," but that he was, as the firstborn Son of God, a second god. God and Logos are not interchangeable terms. For this reason, in John 1:1, God is referred to as *the* God and the Logos as *a* god to show the difference between the two. John deliberately omitted the definite article in the predicate in order to describe who or what the Word was in relation to God, i.e., *a* god, an angelic being, but not *the* God.

It was not difficult for the Gentile mind to picture human salvation as being brought about by the incarnation of the Word in the form of Jesus. The pagans of Asia Minor believed that the Son of God, Hermes, had come down in disguise to dwell among men. The Book of Acts records how in Lystra, Paul and Barnabas were identified with Hermes and Zeus (Acts 14:12). In John's time (after 81 C.E.), the emperor Domitian insisted that he be regarded as God, son of the supreme God, and be addressed as "our Lord and our God." It was, therefore, quite understandable for John to have Thomas adore the allegedly risen Jesus as "my Lord and my God" (John 20:28). This might have been employed as a polemic against Domitian's claim to divinity.

As to the claim that Thomas' alleged exclamation: "My Lord and my God" (literally "The Lord of me and the God of me") is proof of Jesus' divinity, a grammatical analysis of the original Greek will disprove it. It reads in Greek: *Ho kyrios mou kai ho theos mou* ("The Lord of me and the God of me"). Moule states:

In John 20:28 *Ho kyrios mou kai ho theos mou*, it is to be noted that a substantive [e.g., God] in the Nominative case used in a vocative sense [indicates person addressed, e.g. Jesus] and followed by a possessive [e.g., of me] could not be anarthrous [i.e., without the definite article] . . . ; the article before *theos* may, therefore, not be significant.[38]

Because of this grammatical rule, the definite article before *theos* is, in this instance, of no conclusive value for proving that Thomas referred to Jesus as *the* God. A better understanding of John's rendition of Thomas' words may be seen by comparing them with Paul's usage of the words God and Lord: "But for us there is one God, the Father, from whom are all things, and we exist for Him; and one Lord, Jesus Christ, through whom are all things, and we exist through him" (1 Corinthians 8:6). Two separate and distinct entities are spoken of by Paul. Indeed, Thomas' words may be taken literally as an exclamation referring to both: "The Lord of me [Jesus] and the God of me [God]." Alternately, Thomas' words may very well mean that Jesus is referred to as a specific angelic being, who exerts dominion over him ("my lord") as his guardian angel ("my god"), and not to God Himself. In the light of the evidence presented by the New Testament, it is clear that this alleged statement of Thomas' in no way refers to Jesus as the Eternal God of Israel.

Evidence from still another quarter indicates how certain changes in the New Testament text created a climate more conducive to the growth of the doctrine of the Trinity. Archaeological discoveries in Egypt and the Judean desert have provided insight into the use of the Tetragrammaton, the divine name, in the pre-Christian and early Christian periods. A study of pre-Christian Greek Septuagint texts indicates that in all these Greek texts the Tetragrammaton was always written by Jewish scribes in either paleo-Hebrew, square Aramaic script, or in transliteration. This differs considerably from the extant manuscripts of the Septuagint, which are of Christian origin. These all render the Tetragrammaton either *kyrios* ("Lord") or *theos* ("God"). However, it may be assumed that the Septuagint copies used by the New Testament writers were of Jewish origin, and consequently included the Tetragrammaton. Around the end of the first century of the common era, the Christians replaced the divine name with Greek substitutes in the text of the Septuagint and in all quotations from the Septuagint found in the New Testament.

The replacement of the Tetragrammaton with *kyrios* and *theos* in the New Testament has obscured the distinction between the Lord God and the Lord Christ, often making it impossible to distinguish between the two in many passages. As a result, in a number of New Testament citations from the Hebrew Bible, the manuscript traditions are confused as to whether God or Jesus is referred to in the discussion of these quotations. With the removal of the Tetragrammaton and its replacement with the word "Lord," Christian copyists no longer could be sure whether "Lord," referred to God or Jesus. The passage of time compounded the confusion as to which figure was meant. This has often made it impossible for Christians to distinguish between them. It may very well be that the replacement of the divine name played an important part in the eventual development of the doctrine of the Trinity.[39]

As we have seen, the New Testament does not teach the doctrine of the Trinity. However, even if it did, this doctrine would still be false since it does not conform to the teachings of the Hebrew Scriptures. It should be clear for all to see that God is an absolute one who is neither a duality, a trinity, a quaternity, or any other composite being. The transformation of Jesus into part of a triune god is an unfortunate distortion of the biblical text and the Philonic Logos. As a result of misinterpretation, believers have been deceived into worshipping Jesus as the divine Son of God. The missionary expounders of this false doctrine need to become aware of Deuteronomy 27:18: "Cursed be he that makes the blind to wander out of the way," and to desist from continuing with their misleading activities.

1. The phrase "the young child and its mother" (Matthew 2:13–14) shows striking similarity with Isis and her son Horus—the holy mother and child of Egyptian religion. Christianity accommodated itself to paganism by elevating Mary to the status of Mother of God, a place formerly occupied by the ancient Mother Goddess and the Queen of Heaven.

2. Vespasian, who was hailed as *restitutor orbis* ("restorer of the world"), is said to have healed a lame man and given sight to the blind (Tacitus, *History*, vol. 4, 81; Suetonius, *Vespasian*, 7.

3. It is not surprising that because of the obscurity that surrounded the circumstances of the death of Nero, and the very small number of people that had actually seen the corpse, there was a widespread belief that he would return. In 68 C.E. a false Nero caused much consternation and gained many adherents.

4. The Midrash cites Rabbi Abbahu, who explains this verse in Isaiah as follows: "I am the Lord your God: Compare therewith a king of flesh and blood. He reigns, and has a father or a brother or a son. The Holy One—blessed be His name—said: 'I am not so. I am the first, for I have no father; and I am the last, for I have no son; besides me there is no God, for I have no brother'" (Exodus Rabbah 29:5).

5. For *'adonim* used in this way, see also: Genesis 24:9, 10, 51; 39:2–20; 40:1; 42:30, 33; Exodus 21:4, 6, 8; Judges 19:11, 12; Malachi 1:6.

6. The Tetragrammaton: the four-letter name of God, rendered "Lord" or "Jehovah" in many English translations, and in Hebrew as *'Ado-nai*, "the Lord," or *Hashem*, "the Name."

7. See Rashi, Genesis 1:1 as based on Bereshit Rabbah 33:4.

8. See 2 Kings 19:34–35.

9. Some Christian Bibles translate this verse as: "Why is it that you ask my name, seeing it is wonderful?" "Wonderful" is a secondary meaning which is used in the sense of "incomprehensible," "marvelous." It is not to be understood as a proper name identifying the angel. The Hebrew word *peli* ("hidden," "wonderful") indicates that the name is beyond the realm of human knowledge.

10. *Philo*, trans. F. H. Colson and G. H. Whitaker, Loeb Classical Library, vol. 5, *On Dreams*, p. 331.

11. Ibid., pp. 333, 373.

12. Ibid., p. 413.

13. Ibid., vol. 4, *Who Is the Heir*, p. 385.

14. Ibid., vol. 5, *On Dreams*, p. 419.

15. Ibid., p. 423.

16. Ibid., p. 463.

17. Ibid., vol. 4, *The Confusion of Tongues*, p. 45.

18. Ibid., pp. 89, 91.

19. So, according to the most authoritative ancient manuscripts (i.e., Codex Sinaiticus and Codex Vaticanus); only in some later manuscripts, "Son," instead of "god."

20. Albert Barnes, *Barnes' Notes on the New Testament* (Grand Rapids, Kregel Publications, 1966), p. 1569.

21. Ibid.

22. Ibid.

23. Maximillian Zerwick, *Biblical Greek* (Rome: Scripta Ponificii Instituti Biblici, 1963), p. 55, par. 171, p. 57, par. 176.

24. E. C. Colwell, "A Definite Rule for the Use of the Article in the Greek New Testament," *Journal of Biblical Literature* 52 (1933), pp. 12–21.

25. See below p. 174–175 for a discussion of Thomas' alleged statement.

26. Philip B. Harner, "Qualitative Anarthrous Predicate Nouns: Mark 15:39 and John 1:1," *Journal of Biblical Literature* 92 (1973), p. 76.

27. Ibid., p. 75.
28. Ibid., p. 81.
29. Ibid., p. 83.
30. Ibid., p. 83.
31. Ibid., p. 84.
32. Ibid., p. 84.
33. Ibid., p. 84.
34. Ibid., p. 85.
35. Ibid., p. 85.
36. Ibid., p. 87.
37. Ibid., p. 87.
38. C. F. D. Moule, *An Idiom Book of New Testament Greek* (Cambridge, University Press 1977), p. 116.
39. George Howard, "The Tetragram and the New Testament," *Journal of Biblical Literature* 96 (1977), pp. 63–83.

28

A FABLE IS BORN

(Matthew 1:1–16, Luke 3:23–38)

Sometime around the beginning of the common era, a child was born to a couple named Mary and Joseph.[1] Christian missionaries claim that this child was not the son of Joseph, but the Son of God conceived of the Holy Spirit in consort with Mary while she was yet a virgin. This semi-Hebraized version of an Olympian seduction requires further elucidation.

In tracing the genealogy of Jesus, Matthew claims that he was "the son of David" (Matthew 1:1). But how can one reconcile Matthew 1:6, where, in tracing Jesus' descent, it is written, "David the king begot Solomon," with Luke 3:31, where it says concerning his origin, "Nathan, which was the son of David"? Through which son of David was Jesus supposed to descend, Solomon or Nathan? If Jesus was born from the union of the Holy Spirit and a virgin, the genealogical record which traces his ancestry through Joseph back to David is worthless. Christian missionaries might argue that Luke gives Mary's genealogy, but how can they claim this without scriptural evidence, since they profess that the Bible is their sole rule of faith and practice? If either of these records (Matthew 1:1–16 and Luke 3:23–38) is for Mary, where is this explicitly mentioned? According to Isaiah 11:1, the Messiah is called a "shoot" from the stock of Jesse. Even assuming that this is true of Jesus with respect to his descent on his mother's side, such maternal connection does not enter into consideration for succession to the throne of David, which is passed only through the male line: "There shall not be cut off to David a man to sit on the throne of the house of Israel . . ." (Jeremiah 33:17).[2]

When Athaliah sought to destroy the royal seed of David she only killed the king's sons, evidently because the female line had no legal right of succession. Thus, Jehosheba, a royal daughter, could save Joash and hide him in the Temple, where her husband was a priest (2 Kings 11:1–3, 2 Chronicles 22:10–12). The contention that Jesus is to be considered Joseph's adopted son has no bearing on the subject, as an adopted son has no legal rights or claims on his stepfather's lineage. Thus, as an adopted son, Jesus could not inherit his stepfather Joseph's royal lineage. Lineage can only be passed on through the bloodline of the biological father. If Jesus came not to destroy the Law or the Prophets, but to fulfill them (Matthew 5:17), he must adhere to the rules of royal succession as set forth in the Scriptures. God promised David a male heir to the throne, not a female (e.g., Mary as a descendant of David): ". . . I will raise up your seed after you, which shall be of your sons; and I will establish his kingdom" (1 Chronicles 17:11). Even more explicit is God's promise that:

> If you can break My covenant with the day, and My covenant with the night, so that there should not be day and night in their season; then may also My covenant be broken with David My servant, that he should not have a son to reign upon his throne; and with the Levites the priests, My ministers. As the host of heaven cannot be numbered, neither the sand of the sea measured; so will I multiply the seed of David My servant, and the Levites that minister to Me. (Jeremiah 33:20–22)

Mary did not qualify to be heir to the throne and could not pass on what she did not possess.

The incident regarding the inheritance of Zelophehad's daughters (Numbers 27:1–11, 36:1–12) does not apply here since it concerns the transference of physical property and not privileges of lineage. The rights of lineal privilege, e.g., kingship and priesthood, are exclusively passed on through the male line. A princess of the house of David could never aspire to be anointed queen of Israel by virtue of her lineage. Similarly, the daughter of a priest could not participate in the priestly duties surrounding the Temple service. Even if a princess of the house of David married a prince of that family, the male children born to them inherit privileges solely through their father. That is why it is stated: "There shall not be cut off to David a man to sit upon the throne of the house of Israel" (Jeremiah 33:17).

A literal translation of the Greek found in Luke 3 says: "Joseph of the Heli of the Matthat of the Levi of the Melchi . . . of the Judah of the Jacob of the Isaac of the Abraham of the Terah." It is clear from the context that the Greek "of the" is to be rendered "son of." We may therefore conclude that the meaning of Luke 3:23 is that Joseph was the son of Heli and not his son-in-law, as some Christian missionaries would have us believe. To say otherwise is a mere supposition.

There is no genealogical record in the Hebrew Bible which refers to a man as the son of his father-in-law. Saul's words: "Is this your voice, my son David?" (1 Samuel 24:17) cannot be cited as a proof that a son-in-law was considered equal to a son. One is often addressed as "my son" by way of affection or endearment, e.g., Joshua 7:19; 1 Samuel 3:6, 16; 4:16. This is especially true when an older person is addressing a younger person whom he loves. Such was the case with Saul, who had love for David, as stated: ". . . and he [Saul] loved him [David] greatly" (1 Samuel 16:21). But David always remained the "son of Jesse" and was never referred to or considered the "son of Saul."

In this connection note must be taken of the verse: ". . . the children of Barzillai, who took a wife of the daughters of Barzillai the Gileadite, and was called after their name" (Ezra 2:61, Nehemiah 7:63). This is a family name derived from the honoring of an illustrious ancestor—in this case, on the maternal side. However, at no time was the family genealogy traced through the maternal side. The priest who married Barzillai the Gileadite's daughter obviously did not renounce his claim to the priesthood. Accordingly, he and his descendants had to trace their ancestry through his own father, back to Aaron. The Barzillai name was only employed by them as a kind of surname rather than as part of their genuine genealogy.

This unusual instance attests that in any genealogical listing,

Joseph's own paternal ancestry would have to be given. Luke's naming Heli, rather than Jacob, as Joseph's father is simply a variant tradition. He is not Joseph's father-in-law. Moreover, nowhere are Jesus and his brothers and sisters called the "children of Heli," which would be an appropriate parallel to the "children of Barzillai." Jesus is always referred to as the son of Joseph (Matthew 1:16; Luke 3:23, 4:22; John 1:45, 6:42). It is inconceivable, in the patriarchal society in which Jesus was born, that Joseph would have adopted the genealogy of his father-in-law in lieu of that of his own father. For Christian missionary exegetes to propose such a forced interpretation is an act of sheer desperation.

There is no escaping the obvious conclusion that the genealogy of Jesus, as treated in Luke 3:23 and the subsequent verses, is in direct contradiction to the first chapter of Matthew. Luke states: "And Jesus began to be about thirty years old, being, as was the opinion, the son of Joseph, *which was the son of Heli,* which was the son of Matthat, which was the son of Levi, which was the son of Melchi. . . ." In Matthew, where the origin of Joseph is traced back to Solomon the son of David, the enumeration of the ancestors closes in the following manner: ". . . and Eliud the father of Eleazar, and Eleazar the father of Matthan, and Matthan the father of Jacob, and *Jacob the father of Joseph* the husband of Mary, of whom Jesus was born, who is called Christ" (Matthew 1:15–16). While Matthew does not say outright who the father of Jesus was, Luke emphatically states that it was Joseph, "as was the opinion." While Matthew enumerates forty-one generations from Abraham, Luke counts fifty-six. From these contradictory statements the question arises as to who was the husband of Mary. Was it Joseph, the son of Heli, the son of Matthat, as Luke supposes; or was it Joseph, the son of Jacob, the son of Matthan, as Matthew supposes?

Examining the origins of the alleged genealogy of Jesus, we discover that the genealogical record used by Matthew is not taken from the Hebrew Scriptures. A simple reading of the enumerated names will clearly show this. In Matthew 1:8 it is written: ". . . and Asa the father of Josaphat, and Josaphat the father of Joram, and Joram the father of Ozias." This genealogical version is taken directly from the Septuagint, the Greek version of the Bible, and does not accord with what is found in the Hebrew Bible. It is not surprising that the genealogical version found in Matthew parallels the Septuagint. The evangelist, in writing his record, simply went to a Greek translation of the Bible and copied what he found there. He did not base the genealogy on the indisputable record of the Hebrew Scriptures. Comparing Matthew 1:8 with the genealogy of the Davidic dynasty as found in the Hebrew Bible, we find that Asa's son was Jehoshaphat, Jehoshaphat's son was Joram, Joram's son was Ahaziah, Ahaziah's son was Joash, Joash's son was Amaziah, and Amaziah's son was Azariah (Uzziah) (1 Chronicles 3:10–11).

Instead of indisputable evidence, we find the genealogies given for Jesus to be at variance with the true scriptural reading. For unofficial purposes, it was not necessary to name every link in the line of descent when giving one's genealogy. However, if Matthew is presenting us with an official record of the genealogy of Jesus, it is sadly wanting. The rationalization that he excluded evil ancestors, besides it being pure speculation, is hardly acceptable, because an official record is no place for playing favorites. Matthew's genealogical listing is inaccurate and consequently is devoid of any worth.

Neither is Luke's genealogy of Jesus problem-free. Luke inserts a second "Cainan" (the first being the son of Enos [Enosh], who is called Kenan in Genesis 5:9–14 and 1 Chronicles 1:2) between Arphaxad (Arpachshad) and his son Sala (Shelah) (Luke 3:35–36). Cainan (Kenan) is not found in this position in the Hebrew text (Genesis 10:24, 11:12; 1 Chronicles 1:18, 24). Furthermore, Luke's additional use of this name is found neither in the Samaritan Hebrew text of Genesis nor in any of the *targumim*. It is found only in the Septuagint. Evidently, Luke inserted the name Cainan between the names of Sala and Arphaxad on the basis of the Septuagint version. Hence, Luke's record is, like that of Matthew's, taken from a questionable source.[3]

There are still more discrepancies and distortions. The respective genealogical listings given by the evangelists diverge after Solomon and Nathan. They briefly come together again with the mention of Shealtiel and his son Zerubbabel. Matthew lists Shealtiel as the son of Jeconiah but leaves out his grandfather, Jehoiakim, from his record (Matthew 1:11). Luke lists Neri as the father of Shealtiel (Luke 3:27) although the Hebrew text says that Shealtiel was the son of Jeconiah and the grandson of Jehoiakim (1 Chronicles 3:16–17).

Those Christian missionaries who argue that Jesus had a legal right to the throne of David through Joseph, i.e., Matthew's genealogy, although he was adopted and thereby disqualified insofar as inheriting Joseph's lineage was concerned, cannot ignore the curse on Jehoiakim: "Write this man childless, a man that shall not prosper in his days; for no man of his seed shall prosper, sitting upon the throne of David, and ruling any more in Judah" (Jeremiah 22:30). Jehoiakim was to be considered "childless" because none of his descendants were to be considered as having any legal right to inherit the throne of David. Thus, Joseph, a descendant of Jehoiakim, was not an heir to the throne and could not pass on what he did not possess. Besides, there would be many legal claimants by virtue of Davidic descent other than through Jehoiakim: "As the host of heaven cannot be numbered, neither the sand of the sea measured; so will I multiply the seed of David my servant. . ." (Jeremiah 33:22).

Only descendants of Solomon, of whom there surely were many not descended from Jehoiakim, were qualified to sit on the throne of David: "And of all my sons—for the Lord has given me many sons—He has chosen Solomon my son to sit upon the throne of the kingdom of the Lord over Israel" (1 Chronicles 28:5; see also 1 Chronicles 29:1, 24).[4] Since Christian missionaries, following Matthew's genealogy, claim that Jesus was not the natural son of Joseph, they accordingly admit that he was not a descendant of Solomon. However, these Christian missionary apologists also argue that Jesus laid claim to the throne of David as the natural heir through Mary, as allegedly indicated in Luke's genealogy. But as a descendant of Nathan, and not of Solomon, he did not have any claim to the royal throne. The right to the throne has been granted solely to a male descendant of Solomon.

> . . . I [God] will set up your [David's] seed after you, that shall proceed out of your body, and I will establish his [Solomon's] kingdom. He shall build a house for My name, and I will establish the throne of his kingdom forever. I will be to him for a father, and he shall be to Me for a son; if he commits iniquity, I will chasten him with the rod of men, and with the stripes of the children of men; but My mercy shall not depart from him, as I took it from Saul, whom I put away before you. And your house and your kingdom shall be made sure forever before you; your throne shall be established forever. (2 Samuel 7:12–16; see also 1 Chronicles 17:11–14, Psalms 9:29–38)

The Christian missionary apologists also conveniently overlook the fact that since Shealtiel and Zerubbabel were descendants of Jehoiakim, their appearance in Luke's record as direct ancestors of Mary automatically nullifies any claim to the throne by using this record. Thus, Jesus could not inherit the throne of David by the use of Luke's record. Having come together, these two accounts diverge once more after Zerubbabel, with neither evangelical genealogy agreeing with the other or with the Book of Chronicles. The overlapping of the two genealogies, however, is crucial for exposing their inconsistencies and the falseness of their claims. Since the descendants of Jehoiakim cannot sit on the throne of David, Jesus, a descendant of Jehoiakim according to both evangelists, was *ipso facto* unqualified to begin with. In sum, since only specific descendants of Solomon may sit on the Davidic throne, Jesus the descendant of David's son Nathan was unqualified to sit on the throne.

Concerning the naming of the child, Matthew states: ". . . and they shall call his name Emmanuel . . ." (Matthew 1:23). This is supposedly a direct quotation from Isaiah 7:14. However, it is clearly stated in Isaiah 7:14 that "she shall call his name Immanuel,"[5] which indicates that the naming of the child is not a mere mechanical namegiving, but a divine command to his mother. Such being the case, how can Matthew state "they shall call his name" rather than "she shall call his name"? It is obvious, from the context, that Matthew does not refer the "they" to Joseph and Mary. Neither Joseph nor Mary called the child Immanuel (Matthew 1:21, 25). The claim that Isaiah 7:14 refers to Jesus is vitiated by the very words of Matthew. The evangelists are endeavoring, time and again, to link their claim to passages in the Hebrew Bible in order to find support for their contention that Jesus is the Messiah and the fulfillment of what the prophets had to say about the Messiah. Yet details large and small abound which show that this is an impossibility.

An investigation of the memories of those closest to Jesus brings even more surprises. Who more than Mary and Joseph should have remembered the "miraculous" events surrounding the birth of Jesus? One can reasonably expect that when a woman goes through a virgin birth she would remember it, and that a man whose wife remains a virgin after their marriage also does not easily forget it. Yet we are soon to see several strange lapses of memory.

According to Luke, Mary finds Jesus in the Temple teaching the teachers (Luke 2:42–50). She scolds him for causing so much trouble, whereupon he replies with the enigmatic question: "Why is it that you were looking for me? Did you not know that I must be concerned with the affairs of my Father?" Luke's Gospel adds: "And they did not understand the saying which he spoke to them." Mary does not understand; Joseph does not understand. If Mary and Joseph were both visited by angels before their son's birth, how is it that they are so completely surprised only twelve years later? Did not Mary remember that Jesus was supernaturally conceived in a way never experienced by any other creature?

It is inconceivable that Mary would forget Elizabeth saying to her: "Blessed are you among women, and blessed is the fruit of your womb. And why is this [granted] to me, that the mother of my Lord should come to me?" (Luke 1:42–43); and especially her own words: "My soul magnifies the Lord, and my spirit has rejoiced in God my Savior. For He has looked upon the humble state of His slave girl; for, behold, from now on all generations will call me blessed; because the Mighty One has done great things to me; and holy is His name. . ." (Luke 1:46–49). After all this, she still does not know what Jesus meant when he said that he must be concerned with his Father's affairs!

Mary and Joseph did not remember that the wise men worshipped Jesus and presented him with gold, frankincense, and myrrh (Matthew 2:11). They did not recall how an angel appeared to Joseph telling him to go to Egypt with Mary and Jesus (Matthew 2:13), and that Herod slew all the children two years of age and under in Bethlehem (Matthew 2:16). Besides the fact that it "fulfills" Scripture (Hosea 11:1), why did they have to flee to Egypt when, according to Luke 2:39, they went to Nazareth and were not even in the dangerous vicinity of Bethlehem when Herod allegedly had the children slain. Perhaps Matthew's placing them in Egypt in order to fulfill Scripture was too quick for Joseph and Mary to remember, for Luke 2:22 has them in Jerusalem forty days after the birth (cf. Leviticus 12:1–8), and then in Luke 2:39 they return afterwards to Nazareth. Yes, they forgot how the shepherds "made known the saying which had been told to them about this child" (Luke 2:17). Mary and Joseph even forgot how they marveled (ten months after the angelic visitations and one month after the aforementioned events they already were surprised) when Simeon and Anna, the daughter of Phanvel, spoke of Jesus' future while he was yet a mere infant (Luke 2:25–38).

Everything is kept so secretive that in all of the New Testament we find the virgin birth mentioned only by Matthew. Even Jesus' relatives, who come to seize him (Mark 3:21), are not told by Mary that, contrary to what they think, Jesus is not crazy. The Gospel of John explicitly states: "For neither did his brothers believe in him" (John 7:5). Is it conceivable that Mary would not have informed them that Jesus was the Messiah so that they too might believe in him and thereby enjoy salvation? "Did you not know that I must be concerned with the affairs of my Father?" No, Mary and Joseph did not know it. They did not know it because they had never heard of their son's "miraculous" birth. There is no doubt that the story of the virgin birth came into circulation long after the deaths of the principal participants in this drama.

Paul realized the difficulty of trying to explain the discrepancies found in the variant traditions relating to the ancestry, manner of conception, and life of Jesus at a time when there were still living witnesses to the events of Jesus's life. Being aware of the improbability of the claims made by some of his followers, Paul advised the faithful "not to occupy themselves with myths and endless genealogies which give rise to speculations" (1 Timothy 1:4). The believer must rely on faith alone. The "myths and endless genealogies" were, nevertheless, committed to writing in later years when there was no longer anyone who could dispute the veracity of the claims made by the evangelists. It was now left to the devices of the Christian apologists to explain away the divergent "myths and endless genealogies" of the Christian tradition as recorded by the evangelists. The Christian believer is thus compelled to gloss over the very words of the Gospels, and rely on explanations and rationalizations which stretch the imagination to the utmost limits.

1. Matthew's dating of the birth of Jesus as occurring during the reign of Herod the Great (d. 4 B.C.E) conflicts with the date given by Luke, who synchronizes the birth with the census of Quirinius in 6 C.E. (Luke 2:1–6). Historians generally agree that Luke's dating is too late.

2. This indicates that the Davidic dynasty will be restored in the future, i.e., after Elijah comes to restore genealogical knowledge.

3. This is an example of a major difference between Judaism and missionary Christianity. The New Testament writers accepted the Greek Septuagint version rather than the Hebrew text as their biblical source. As a result, Jews and Christian missionaries do not use the same biblical text, which leads to conflicting conclusions as to the meaning of the Scriptures.

4. Maimonides expresses this biblical teaching as follows: "Part of this article of faith [i.e., the belief in the Messiah] is that there can be no king for Israel except from the house of David and through the seed of Solomon alone; and whoever opposses this family denies God, may He be blessed, and the words of His prophets" (Maimonides, *Commentary on the Mishnah,* Sanhedrin, chap. 10, s.v. "The Twelfth Article of Faith").

5. The Septuagint has ". . . and *you* shall call his name Emmanuel."

29

PROPHECY AND FULFILLMENT IN THE NEW TESTAMENT: RACHEL WEEPING FOR HER CHILDREN

(Matthew 2:16–18)

Then when Herod saw that he had been tricked by the magi, he became very enraged, and sent and slew all the male children who were in Bethlehem and in all its environs, from two years old and under, according to the time which he had ascertained from the magi. Then that which was spoken of through Jeremiah the prophet was fulfilled, saying: "A voice was heard in Ramah, weeping and much wailing, Rachel weeping for her children; and she refused to be comforted, because they were no more."

(Matthew 2:16–18)

Eager to show fulfillment of prophecy in the life of Jesus, Matthew refers to Jeremiah 31:15 as a proof-text that Rachel wept for the allegedly slain children of Bethlehem. (It is strange that so outstanding an event was not reported by the historian Josephus.) However, an examination of this quotation within its biblical context plainly shows us that it does not refer to slain, but rather to captive children.

> Thus says the Lord: A voice is heard in Ramah, lamentation, and bitter weeping, Rachel weeping for her children; she refuses to be comforted for her children, because they are no more. Thus says the Lord: Refrain your voice from weeping, and your eyes from tears; for your work shall be rewarded, says the Lord; and they shall come

back from the land of the enemy. And there is hope for your future, says the Lord; and your children shall return to their own border. I have surely heard Ephraim bemoaning himself: "You have chastised me, and I was chastised, as an untrained calf; bring me back and I shall be restored, for You are the Lord my God. For after I was turned, I repented, and after I was instructed, I smote upon my thigh; I was ashamed, and also humiliated, because I bore the disgrace of my youth." (Jeremiah 31:15–19)

The exiled Ten Tribes are collectively referred to by the name Ephraim, the leading northern tribe. Ephraim was the son of Joseph, whose mother was Rachel. If Jeremiah's prophecy was meant to be connected with the alleged massacre of the innocent children of Bethlehem, it would not have been Rachel weeping, but Leah, the ancestress of the tribe of Judah, in whose tribal area that town is situated. This is the substance of which New Testament fulfillment of prophecy is made. Let the believer beware.

30

THE NAZARENE

(Matthew 2:23)

And he [Joseph, along with Mary and Jesus] came and resided in a city called Nazareth, that what was spoken through the prophets might be fulfilled: "He will be called a Nazarene."

(Matthew 2:23)

At no point in the Hebrew Scriptures is the Messiah referred to as a Nazarene. Despite Matthew's statement, there is no prophecy which mentions that the Messiah will be an inhabitant of Nazareth. In fact, the town of Nazareth is never mentioned in the Hebrew Bible.

It has been speculated that what Matthew is referring to is the description of the Messiah as a *netser* ("shoot"), i.e., a new, flourishing growth from the Davidic line. This term first appears in Isaiah: "And there shall come forth a shoot out of the stock of Jesse, and a branch out of his roots shall bear fruit" (Isaiah 11:1). But despite Isaiah's use of the term, it is nowhere indicated that the Messiah would actually be called *netser*.

Neither can it be said that Matthew is referring to the Messiah as being a Nazarite, for nowhere in the Hebrew Scriptures is it stated that the Messiah will ever take the Nazarite vow. Furthermore, the spellings of the words Nazarite, נזיר (*nazir*), and Nazarene, נצרי (*notsri*), are not the same in Hebrew. Whether the evangelist is comparing Nazarene and *netser* or Nazarene and Nazarite is inconsequential, for there is no basis in fact for either claim. At best, Matthew is indulging in a play on words. There is no reason for giving credence to this New Testament "fulfillment."

31

THE POOR MEMORY OF JOHN THE BAPTIST

(Matthew 3:11, 13–17; Mark 1:7–11; Luke 3:16, 21–22; John 1:26–34)

"As for me [John], I baptize you in water for repentance, but he who is coming after me is mightier than I, and I am not fit to remove his sandals. He will baptize you with holy spirit and fire. . . ." Then Jesus came from Galilee to the Jordan to John in order to be baptized by him. But the latter tried to prevent him, saying: "I have need to be baptized by you, and you are coming to me?" But Jesus answering said to him: "Let it be so now, for in this way it is fitting for us to fulfill all righteousness." Then he permitted him. After being baptized Jesus immediately came up from the water; and behold, the heavens were opened up, and he saw God's spirit descending like a dove, coming upon him. And behold, a voice out of the heavens, saying: "This is My Son, the beloved, in whom I am well pleased."

(Matthew 3:11, 13–17)

The evangelists report that when Jesus came to be baptized by John the Baptist, the latter realized that Jesus was greater than he was (Matthew 3:11, 13–17; Mark 1:7–11; Luke 3:16, 21–22; John 1:26–34). At first John hesitated, but after receiving assurance that it was proper, he complied with Jesus' request for baptism. While he was being baptized, the Synoptic Gospels record, the spirit of God descended upon Jesus in the form of a dove, but this was witnessed exclusively by Jesus. Only the Gospel of John actually claims that John the Baptist also saw the spirit of God descend upon Jesus in the form of a dove (John 1:32–34). It is no wonder that, according to the fourth Gospel, John the Baptist felt confirmed in his belief that Jesus was superior to himself (John 1:36). There could be no doubt in John's mind that Jesus was the Messiah, the very Son of God. Accordingly, the Gospel of John makes no mention of any uncertainty on the part of John the Baptist as to who Jesus was.

Shortly after the baptism, John the Baptist was thrown into prison by Herod Antipas. Matthew and Luke indicate that while in prison, John forgot what he had said, seen, and heard just a short time before. These two evangelists relate that while in prison, John was visited by his disciples, who informed him of Jesus' accomplishments. Rather than accept this report at face value, John sent two of his disciples to inquire as to whether Jesus was the Messiah (Matthew 11:2–3, Luke 7:19–20). How could John have forgotten so quickly who Jesus was? Did he not identify Jesus as the "Lamb of God" before all the people assembled at the Jordan River (John 1:29)? It would have been impossible for John to forget who Jesus was had he actually witnessed the spirit of God descending upon him and heard the accompanying heavenly verification of Jesus' chosen position, as recorded in the fourth Gospel. Who could ever forget such a sight? Yet the John the Baptist of the Synoptic Gospels did forget. Is it not strange that he had to ask his disciples to verify who Jesus actually was?

Apparently, the John the Baptist of Matthew's and Luke's tradition was not too sure of who Jesus was (Matthew 11:3, Luke 7:19). They report that John had to be convinced once more of who Jesus was supposed to be, even after what he had sup-posedly witnessed at the Jordan River. There is no indication in the Gospels that John underwent any torture while in prison which might have impaired his memory. Indeed, John was in complete control of himself when he sent his disciples to Jesus. It would also seem quite plausible that before his imprisonment John would have informed at least some of his disciples about Jesus, and word would then have spread to all of them that he had met the Messiah at the Jordan River. According to the fourth Gospel, two of his followers on hearing such news from John left him to follow Jesus (John 1:35–37). Why did the John the Baptist of Matthew and Luke need a new confirmation of something that had earlier been shown so clearly to him? Satisfactory answers must first be supplied before the alleged testimony of John the Baptist can be used as evidence that Jesus is the Messiah.

32

SATAN'S TEMPTATION

(Matthew 4:1–11, Mark 1:13, Luke 4:1–13)

While Mark, the earliest of the Gospels, simply states that Jesus was tempted by Satan (Mark 1:13), Matthew (Matthew 4:1–11) and Luke (Luke 4:1–13) elaborate the story. It is claimed that during Jesus' alleged forty days' sojourn in the desert, following his baptism by John, Satan tempted him with promises of an earthly kingdom if Jesus would only worship him.

However, if Jesus is part of God, how could he possibly sin, and how could Satan possibly hope to tempt him? Satan's words would be absolutely meaningless. Surely, even the earthly Jesus was incapable of committing as sinful an act as the worshipping of Satan. Indeed, unlike a mere mortal, it was decreed that the Jesus of missionary Christianity follow exactly the life outlined for his earthly existence by the very godhead of which he was an integral part. In assuming a human body, the Jesus of Christian missionary theology knew what God's purpose for the future of mankind was and what was expected of him in order to bring this about. Did Jesus, the perfect god-man, have free will to sin while on earth? Obviously not! Had he failed to carry out God's plan, the entire timetable would have been eternally disrupted. Lacking free will to do as he pleased, Jesus could not truly have been tempted.

Neither could Satan, as one of God's creations, promise Jesus, who was already divine and in control of the universe, a mere earthly kingdom as a reward for worshipping him. As puffed up with pride as one might envision Satan to be, he is certainly not stupid. He knew Jesus was not a mere human, given to flattery and subject to the temptations of the flesh. Jesus was not one who would accept worthless promises. Even if we suppose that Satan did make Jesus the most extravagant of offers, as reported by the New Testament, it would not in the least have been a temptation to the divine Jesus of missionary Christianity. In view of the claim by Christian missionary theology that Jesus was offered an earthly kingdom by God: "Ask of Me, and I will give the nations for your inheritance, and the ends of the earth for your possession" (Psalms 2:8), can anyone believe that a member of the Trinity would have difficulty in choosing between the two opposing offers? Certainly Satan would not have wasted his time on such a futile endeavor. It is obvious that the account of Satan's attempt to tempt Jesus cannot be reconciled with the overall view of Jesus as held by the Christian missionaries.

Of Jesus it is said: "For because he himself has suffered and has been tempted, he is able to come to the aid of those who are tempted" (Hebrews 2:18). But if Jesus was God as well as man at the time of his temptation by Satan, how is this verse, and indeed the entire temptation episode, to be reconciled with the belief expressed by the author of James? He states: "Let no one say when he is tempted: 'I am being tempted by God'; for God cannot be tempted by evil, and He Himself does not tempt anyone" (James 1:13). If according to James "God cannot be tempted by evil," then the Jesus who the missionaries claim is God cannot have been tempted by Satan. The entire Gospel episode of Satan's temptation of Jesus must therefore have not occurred.

33

JESUS MOVES FROM NAZARETH TO CAPERNAUM

(Matthew 4:13–16)

And having left Nazareth he came and took up residence in Caper-naum beside the sea in the districts of Zebulun and Naphtali in order that there might be fulfilled what was spoken through Isaiah the prophet, saying: "The land of Zebulun and the land of Naphtali, by the way of the sea, on the other side of the Jordan, Galilee of the Gentiles. The people sitting in darkness saw great light, and those sitting in the region and shadow of death, light rose up to them."

(Matthew 4:13–16)

Matthew declares that Jesus' moving from Nazareth to Caper-naum to begin his ministry was the fulfillment of a prophecy. The fallaciousness of this assertion will become clear by com-paring what Matthew says with the actual words of the prophet. The statements which Matthew is citing appear in Isaiah as follows:

For is there no gloom to her that was stedfast? Now the former has lightly afflicted the land of Zebulun and the land of Naphtali, but the latter has dealt a more grievous blow by the way of the sea, beyond the Jordan, in the district of the nations. (Isaiah 8:23)

The people that walked in darkness have seen a great light; they that dwelt in the land of the shadow of death, upon them has the light shined. (Isaiah 9:1)

Matthew, in the process of quoting these two verses together, omits those parts which, if left in place, would totally invalidate his claim. Based on Matthew's connection of these two verses, the Christian translations of the Bible list them as Isaiah 9:1 and 9:2 respectively. These two verses from Isaiah, however, do not belong in conjunction with each other. In the Hebrew Bible, what is Isaiah 9:1 in the Christian versions of the Scriptures, with its reference to Naphtali and Zebulun, is to be found as the last verse of the eighth chapter, Isaiah 8:23, while what is Isaiah 9:2 in the Christian versions of the Scriptures is the beginning of the ninth chapter, Isaiah 9:1, in the Hebrew Bible. Reading these verses it becomes obvious that what is Isaiah 9:1 in the Christian versions belongs to the material in the eighth chapter of the Hebrew Bible, in which Isaiah speaks about the destruction, not long before, of the kingdom of Israel by the Assyrians. What is Isaiah 9:2 in the Christian versions represents a complete change, not only in subject matter, but also in form, as it is written in poetry, whereas the verse the Christians consider to be Isaiah 9:1 is written in prose.

The Hebrew division is the logical separation of the two chapters. The combination of the two verses in the same chapter by the Christian translators is due to the fact that the two quotations appear together in Matthew. The evangelist was so anxious to have as much of Jesus' career be part of the prophetic prediction that he combined the reference to Zebulun and Naphtali and the reference to the light and darkness to facilitate the claim that these were predictions of the beginning of Jesus' ministry. There is no need to disprove this claim, as Matthew's mistreatment of these two verses is self-evident.

34

JESUS AND DIVORCE

(Matthew 5:32, 19:8–9; Mark 10:2–12; Luke 16:18)

But I say to you that everyone who divorces his wife, except on account of fornication, makes her commit adultery; and whoever marries a divorced woman commits adultery.

(Matthew 5:32)

Matthew's Jesus declares that there is only one legitimate reason for divorce, and that is adultery. He claims that the reason this command is not included in the laws of the Torah is: "Because of your hardheartedness, Moses permitted you to divorce your wives; but from the beginning it has not been this way" (Matthew 19:8). He then reasserts, once more, that "whoever divorces his wife, except for fornication, and marries another commits adultery" (Matthew 19:9). Mark's Jesus is even more restrictive, declaring that under no circumstances is divorce to be granted: "Whoever divorces his wife and marries another commits adultery against her; and if she divorces her husband and marries another, she is committing adultery" (Mark 10:11–12). The same harsh criterion is set by Luke's Jesus: "Everyone who divorces his wife and marries another commits adultery; and he who marries one who is divorced from a husband commits adultery" (Luke 16:18).

The validity of Jesus' command concerning divorce, as presented in Mark and Luke, is upheld by Paul: "But to the married I give instruction, not I, but the Lord, that a wife should not leave

199

her husband but if she does leave, let her remain unmarried, or else be reconciled to her husband, and that a husband should not send his wife away." (1 Corinthians 7:10–11). Moreover, in Romans 7:3, Paul states that if a woman marries another man while her first husband is still living, she is an adulteress.

Contrary to Matthew's record, which allows only adultery as a reason for divorce, Jesus' words, as recorded by Mark and Luke, do not permit divorce under any circumstances. The addition or omission of adultery is an extremely important difference and leaves unanswered the question as to which statement, if any, is the actual teaching of Jesus. Paul supports the extremely rigid, legalistic declaration as found in Mark and Luke. He also directly attributes to Jesus this legislation, whose restriction goes beyond the law of divorce as stated in the Law of Moses. Jesus' law on divorce, in any form, is an impractical legalism which, on examination, is found to be nonviable in society. It is no wonder that throughout history the followers of Jesus, in one way or another, have disregarded his command.

35

TURNING THE OTHER CHEEK

(Matthew 5:39, Luke 6:29)

Do not resist him that is wicked; but whoever slaps you on your right cheek, turn to him the other also.

(Matthew 5:39)

To him that strikes you on the cheek, offer the other also.

(Luke 6:29)

Christian missionaries are fond of using these verses as an illustration of the extraordinary pacifistic teachings of Jesus. However, this sublime dictum was not practiced by Jesus himself. According to the Gospels, Jesus preached turning the other cheek, loving one's neighbor and praying for them, and forgiving those who wrong you. The fact of the matter is that he himself never turned the other cheek. Jesus responded to his opponents, not with passive resistance, but by answering criticism with criticism, reviling and threatening his adversaries (e.g., Matthew 15:1–20). Jesus never forgave anyone who wronged or criticized him. He only forgave those who wronged others. On the cross, in a verse not found in the earliest New Testament manuscripts, he allegedly offered a general forgiveness of everyone: "Father, forgive them, for they do not know what they are doing" (Luke 23:34). However, when an opportunity to personally forgive others presented itself he always declined. For example, instead of forgiving Judas for betraying him he said: "But woe to that man through whom the Son of Man is betrayed! It would have been good for that man if he had

201

not been born" (Matthew 26:24). In John 18:22–23, we find that Jesus, when beaten by an officer, instead of offering quietly his other cheek argues with him:

> But having said these things, one of the officers standing by gave Jesus a slap, saying: "Is that the way you answer the high priest?" Jesus answered him: "If I have spoken wrongly, bear witness concerning the wrong; but if rightly, why do you hit me?"

For his part, Paul did not submit meekly to the high priest Ananias' order that he be smitten on the mouth. He did not offer his cheek in compliance with Jesus' command. Instead, Paul swore at Ananias in direct contradiction of another of Jesus' alleged commandments: "Bless those who curse you, pray for those who mistreat you" (Luke 6:28), and his own statement: "Bless those who persecute you; bless, and do not curse" (Romans 12:14).

> And the High Priest Ananias commanded those standing beside him to strike him on the mouth. Then Paul said to him: "God is going to strike you, you whitewashed wall. And do you sit to judge me according to the Law, and in violation of the Law order me to be struck?" (Acts 23:2–3)

Is it no wonder that the dictum to turn the other cheek, attributed to Jesus, is more spoken about than complied with?

36

IS CHRISTIANITY ENTIRELY GOOD? THE NEW TESTAMENT PERSPECTIVE

(Matthew 7:15–20, Luke 6:43–45)

Beware of the false prophets who come to you in sheep's clothing, but inwardly are ravenous wolves. You will know them by their fruits. Grapes are not gathered from thorns, nor figs from thistles, are they? Thus, every good tree bears good fruit, but the rotten tree bears bad fruit. A good tree cannot produce bad fruit, nor can a rotten tree produce good fruit. Every tree that does not bear good fruit is cut down and thrown into the fire. So then, you will know them by their fruits.

(Matthew 7:15–20; see also Luke 6:43–45)

In these verses, Jesus vigorously affirms that what is good cannot possibly produce evil, and conversely, that what is evil cannot possibly produce good: "A good tree cannot produce bad fruit, nor can a rotten tree produce good fruit." Viewed from this perspective, Christianity cannot be considered wholly good since so many wrongs have issued from its domination in many lands throughout extended periods in history. To argue, as many Christian missionary apologists do, that the evils resulting to the world in the wake of Christianity are not really of Christian origin is tantamount to claiming that the bad fruits growing on a tree were not produced by the tree. No amount of explaining can absolve Christianity from the innumerable wrongs stemming from the hegemony it has exercised over vast areas in the course of its tortuous history.

Matthew also records Jesus as saying:

Not everyone who says to me: "Lord, Lord," will enter the kingdom of the heavens, but he who does the will of my Father who is in the heavens. Many will say to me on that day: "Lord, Lord, did we not prophesy in your name, and in your name cast out demons, and in your name perform powerful works?" And then I will declare to them: "I never knew you; depart from me, you who practice lawlessness." (Matthew 7:21–23)

How aptly this applies to Christianity in general, which has spoken in the name of Jesus and in his name "performed powerful works." Could Jesus possibly accept Christianity as his own? To be true to his own dictum that bad fruit can never be produced by a good tree, Jesus would disown and reject Christianity for all the evil it has perpetrated in his name. Yet even though he might reject Christianity, many of the horrors it has subjected the world to are the direct result of his teachings. Yes, indeed, "You will know them by their fruits."

37

THE DROWNING OF THE HERD OF SWINE

(Matthew 8:30–32, Mark 5:11–13, Luke 8:31–33)

Now there was at a distance from them a herd of many swine feeding. And the demons began to entreat him, saying: "If you are going to expel us, send us into the herd of swine." And he said to them: "Go away!" And they came out, and went into the swine, and behold, the entire herd rushed down the steep bank into the sea, and died in the waters.

(Matthew 8:30–32)

Now there was a big herd of swine feeding there on the mountain side. And they entreated him, saying: "Send us into the swine so that we may enter them." And he gave them permission. And coming out, the unclean spirits entered the swine; and the herd rushed down the steep bank into the sea, about two thousand of them; and they were drowned in the sea.

(Mark 5:11–13)

And they were entreating him not to command them to depart into the abyss. Now there was a herd of many swine feeding there on the mountain; and the demons entreated him to permit them to enter the swine. And he gave them permission. And the demons came out from the man and entered the swine; and the herd rushed down the steep bank into the lake, and were drowned.

(Luke 8:31–33)

Jesus did not have the supernatural powers to do what is claimed for him in the incident of the drowning of the swine herd. However, this is beside the point, since the evangelists contend that he did. In view of this, let us investigate the implications of this tale. By allowing the demons to enter and take possession of the herd of swine, Jesus was at fault for causing the death of the swine. To rationalize this act by asserting that certain unstated factors were involved has no basis in the Gospel presentation. There is no reason to accept the assumptions of Christian missionary commentators that either the owners of the swine were Jewish and thus were guilty of disobeying the Torah, or that the swine were owned by a Gentile in defiance of his Jewish neighbors.

It is doubtful that demons can be destroyed by drowning. Therefore, the demons under discussion here must have continued to exist doing evil. Yet the innocent herd was killed. Jesus, as the all-knowing god-man, must have had foreknowledge of what the demons would do once they entered the unclean animals. It might be argued that a man is worth more than a herd of swine, but to rid the man of demons it was not necessary to transfer the demons to another life-form. According to the New Testament, Jesus could expel demons from people without having to place them into another life-form (Matthew 9:33; Mark 1:39, 7:26–30; Luke 8:2, 13:32). In addition, the death of the animals was not necessary to confirm to the man (two men according to Matthew 8:28) that he was now rid of the demons; he would have sensed the difference. Moreover, Mark 1:34 asserts that Jesus had such power over demons that they could not speak without his permission. Indeed, the demons needed his permission to enter the swine (Matthew 8:31, Mark 5:12, Luke 8:32). Since the demons, unlike humans, had no free will, but were subjected to Jesus' will, he was culpable for the wanton death of the swine by reason of his giving permission for the demons to enter and take possession of the swine. We must, thus, accept the inescapable conclusion that Jesus was indeed responsible for the violent death of the swine.

38

JESUS' OUTLOOK ON VIOLENCE
(Matthew 10:34–35; Luke 12:49–53, 19:27)

Admittedly, the use of violence is not always an act of evil, but if Jesus was the person spoken of by Isaiah as the one who "had done no violence" (Isaiah 53:9), then he could never have used any violence. But such is definitely not the case, as he most certainly did commit acts of violence when he attacked the merchants (Matthew 21:12, Mark 11:15–16, Luke 19:45, John 2:15), cursed a fig tree for not bearing fruit out of season (Matthew 21:18–21, Mark 11:13–14), and permitted demons to enter the swine herd causing their death (Matthew 8:32, Mark 5:13, Luke 8:33). Indeed, if Jesus was truly the submissive servant of the Lord as depicted by Isaiah, he could not have uttered such violent words as: "Do not think that I came to bring peace on the earth; I did not come to bring peace, but a sword. For I came to set a man against his father, and a daughter against her mother, and a daughter-in-law against her mother-in-law." (Matthew 10:34–35).

Luke continues this theme of Jesus' call to violence:

> I have come to cast fire upon the earth; and how I wish it were already kindled! But I have a baptism to undergo, and how distressed I am until it is accomplished! Do you suppose that I came to grant peace on earth? I tell you, no, but rather division; for from now on five members in one household will be divided, three against two, and two against three. They will be divided, father against son, and son against father; mother against daughter, and daughter against mother; mother-in-law against daughter-in-law, and daughter-in-law against mother-in-law. (Luke 12:49–53)

Here, Jesus, who supposedly committed no act of violence, proudly avows that his is a mission which will cause discord, disturb the universal peace, and bring war to the world. It was during this "first coming" that he calmly called for his opponents to be brought before him for summary execution: "But these enemies of mine who did not want me to reign over them, bring them here, and slay them in my presence" (Luke 19:27). Is this love? Is this compassion? Is this nonviolence?

39

WHO SHALL SEE THE SECOND COMING OF JESUS?

(Matthew 16:28, Mark 9:1, Luke 9:27)

Truly I say to you, there are some of those who are standing here who will not taste death at all until they see the Son of Man coming in his kingdom.

(Matthew 16:28; see also Mark 9:1, Luke 9:27)

The early Christians expected Jesus to return shortly, as Paul states: "And the God of peace will crush Satan under your feet shortly" (Romans 16:20). The author of Hebrews writes: "For yet in a very little while, he who is coming will come, and will not delay" (Hebrews 10:37). The author of Revelation attributes the following statements to Jesus:

Do not seal up the words of the prophecy of this book, for the time is near. (Revelation 22:10)

Behold, I am coming quickly, and my reward is with me, to render to each one as his work is. (Revelation 22:12)

Yes, I am coming quickly. (Revelation 22:20)

Indeed, Mark's Jesus, after listing all the tribulations the world must go through before he returns a second time (Mark 13:5–29), declares: "Truly I say to you, this generation will not pass away until all these things take place" (Mark 13:30).

209

Now, some two thousand years later, it is apparent that the quick return of Jesus expected by the early Christians never came to pass. The promise that Jesus would return within a short time after the resurrection to establish his kingdom can never be fulfilled.

It is argued, in accordance with 2 Peter 3:8–9, that while the period of time that has elapsed since the death of Jesus is of long duration in human terms, it is actually a short interval when measured by God's standards. This argument, in turn, is based on Psalm 90:4: "For a thousand years in Your sight are but as yesterday when it is past, or as a watch in the night." This explanation is entirely without validity, because what is involved here is not merely a question of the interpretation of the word "quickly" as used in such verses as Revelation 22:12, 20. Jesus' promise of his quick return includes prolonging the lifetime of certain individuals until he returned (Matthew 16:28). Yet all of Jesus' early followers tasted death, none surviving until this day, and Jesus' promise to them of his second coming never materialized. Jesus' vain promise and his followers' vain hopes are both expressed in Revelation: "He who testifies of these things says: 'Yes, I am coming quickly.' Amen. Come, Lord Jesus" (Revelation 22:20). But the truth is that Jesus is never coming back.

40

JESUS' TRIUMPHAL ENTRY INTO JERUSALEM

(Matthew 21:8–11, Mark 11:8–10, Luke 19:36–38, John 12:12–13)

And most of the multitude spread their garments in the road, and others were cutting branches from the trees, and spreading them in the road. And the multitudes going before him and those who followed were crying out, saying: "Hosanna to the son of David; blessed is he who comes in the name of the Lord; hosanna in the highest!" And when he had entered Jerusalem, all the city was stirred, saying: "Who is this?" And the multitudes were saying: "This is the prophet Jesus, from Nazareth in Galilee."

(Matthew 21:8–11)

And many spread their garments in the road, and others cut leafy branches from the fields. And those who went before and those who followed were crying out: "Hosanna! Blessed is he who comes in the name of the Lord; blessed is the coming kingdom of our father David; hosanna in the highest!"

(Mark 11:8–10)

And as he was going, they were spreading their garments in the road. As he was now getting near the descent of the Mount of Olives the whole multitude of the disciples started to rejoice and praise God with a loud voice for all the powerful works they had seen, saying: "Blessed is the King who comes in the name of the Lord; peace in heaven and glory in the highest!"

(Luke 19:36–38)

211

> *On the next day the great multitude who had come to the feast, when they heard that Jesus was coming to Jerusalem, took the branches of the palm trees, and went out to meet him, and began to cry out: "Hosanna! Blessed is he who comes in the name of the Lord, and the King of Israel."*
>
> (John 12:12–13)

If, as the Gospels relate, Jesus was crucified on a Friday, then he was in two different geographic locations at the same time earlier that week. Before his alleged triumphal entry into Jerusalem, the fourth Gospel has Jesus stay over night at Bethany (John 12:1, 12). The Synoptic Gospels, however, insist that Jesus proceeded directly to Jerusalem (Matthew 21:1, Mark 11:1, Luke 19:28–29), arriving, according to Mark, late in the afternoon. Thereupon, Mark relates, he briefly entered the Temple and then went to Bethany, where he stayed overnight (Mark 11:11–12). Returning to Jerusalem the next day, he made his assault on the Temple. However, according to Matthew and Luke, he made his attack on the Temple right after his triumphal entry into Jerusalem, not the next day. John has the Temple attack occur at a completely different time (cf. John 2:13–16 with John 12:12–13).

Matthew informs us that when Jesus entered Jerusalem, the entire populace became excited (Matthew 21:8–11). In a land that was seething with rebellion, the Romans were constantly on the lookout for any signs of insurrection. This was especially true before Passover, the festival of freedom from bondage. Therefore, it is highly unlikely that they neglected a messianic procession crying: "Hosanna to the son of David; blessed is he who comes in the name of the Lord; hosanna in the highest!" (Matthew 21:9; see also Mark 11:9–10, Luke 19:38, John 12:13). Indeed, it is strange that the Romans failed to respond to Jesus' violent actions in the Temple. Under the political and social conditions then prevailing in Judea, such an entrance as Jesus made into Jerusalem should have been unquestionably taken as an outright insurrection. Jesus knew very well that to the people at large, a messianic declaration was a call to revolt against the Romans.

It is clearly stated in Luke's narrative that it was Jesus' own disciples who initiated this messianic procession: "As he was now getting near the descent of the Mount of Olives the whole multitude of the disciples started to rejoice and praise God with a loud voice for all the powerful works they had seen" (Luke 19:37). Hence, this procession was not a spontaneous outburst on the part of the common people, but a carefully calculated move on the part of Jesus and his disciples designed to promote political agitation. At the end of their accounts, the evangelists present Jesus as innocent as a lamb before Pilate. In turn, Pilate is portrayed as flinching from condemning the guiltless Jesus: "For he knew that because of envy they had handed him over" (Matthew 27:18, Mark 15:10). It is even claimed that he wanted to release Jesus (Luke 23:20, John 19:12). In truth, considering that it was Pilate's responsibility to be aware of any and all incidents which might lead to insurrection, he must have been informed of the open messianic display and tumult caused by Jesus' triumphal entry into the city. He should, thus, have considered Jesus a rebel deserving of death as a political criminal, and should have dealt with him accordingly. This fact was totally disregarded by the evangelists, who were apparently seeking to curry favor for Christianity with the Roman authorities.

Is it not strange that during the various inquiries at which Jesus is alleged to have been examined, no mention was made by his enemies of his pretentious entry into Jerusalem? Surely, had the incident occurred it would have been used against him at one inquiry or another. Evidently, the Gospel writers felt that it was best not to mention the incident, as it constituted a provocation against Roman authority, and they wished to portray Jesus as a peaceful, nonviolent person who was not guilty of any wrongdoing.

41

VIOLENCE IN THE TEMPLE

(Matthew 21:12–13, Mark 11:15–17, Luke 19:45–46, John 2:13–16)

And Jesus entered into the Temple and cast out all those who were selling and buying in the Temple, and overturned the tables of the moneychangers and the seats of those who were selling doves. And he said to them: "It is written, 'My house shall be called a house of prayer'; but you are making it a robbers' den."

(Matthew 21:12–13)

And they came to Jerusalem. And he entered into the Temple and began to cast out those who were selling and buying in the Temple, and overturned the tables of the moneychangers and the seats of those who were selling doves; and he would not allow anyone to carry a utensil through the Temple. And he was teaching and saying: "Is it not written, 'My house shall be called a house of prayer for all the nations'? But you have made it a robbers' den."

(Mark 11:15–17)

And he entered into the Temple and began to cast out those who were selling, saying to them: "It is written, 'And My house shall be a house of prayer,' but you have made it a robbers' den."

(Luke 19:45–46)

And the Passover of the Jews was near, and Jesus went up to Jerusalem. And he found in the Temple those who were selling oxen and sheep and doves, and the moneychangers seated. And he made a whip of ropes, and drove them all out of the Temple, with the sheep and the oxen; and he poured out the coins of the moneychangers and overturned their tables. And to those who were selling the doves he said: "Take these things away; stop making my Father's house a house of merchandise."

(John 2:13–16)

The evangelists disagree as to exactly when Jesus carried out his attack on the Temple. Matthew and Luke have one time, Mark another, and John still a third. John's account indicates that the incident occurred on an earlier visit to Jerusalem than the one recorded in the Synoptic Gospels. However, the evangelists do agree that Jesus attacked the commercial activity in the Temple courtyard by violent means. Whip in hand, he attacked the merchants in the Temple area, causing a fracas. He overturned the tables of the moneychangers and the seats of those selling doves, and drove out of the Temple courtyard not only those who sold, but even those who were buying animals, along with the sheep and oxen. Jesus' action was a direct assault, planned in advance, and accompanied by a determined show of force. On his first day in Jerusalem, Jesus entered the Temple courtyard and "looked around at everything," then left (Mark 11:11). The following day he returned to begin his surprise assault. Contrary to Mark, Matthew and Luke say that Jesus, on first arriving in the city, proceeded directly to the Temple. They do not mention the earlier Temple visit. These two evangelists give the impression that Jesus' assault took place as a spontaneous reaction when he first entered the Temple. This difference is significant in that Mark's account indicates that Jesus carefully studied the situation before making his plans. It was only then that he returned and disrupted the commercial activity in the Temple courtyard. Mark's account, in particular, indicates that Jesus deliberately initiated the attack, and reveals the violence of his actions. Moreover, Jesus' disciples must have assisted him, as it would have been impossible for Jesus to have accomplished it all alone. Mark writes that Jesus took such complete control of the Temple courtyard that he prevented its use as a throughfare: "And he would not allow anyone to carry a utensil through the Temple" (Mark 11:16). Such control could only have been attained with the aid of his followers. It appears that Matthew and Luke attempted to suppress the information concerning the extent of Jesus' actions so as to minimize the impression that Jesus was a man of violence. The record of Jesus' violence, however, speaks for itself.

The Synoptic narratives quote Jesus as chastising the merchants with a statement which is actually a combination of phrases, taken out of context, from two separate biblical verses, Isaiah 56:7 and Jeremiah 7:11. On the other hand, John's narrative of this incident does not rely on biblical quotations. What Jesus actually said, if this incident happened at all, is a minor issue when compared to that of his use of violence.

It is curious that during the various inquires at which Jesus is alleged to have been examined, no mention was made by his enemies of the violent attack on the commercial activity going on in the Temple. Surely, if the incident had occurred, it would have been used against him at one inquiry or another. One can understand that from the Gospel writers' point of view, it was best not to mention the incident beyond the bare essentials since it showed Jesus' violent nature. The disruption of essential commerce needed for exchanging heathen coins depicting idolatry for ones that could be donated to the Temple, and for the purchase of sacrificial animals, was a provocation which disrupted not only the orderly Temple service but posed a threat to peace, and would automatically involve the Roman authorities. The evangelists, wishing to portray Jesus as a peaceful, nonviolent person who was not guilty of any wrongdoing, suppress any mention of this incident at the inquiries into his behavior. The evangelists, while showing what they consider to be Jesus' righteous indignation at the greed of his enemies, deliberately neglect to mention the violent aspects of his attack. They do this to preserve their overall portrayal of Jesus as a man of love and peace. In reporting on the inquiries, the evangelists want to emphasize their conception of Jesus, the man of peace, unjustly condemned by his enemies. Writing about these proceedings, they remain completely silent concerning his use of violence just a few days prior to his arrest. The evangelists must have realized that it did not matter whether Jesus was right or wrong in violently attacking the merchants. Violence is violence! Mark, the earliest Gospel writer, provides a slight insight, suppressed in the other Gospels, which gives us an inkling of the riotous and ruthless action that took place in the Temple on that day. If Jesus did not plan that the Temple attack and his earlier provocative entrance into Jerusalem would be the means of starting a revolt, this would indicate that he was ignorant of the political and social conditions in Judea, an unlikely possibility. On the other hand, it would have been ridiculous for the Romans and the Jews, who witnessed such activities, to think they were anything but the initial stages of a serious attack on the Roman domination of Judea.

42

THE CURSING OF THE FIG TREE
(Matthew 21:18–22; Mark 11:12–14, 20–25)

In the morning, as he was returning to the city, he became hungry. And seeing a lone fig tree by the road, he went to it, and found nothing on it except leaves only; and he said to it: "No longer shall there ever be any fruit from you." And the fig tree withered instantly. And seeing this, the disciples marveled, saying: "How did the fig tree wither instantly?" And Jesus answered and said to them: "Truly I say to you, if you have faith, and do not doubt, you shall not only do what was done to the fig tree, but even if you say to this mountain: 'Be lifted up and cast into the sea,' it shall happen. And everything you ask in prayer, believing, you shall receive."

(Matthew 21:18–22)

And on the next day, when they had departed from Bethany, he became hungry. And seeing at a distance a fig tree that had leaves, he went to see if perhaps he would find anything on it; and when he came to it, he found nothing but leaves, for it was not the time of figs. And he answered and said to it: "May no one ever eat fruit from you again!" And his disciples were listening. . . . And when they were passing by early in the morning, they saw the fig tree withered up from the roots. And Peter, having remembered it, said to him: "Rabbi, behold, the fig tree which you cursed has withered." And Jesus answered saying to them: "Have faith in God. Truly I say to you that whoever says to this mountain: 'Be lifted up and cast into the sea,' and does not doubt in his heart, but believes that what he says is going to happen; it shall be granted him. Therefore I say to you, all things for which you pray and ask, believe that you have received them, and they shall be granted you. And whenever you stand praying, forgive, if you have anything against anyone; in order that your Father also who is in the heavens may forgive you your transgressions."

(Mark 11:12–14, 20–25)

While on the road to Jerusalem, Jesus became hungry (Matthew 21:18, Mark 11:12), and, seeing a fig tree with leaves, he approached it but found no fruit on it, "for it was not the time of figs" (Mark 11:13). He cursed the fig tree and it withered either instantly (Matthew 21:20) or by the next morning (Mark 11:20–21).

It is the nature of the fig tree that even before the tree is covered with leaves, the *paggim* ("green figs") begin to develop and continue to grow during the summer months. The first ripe figs sometimes appear in the early summer (Song of Songs 2:13), many weeks after the leaves have appeared. Therefore, even if there had been figs, as Jesus had expected, it was too early in the season for them to be ripe for eating. Moreover, a tree, lacking a mind and conscience of its own, cannot be treated as deceptive, and certainly cannot be held responsible for not producing fruit. Why then the violent action against the tree? According to the Torah, not even during the exigencies of war is one permitted to chop down a fruit-bearing tree (Deuteronomy 20:19). That Jesus, in violation of the Torah, destroyed a tree he considered capable of bearing fruit is indicated by his statement: "May no one ever eat fruit from you again!" (Mark 11:14), alternately expressed as: "No longer shall there ever be any fruit from you" (Matthew 21:19).

When questioned by his disciples about his actions, Jesus said he did it to show what can be done by faith (Matthew 21:21–22; Mark 11:22–24). But how does wanton destruction demonstrate faith? No moral lesson is clearly stated or even alluded to in this destructive act. If Jesus was all-powerful and all-loving, would it not have been proper for him to command the tree to give forth fruit rather than to command it to wither and die? While he advises his followers to forgive those with whom they have had differences: "And whenever you stand praying, forgive, if you have anything against anyone" (Mark 11:25), he did not practice what he himself preached. In any case, whatever the reason for Jesus' action, it was an act of violence, which is not in conformity with the picture of the nonviolent suffering servant of the Lord as portrayed in Isaiah 53:9.

43

WHICH ZECHARIAH?

(Matthew 23:35)

. . . so that there may come upon you all the righteous blood poured out upon the earth from the blood of righteous Abel to the blood of Zechariah son of Barachiah, whom you murdered between the Temple and the altar.

(Matthew 23:35; see also Luke 11:51)

Matthew's Jesus made an egregious error which illustrates the inaccuracy of the evangelical account. The Hebrew Scriptures inform us that it was Zechariah, the son of Jehoiada the priest, who was slain by the altar (2 Chronicles 24:20–21). Any attempt to reconcile this discrepancy, by which Zechariah, the son of Jehoiada the priest, and Zechariah, the son of Berechiah (Zechariah 1:1), are to be viewed as identical, is completely without foundation. Zechariah, the son of Jehoiada, was slain in the days of Joash, king of Judah (ca. 840 B.C.E.), while the prophet Zechariah, the son of Berechiah, did not prophesy until the second year of Darius (ca. 520 B.C.E.), which followed the return from the Babylonian captivity. There is absolutely no reason to believe that Zechariah, the son of Berechiah, the son of Iddo, died in the manner described. The Scriptures do not indicate when, where, or how Zechariah, the son of Berechiah, died. However, it is obvious that the death described by Matthew was suffered by another person, Zechariah, the son of Jehoiada.

Matthew may have confused a similar account related in the writings of the Jewish historian, Flavius Josephus, where we are told in *The Jewish War* how a man named Zecharias, son of Baris

220

(or Bariscaeus), was slain in the Temple by the Zealots (ca. 68 c.e.).[1] The incident quoted by Matthew could not have been known to Jesus, having occurred years after his death. The evangelist put these words into Jesus' mouth, utilizing the information from Josephus as a basis for his story. In narrating this incident, Luke only mentions the name of Zechariah without specifying who his father was (Luke 11:51).[2]

1. Flavius Josephus, *The Jewish War*, Book 4, 338; trans. H. St. J. Thackeray, Loeb Classical Library, vol. 3, pp. 99–101.
2. For information concerning the implications of Jesus' blood libel against the Jews mentioned in Matthew 23:35, see below Chapter 59, "Jesus And Forgiveness."

44

CONFUSED TRADITIONS

(Matthew 26:6–7, Mark 14:3, Luke 7:37–38, John 12:2–3)

Now when Jesus was in Bethany in the house of Simon the leper, a woman came to him with an alabaster vial of costly perfume, and she poured it upon his head as he reclined.

(Matthew 26:6–7)

And behold, there was a woman in the city who was a sinner; and when she learned that he was reclining in the Pharisee's house, she brought an alabaster vial of perfume, and standing behind him at his feet, weeping, she began to wet his feet with her tears, and kept wiping them with the hair of her head, and kissing his feet, and anointing them with the perfume.

(Luke 7:37–38)

Therefore they made him a supper there, and Martha was serving, but Lazarus was one of those reclining together with him. Mary, therefore, took a pound of costly, genuine spikenard ointment, and anointed the feet of Jesus, and wiped his feet with her hair; and the house was filled with the fragrance of the ointment.

(John 12:2–3)

Mark 14:3 is in basic agreement with Matthew, but Luke's version of the same event differs in quite a number of details. There is no doubt that Luke, though he changes the time and location of the event, is depicting the same occurrence (Luke 7:44). However, the information given by the various versions

222

found in the Synoptic Gospels does not coincide with the same story as described by John.

Only Luke says that the woman was a sinner. The Synoptic Gospels say she anointed Jesus with perfume, while John says it was spikenard ointment. Matthew and Mark say the woman anointed Jesus' head; Luke and John say she anointed his feet. There is a decided lack of agreement between the four evangelists.

45

THIRTY SILVER PIECES

(Matthew 26:14–15)

Then one of the twelve, the one called Judas Iscariot, went to the chief priests and said: "What are you willing to give me to deliver him to you?" And they paid him thirty silver pieces.

(Matthew 26:14–15)

Matthew is the only evangelist to mention the specific sum allegedly paid for the betrayal of Jesus. The reason for this is because one of the tasks he sets for himself is to show the interconnection between his narrative and biblical prophecy. Accordingly, Matthew violently wrenches a verse out of its context in the Book of Zechariah in order to show that the sum paid to Judas was foretold in the Hebrew Scriptures. The prophet says: "And I said to them: 'If it seems right to you, give me my wages, but if not, keep them.' So they weighed for my wages thirty pieces of silver" (Zechariah 11:12). Zechariah speaks here of himself. As the divinely appointed shepherd of Israel, he requests his wages of the people, who then allot him this meager sum. This verse cannot be connected in any reasonable way with Judas Iscariot. Matthew's credibility is further weakened by the fact that the paltry sum of thirty silver pieces would not have been enough for Judas to acquire a field, as described in Acts 1:18. Interestingly, the author of Acts does not mention the amount of money involved. Matthew is plainly misusing Zechariah's words to serve his own purposes.

46

THE LAST SUPPER

(Matthew 26:17–30, Mark 14:12–26, Luke 22:7–39, John 13:1–18:1)

It was on the evening prior to his crucifixion that Jesus gathered together his disciples for a last meal. This meal is generally referred to as the Last Supper. Was the Last Supper the *seder*, the paschal meal eaten on the night of Nisan 14 (Synoptic Gospels) or another meal on Nisan 13 (fourth Gospel)? Two variant traditions exist in the New Testament as to whether to identify the Last Supper with the paschal meal or a regular meal. The author of John makes no reference to the Passover ceremonial bread *(matsah)* and wine, which Jesus allegedly used to represent his body and blood (Matthew 26:26–28, Mark 14:22–24, Luke 22:19–20). He does not connect the Last Supper with the *seder*, stating instead that the Passover festival began on the night following the daylight hours[1] during which Jesus was crucified:

> They [the priests] did not enter into the judgment hall in order that they might not be defiled, but might eat the Passover. (John 18:28)

> Now it [the day of the crucifixion] was the day of preparation for the Passover. (John 19:14)

Thus, John reports that Jesus died on the afternoon preceding Passover. The Last Supper, according to him, took place the evening before that of the *seder* feast.

No matter how Christian missionaries may explain John's account in order to harmonize it with the Synoptic Gospels, the

225

evidence for two variant traditions overwhelms all opposition. Too many problems surface which cannot be ignored or reconciled. If this meal was indeed a *seder*, we must then conclude that Jesus and his disciples did not observe the Torah injunctions against transacting business on a festival (Exodus 12:16, Leviticus 23:6–7; Numbers 28:17–18, Nehemiah 10:30, 32). Observant Jews would never handle money or conduct business transactions on a festival, yet John states: "For some [of the disciples] were supposing, because Judas had the money box, that Jesus was saying to him: 'Buy the things we have need of for the feast'; or else, that he should give something to the poor" (John 13:29). The disciples thought Judas had been instructed by Jesus to go and purchase things needed for the feast, but were not startled by what they presumed to be his order. Are we to assume that they were not observant of the Torah regulations, and that on the very *seder* night their leader, Jesus, was capable of ordering one of them to violate a fundamental commandment of God? How could the disciples even think that he who came to fulfill all the Law (Matthew 5:17) would ask anyone to violate that very Law? Furthermore, they must have known that Judas would find no shops open. Preparations for the paschal meal and the Passover festival, in general, would have been made prior to the holiday and not during the ceremony itself.

Did Judas, on Jesus' orders, go out to give charity? Some disciples thought this possible. But no observant Jew would give money, or ask someone to give it, on a festival. We must presume either that this was not the *seder* or that Jesus, lacking any regard for the Law of God, was capable of sending Judas out on an errand which violated that Law. Under such circumstances Jesus could not be the Messiah.

---

1. The days of the Jewish calendar run from the evening of one day to the evening of the next.

47

DID JESUS OFFER HIMSELF AS A WILLING SACRIFICE FOR MANKIND'S SINS?

(Matthew 26:39, Mark 14:35–36, Luke 22:41–44)

Christian missionaries claim that Jesus came into the world expressly to offer himself as a willing sacrifice to atone for mankind's sins. If that was the case, why did he hesitate and pray for the reversal of the fate prescribed for him? "And going a little way forward, he fell upon his face praying and saying: 'My Father, if it is possible, let this cup pass from me. Yet, not as I will, but as you will' " (Matthew 26:39; see also Mark 14:35–36, Luke 22:41–44). Furthermore, why did Jesus, the god-man, need an angel to strengthen him: "Then an angel from heaven appeared to him, strengthening him" (Luke 22:43). If he supposedly had full knowledge of why he had to die, and of the resulting rewards that would accrue to him, he should not have been in any need of a reassuring angel. Did this god-man have to be reminded of his role and of its rewards? Even the human side of his being should have been governed by this knowledge. He should have gone to his death in a state of inner joy rather than with feelings of despair and failure. We find that Jesus was in a state of agony (Luke 22:44) in which he tearfully cried out to be saved from death (Hebrews 5:7). Jesus' alleged exclamation: "Yet, not as I will but as you will," undoubtedly indicates that had it been his choice, he would not have undergone execution. Although he seems to have submitted to God's will, in his final moments of life Jesus expressed feelings of frustration and abandonment: "My God my God, why have you forsaken me?"

227

(Matthew 27:46, Mark 15:34).[1] We must conclude that at that last critical moment, he did not wish to die and become a willing sacrifice for the sins of mankind.

1. Although Luke and John record different versions of Jesus' last words (Luke 23:46, John 19:30), they do not alter the feeling of Matthew's and Mark's version, which is one of despair, frustration, and abandonment.

48

THE TRIAL OF JESUS

(Matthew 26:57–27:24, Mark 14:53–15:15, Luke 22:54–23:24, John 18:12–19:16)

The evangelical accounts of the trial proceedings against Jesus present the reader with four varied versions of those crucial events. While certain features of their respective reports are similar, there are enough irreconcilable differences to question the veracity of their accounts.

Briefly put, here are some questions that must be answered before one accepts the accounts of the trial proceedings as true:

1. Was Jesus, after his arrest in Gethsemane, first taken to the then high priest Caiaphas (so identified in Matthew 26:3, John 18:13), as indicated in Mark 14:53 and Luke 22:54, or was he first taken to Caiaphas' son-in-law, Annas, as John states (John 18:13)?
2. Was there a Jewish trial before the entire Sanhedrin, as in Matthew 26:59 and Mark 14:55, or merely an inquiry by the Sanhedrin, as in Luke 22:66–71, or just private interrogations, first by Annas (John 18:13) and then by Caiaphas (John 18:24), as only John writes?
3. Was there an additional morning meeting of the Sanhedrin convened expressly to confirm the decision of the night before, as in Matthew 27:1 and Mark 15:1, but which is not mentioned at all in either Luke or John? Is it not strange that in their respective narratives, Luke and John leave no time for this event to have occurred?
4. Did the Jewish trial take place on Passover, as in the Synoptic Gospels (Matthew 26:18–20, Mark 14:16–18, Luke

22:13–15), contrary to Jewish religious tradition and practice, which forbids trials on festivals, or was it the day before Passover, as in John's Gospel (John 18:28, 19:14)?

5. Did the trial before the Sanhedrin take place at night, as in Matthew and Mark—something which is contrary to Jewish religious tradition and practice, which forbid trials at night—or did the proceedings before the Sanhedrin take place *only* in the morning, as in Luke 22:66?

6. Shall we consider valid Luke's version, which has Pilate interrupt his own Roman trial proceedings in order to send Jesus to Herod Antipas, a Jew, for judgment (Luke 23:7)? Can one believe that Pilate would compromise his own power by sending Jesus to Herod Antipas, who, at that time, was not only himself subject to Rome but was still Pilate's enemy (Luke 23:12)?

7. Did the witnesses testify that Jesus said *"I am able* to destroy this Temple"* (Matthew 26:61) or *"I will* destroy this Temple made with hands" (Mark 14:58)? In other words, did Jesus claim, according to the accusations recorded by the evangelists, ability or clear intent?

8. Did the high priest ask Jesus if he was the "Son of God" (Matthew 26:63, Luke 22:70) or the "Son of the Blessed" (Mark 14:61)?

9. It is difficult to believe that Pilate, possessing enough military might to enforce any decision he desired, was compelled by a Jewish mob to order the execution of Jesus, whom he knew to be innocent (Matthew 27:18, 20, 24; Mark 15:10, 14–15; Luke 23:14, 20, 24; John 19:12). We are told that he accepted the mob's demand for the release of a known rebel, Barabbas, who had led an insurrection against Roman rule (Matthew 27:16, 20–21, 26; Mark 15:7, 15; Luke 23:18–19). If this was the case, Pilate certainly had more to fear from the imperial wrath than from the Jewish accusation that if he released Jesus, he was not a friend of the emperor (John 19:12). Are we to believe the ludicrous situation the evangelists describe?

The factual discrepancies found in the various trial accounts produce a host of questions affecting the reliability of the evangelical records. We are confronted with a crucial New Testament event which is full of questionable information. This, however, is an ever-present phenomenon of evangelical reporting that is not confined to the trial episode alone.

49

HOW FALSE WERE THE "FALSE WITNESSES"?

(Matthew 26:59–61, Mark 14:55–59)

Mark states that the Jewish religious authorities sought testimony which could condemn Jesus to death: "Now the chief priests and the whole Sanhedrin were seeking testimony against Jesus to put him to death, and they were not finding any" (Mark 14:55). Matthew aggravates this allegation, claiming that the authorities deliberately sought false testimony: "Now the chief priests and the whole Sanhedrin were seeking false testimony against Jesus in order that they might put him to death" (Matthew 26:59). These two evangelists then present their respective versions of the witnesses' testimony. Mark writes: "And some stood up and began to give false testimony against him, saying: 'We heard him say: "I will destroy this Temple made with hands and in three days I will build another not made with hands" ' " (Mark 14:57–58). In his version Matthew writes: "But later on two came forward and said: 'This man stated: "I am able to destroy this Temple of God and to rebuild it in three days" ' " (Matthew 26:60–61). Matthew alters the charge, which the witnesses in Mark ascribe to Jesus. In his Gospel, the intention to destroy the Temple is now modified to one of ability to perform the act, that is, from "I will" to "I am able." Matthew also gives the exact number of witnesses as two, whereas Mark merely says "some" gave testimony.

Luke's Gospel omits completely the accusation that Jesus had threatened to destroy the Temple. According to him, Jesus was tried only on the charge of being the "Christ" or the "Son of God" (Luke 22:67–71). However, in Acts, attributed to Luke,

Stephen is accused of saying that Jesus would destroy the Temple (Acts 6:14). John, writing much later, states that Jesus actually made a declaration quite similar to that which Matthew and Mark report as false testimony: "Destroy this Temple, and in three days I will raise it up" (John 2:19).

It is not surprising that Matthew and Mark do not agree on the exact wording of the testimony given by the witnesses. The fact is that rarely do the evangelists use the same wording in transcribing their respective versions of events and quotations. As a result, it is impossible to say with certainty that the two witnesses definitely gave false testimony. Even the evangelists cannot agree as to what the alleged false statement was supposed to have been. There is also no reason to believe that each evangelist is recording, in turn, what was the respective false testimony of the two witnesses. In fact, Matthew's Gospel indicates that there was no disagreement between their testimonies (Matthew 26:60–62). As already mentioned, John quotes Jesus as stating: "Destroy this Temple, and in three days I will raise it up." This shows that, according to John, there was a factual basis for the testimony (cf. Mark 13:2, Acts 6:14). One could never get this impression from either Matthew or Mark. They do not mention Jesus as ever making such a statement. According to their description of the events, the witnesses devised the entire story. Yet from John we see not only that Jesus said something quite similar to the testimony, but, given the inconsistent manner in which the evangelists transmit quotations, that there is a strong possibility that the witnesses may very well have quoted Jesus correctly and that, in actuality, it is the evangelists who distorted the record. One thing is certain. It suited the evangelists to accuse the witnesses and the Sanhedrin of perversity.

In the final analysis, whether the evidence represents fact or fancy is not important. What is most significant is that nothing attributed by the witnesses to Jesus would have been considered blasphemous by a Jewish court. Perhaps his claim was foolish and pretentious, but it was not one justifying his condemnation to death. Therefore, if there was any falsehood involved, it was on the part of Matthew and Mark seeking to condemn the Jewish leadership. It is likely that the inconsistencies in testimony are due to the prejudicial evangelical writers rather than to the witnesses. In principle, even John agrees with the witnesses that Jesus said he could rebuild the Temple after three days. Whether Jesus said: "I will" (according to Mark), "I am able" (according to Matthew), or "If you" (according to John), his declaration, in any form given, is merely an idle boast for which no one is liable to the death penalty. This testimony could never have been used to condemn Jesus. Having insufficient information as to what actually transpired in the time period that elapsed between the capture and the execution of Jesus, the evangelists fabricated a tale based on legendary material. This segment of their record cannot be accepted as historically accurate.

50

THE DEATH OF JUDAS ISCARIOT
(Matthew 27:3–5)

Then when Judas, who had betrayed him [Jesus], saw that he had been condemned, felt remorse and returned the thirty silver pieces to the chief priests and the elders, saying: "I sinned when I betrayed righteous blood." But they said: "What is that to us? See to that yourself!" And he threw the silver pieces into the Temple and departed, and went off and hanged himself.

(Matthew 27:3–5)

Judas Iscariot is portrayed by Matthew as repenting his deed. In his remorse, Judas attempted to return the thirty silver pieces to the Jewish officials, but they refused to accept them. He then threw the silver pieces down, went out, and hanged himself.

This tale suffers from the suspicion that the evangelist is once more trying to introduce a biblical illustration to enhance his narrative. In this instance, it is the thirty pieces of silver mentioned in Zechariah 11:13. In addition, there is a tradition of Judas' death, given in Acts, which is totally at variance with that of Matthew: "This man acquired a field with the wages of his wickedness; and falling headlong, he burst open in the middle and all his intestines were poured out" (Acts 1:18). According to this tradition, Judas felt no remorse whatsoever, did not return the money, and certainly did not commit suicide. He lived at least long enough to use the money he received to purchase a parcel of land. His subsequent death is attributed to a violent fall while on his property.

235

51

THE POTTER'S FIELD

(Matthew 27:7–10)

And they counseled together and with the money bought the potter's field as a burial place for strangers. Therefore that field has been called the Field of Blood to this day. Then that which was spoken through Jeremiah the prophet was fulfilled, saying: "And they took the thirty silver pieces, the price of the one whose price had been set by the sons of Israel, and they gave them for the potter's field, as the Lord directed me."

(Matthew 27:7–10)

When Judas attempted to return the price paid for his betrayal of Jesus, the priests refused to accept it. He then threw it down and left the Temple. The priests, feeling that money used as payment for a treacherous act could not be put into the Temple treasury, purchased a burial place for strangers with it: "Therefore that field has been called the Field of Blood to this day."

In Acts there is a variant tradition concerning the manner in which the field was named:

This man acquired a field with the wages of his wickedness, and falling headlong he burst open in the middle, and all his intestines were poured out. And it became known to all the inhabitants of Jerusalem; so that in their own language that field was called Akeldama, that is, Field of Blood. (Acts 1:18–19)

In this variant tradition, the field was not named as a result of the priests buying it for use as a burial place for strangers, but rather because Judas met a bloody death there.

236

Matthew's biblical quotation is erroneous. There is no such statement to be found in the Book of Jeremiah. The quotation is actually Matthew's own creation, based on Zechariah 11:12–13, not Jeremiah. Matthew's error may have come about because Jeremiah at one point tells a parable about a potter and his clay (18:1–6) and at another point speaks about a field (32:6–9). Nevertheless, the evangelist's mistake, whether due to confusion or deliberate manipulation of the text, is inexcusable. In addition, there is absolutely no relationship between the passages found in Jeremiah and Zechariah and Matthew's passage. The prophets' message and Matthew's passage are mutually exclusive, not parallel as the evangelist would have us believe.

52

THE RESURRECTION

(Matthew 28:6–7, Mark 16:6, Luke 24:6, John 20:9)

A major difficulty facing a study of the alleged resurrection of Jesus is that all the information concerning it comes from the New Testament, a book which contains many inaccuracies. The accounts of what occurred in the days following the crucifixion form some of the most dubious chapters in the entire New Testament. This is due, in part, to the fact that the authors of the New Testament, and especially the evangelists, wrote many years after the death and burial of Jesus. Let us examine the web of events surrounding the life and death of Jesus as woven together by the authors of the Gospels, and we shall discover that many of its strands contradict the very belief they endeavor to promote.

Belief in the resurrection of Jesus, so crucial to the theology of missionary Christianity, is based on unsubstantiated evidence. The Gospel accounts of the resurrection are not the result of objective observations by trustworthy eyewitnesses. As a result, the veracity of the resurrection accounts is highly questionable. The Christian missionary response to divergences and contradictions found in the Gospels is that they are irrelevant. The missionaries claim that it is of no importance that the Gospels vary in so many details. After all, no two people see the same incident in the same way. Each of the evangelists, it is said, saw the resurrection event from a different perspective. The important thing, Christian missionary apologists contend, is that the evangelists agree on the essential fact of the resurrection. But herein lies a basic fallacy in the Gospel narratives of the resurrection. The evangelists could not see the resurrection event from different perspectives since they did not personally witness the resurrection. In fact, although Peter is alleged to have stated: "This Jesus God resurrected, of which we are all witnesses" (Acts 2:32), not one witness is produced who saw the resurrection. A careful reading of the text indicates that the Gospel writers can only attest to several accounts which exist concerning the events surrounding the body's disappearance. They cannot attest to the reason for its disappearance or what was the nature of its final disposition. They knew nothing more than that on Sunday morning the tomb was empty. No one saw Jesus rise from the dead. The disappearance of the body does not mean that there was a resurrection. The empty tomb explains nothing.

Matthew offers a typology from the Book of Jonah (Jonah 2:1, 1:17 in some versions) to bolster the belief that Jesus would rise on the third day. He quotes Jesus as saying to the scribes and Pharisees: "For just as Jonah was three days and three nights in the belly of the sea monster, so will the Son of Man be three days and three nights in the heart of the earth" (Matthew 12:40). This typology supposedly foreshadows the burial and the resurrection of Jesus. Yet it contains an essential difference in comparison with Matthew's resurrection account. This difference destroys Matthew's attempt at an analogy. According to all four Gospels the crucifixion took place on a Friday and the resurrection on the following Sunday.[1] From this it would seem that Jesus was buried for three days (Friday, Saturday, Sunday). Thus, Luke writes that according to prophecy, Jesus was to rise on the third day: "Then he opened their minds to understand the Scriptures, and he said to them: 'Thus it is written, that the Christ should suffer and rise from the dead the third day' " (Luke 24:45, 46; see also Matthew 16:21; Mark 8:31, 10:34; Luke 9:22, 18:33). While it is true that according to Jewish law part of the day is equivalent to a full day, Matthew's Jesus promised to be buried specifically for three days and *three nights.* By the use of the phrase "three days and three nights," Matthew's Jesus indicated that he expected to be buried for three consecutive periods between dawn and dark (day) and dark and dawn (night), or approximately seventy-two hours. The Scriptures employ the phrase "three days" in a more general sense than that expressed by "three days and three nights." For example, "three days does not necessarily include the period of day or night at either the beginning or end of the total time to be indicated. Therefore, when the phrase "three days" is meant to specifically include three days and three nights, and this is not evident from the text, it must be stated as such: ". . . neither eat nor drink three days, night or day. . ." (Esther 4:16). However, when the phrase "three days and three nights" is stated, it includes either all three days and all three nights or can be deficient in only parts of a day or night at the beginning or end of the entire period, but never of a full segment of day or night out of twenty-four hours (1 Samuel 30:11–13).

Although Jesus did not have to be buried exactly seventy-two hours, he did have to be buried at least on parts of three days and three nights. Jesus died on a Friday at the ninth hour, which corresponds to about 3 p.m. The claim is made that Jesus rose three days later, on a Sunday. This would mean that he was buried during the daylight hours of three different days. If this was true, he was buried for only two nights.

The Gospel of John indicates that Jesus' promise to rise after being buried three days and three nights was never fulfilled. According to Matthew the women came to the tomb "as it began to dawn toward the first day of the week" (Matthew 28:1), Mark says "they came to the tomb when the sun had risen" (Mark 16:2), and Luke says it was "at early dawn that they came to the tomb" (Luke 24:1). But in John it clearly states that it was not yet dawn when the body of Jesus disappeared from the tomb: "On the first day of the week Mary Magdalene came early to the tomb, while it was still dark, and saw the stone already taken away from the tomb" (John 20:1). Thus, John says that Jesus, having risen before the dawn of Sunday morning, was buried for only two days and two nights, i.e., one full day (Saturday), part of another (Friday), and two nights (Friday and Saturday nights). This contradicts the assertion that in fulfillment of prophecy, Jesus was buried three days and three nights. The

New Testament evidence simply does not add up to three days, i.e., daylight hours, and three nights, as specifically promised by Jesus. Therefore, Jesus did not fulfill his very own prediction.

Luke records that one of the two thieves crucified with Jesus cast doubt on his claim to be the Messiah (Luke 23:39). Disagreeing with this, Matthew and Mark have not one but both of the thieves reviling Jesus (Matthew 27:44, Mark 15:32).[2] But there is no end to the inconsistencies, for Luke has Jesus promise the thief who, in this version, did not revile him that "today you shall be with me in paradise" (Luke 23:43). This promise could not be true if one is to believe Mark, who states that Jesus rose on the first day of the week (Mark 16:9).[3] That was three days later (Luke 24:46)! In addition, Mark and Luke indicate that Jesus "was taken up into heaven" at a date sometime after the crucifixion (Mark 16:19, Luke 24:51). Moreover, John says that after the resurrection Jesus said to Mary Magdalene: "Touch me not for I have not yet ascended to the Father" (John 20:17). Jesus' promise to the thief is completely untenable.

Which of Jesus' followers came to the tomb? Matthew says that Mary Magdalene and another woman named Mary came to view the grave (Matthew 28:1). Mark relates that Mary Magdalene, Mary the mother of James, and Salome came to the tomb (Mark 16:1). Luke has Mary Magdalene, Joanna, and Mary the mother of Jesus, as well as "other women," at the tomb (Luke 24:10). John writes that Mary Magdalene came to the tomb, and it can be seen from the context that she was alone and not with any "other woman" (John 20:1).

How many angels did Jesus' followers find at, or in, the tomb, one or two? Who rolled away the stone from before the tomb? Where were the angels when first seen? Which of Jesus' followers entered the tomb, and when did they do so? Which evangelical version is correct? Matthew says that when Mary Magdalene and Mary arrived at the tomb an angel "approached and rolled away the stone and sat upon it," to the accompaniment of a great earthquake (Matthew 28:2). Mark claims that when the women arrived at the tomb they found the stone already rolled away, and no mention is made of an angel moving it for them or of a great earthquake (Mark 16:4). Luke also reports that the women found the stone already rolled away from the tomb, making no mention of its being moved by an angel or of an earthquake (Luke 24:2). John states that Mary Magdalene found the stone already removed from the entrance when she arrived at the tomb. Mark claims that when "they entered into the tomb they saw a young man sitting on the right side wearing a white robe" (Mark 16:5). Luke says that when they entered into the tomb "two men stood by them in flashing clothing" (Luke 24:4). Well, which is it, Mark or Luke, one angel or two, sitting or standing? But if this is not confusing enough, John gives us a little of both versions plus some additional contradictions. John says that Mary Magdalene ran to Simon Peter and the beloved disciple when she saw that the stone was rolled away from the tomb's entrance (John 20:1–2). She does not make any mention to them of seeing angels or experiencing an earthquake but expresses her feeling that evildoers had removed the body. John indicates that Mary Magdalene first looked into the tomb when she came back a second time. It was only then, John reports, that she saw "two angels in white sitting, one at the head and one at the feet, where the body of Jesus had been lying" (John 20:12). However, this occurred after the disciples left and not on an earlier visit to the tomb as in the other versions.

Where was Jesus while all this was going on?

Matthew 28:6: "He is not here, for he was raised up."

Mark 16:6: "He was raised up, he is not here."

Luke 24:6: "He is not here, but he was raised."

John 20:14: "She turned back, and saw Jesus standing."

And we thought he was supposed to be in heaven with the thief!

Let us now return to the problem involving angels. In Matthew the angel says, "go quickly and tell his disciples" (Matthew 28:7). In Mark the angel says, "tell his disciples and Peter" (Mark 16:7). But according to Luke they went to tell the disciples without being commanded to do so by the angels (Luke 24:9).

John has Mary Magdalene tell the disciples what has happened before she sees the angels (John 20:2, 11–12). She further informed them that "we do not know where they have laid him." John, therefore, contradicts the claim that the angels provided the knowledge of the resurrection (Matthew 28:6, Mark 16:6, Luke 24:6). According to John, Jesus himself, not an angel, informs Mary Magdalene of his forthcoming ascension (John 20:17–18).

Where did Jesus appear to Mary Magdalene after his death? Matthew states that Jesus first appeared to Mary Magdelene and Mary after they had left the tomb and were on the road returning to Jerusalem to tell his disciples about the empty tomb: "Behold, Jesus met them, saying: 'Hello.' And they approached and took hold of his feet and worshipped him" (Matthew 28:9). However, according to John, Jesus first appeared to Mary Magdalene while she was alone at the tomb, and he said to her: "Touch me not, for I have not yet ascended to the Father" (John 20:17). In this scene, Mary Magdalene, one of Jesus' most intimate followers, did not recognize him when he appeared to her, and had to be informed by the man she met at the tomb that he was Jesus (John 20:14–16). Disagreeing with John, Matthew says that an angel, not Jesus, was present at the tomb and told the two women, of whom Mary Magdalene was one, that Jesus had risen (Matthew 28:5–7). No room is left in Matthew's narrative for them both, or Mary Magdalene alone, as in John's version, to have met Jesus at the tomb. Mark merely records that Jesus appeared to Mary Magdalene first, but no geographic location is given for this meeting (Mark 16:9). Luke's version does not mention an appearance by Jesus to Mary Magdalene, or any other woman, and leaves no room for one to have occurred (Luke 24:9–10). The author of John alleges that Mary Magdalene, while alone at the tomb, grabbed Jesus by the feet (John 20:17), but Matthew's version has both Marys, while on the road to Jerusalem, grab his feet (Matthew 28:9). Strangely enough, although John's Jesus admonishes Mary Magdalene for touching him, Matthew's Jesus says nothing to the two Marys about their holding on to him. Exactly where and to whom did Jesus appear—near the

tomb to Mary Magdalene alone (John), on the road to both
Marys (Matthew), at an undisclosed location to Mary Magdalene
alone (Mark), or to neither one (Luke)? Did they or did they not
touch him? What is one to believe about the veracity of any of
this? Confusion and unreliable evidence are the substance of this
alleged postresurrection appearance.

Only Matthew mentions the Jewish officials sending a contingent of soldiers to guard the tomb (Matthew 27:65–66). He writes
that the Jewish enemies of Jesus, knowing of the latter's promise
to rise from the dead on the third day, ask Pilate to send soldiers
to guard the tomb. Is it not strange that Matthew should insist
that Jesus' enemies not only knew of his promise but that they
believed it as well?

The request of the Jewish officials that the tomb be guarded
allegedly took place on the day following the crucifixion, which
was the Sabbath and the first day of Passover (Matthew
27:62–64). In response to the request Pilate said to the officials:
"You have a guard. Go make it as secure as you know how"
(Matthew 27:65). Because of the holiness of the day, these
soldiers could not have been organized and sent to the tomb by
the Jews before the end of the Sabbath. Enough time, therefore,
would have elapsed between the end of the Sabbath and the
arrival of the soldiers for Jesus' body to have been quickly
removed by some of his followers. In any case, the soldiers
would have been poor witnesses to the events, for how could
they know "all the things that had happened" (Matthew 28:11)
when, according to Matthew 28:4, they fainted on seeing the
angel? If there was a contingent of soldiers, they found the tomb,
on their arrival, already open and the body gone. Subsequently,
the early Christians developed the story to include "miraculous"
events as an answer to the Jews, who correctly surmised that
some of Jesus' confederates were directly implicated in the
body's disappearance.

Matthew advances a rather unlikely explanation of the general
disbelief of the Jews in the resurrection story (Matthew 28:12–
15). He says that the Jewish officials bribed the soldiers sent to
guard the tomb to say that they had fallen asleep and that while

they slept, Jesus' disciples stole the body. Sleeping while on guard duty is an extremely serious offense for soldiers to commit, and it is unlikely that the soldiers would have let themselves be bribed into admitting something which could lead to their execution. Even though the Jewish officials promised to protect them from the consequences if Pilate heard that they had slept on duty, it is doubtful that the soldiers, be they Jewish or Roman, would have risked the chance. Pilate, harsh, brutal, and insensitive, was simply not the man the soldiers could expect to overlook a flagrant breach of their assigned duty.

The facts of how the body disappeared were branded as a lie by Matthew. His fabrication was necessitated by the need to preserve the Christian belief in the risen Christ. As a good Pauline Christian he agreed with Paul's admonition that without the resurrection "your faith is worthless" (1 Corinthians 15:17). Christianity is based not on the life and death of Jesus, but on the alleged resurrection. Since the facts would nullify the Christian faith, Matthew disqualifies the testimony of those Jews who knew the truth, accusing them of scheming and lying.

It has been argued that the absence of the body but the presence of linen wrappings shows that Jesus rose from the dead. Actually, only Luke and John (Luke 24:12, John 20:5) mention the finding of linen wrappings in the tomb. John adds a "cloth which was upon his head" (John 20:7). In any case, Luke and John prove nothing since the finding of these articles could as easily be the result of a hasty departure from the tomb by Joseph of Arimathaea and Nicodemus. If linen wrappings were really found in the tomb, they were either leftover extras or additional ones brought by Nicodemus. In the rush to prepare for the burial, Joseph of Arimathaea would not have had time to measure off the exact amount of linen needed for wrapping the body. It is also conceivable that Nicodemus, unaware of what preparations Joseph of Arimathaea had made, may have also brought linen wrappings along with spices for the burial. In the rush to leave as quickly as possible, these linen wrappings were left behind.

The two most crucial New Testament witnesses of the final

disposition of the body, Joseph of Arimathaea and Nicodemus (the latter only mentioned by John), are never mentioned again once the initial burial was complete. Reconstructing events as they actually occurred is difficult since the sparse New Testament information is burdened by legend, distortion, and censorship. In all likelihood, immediately after the Sabbath these two men, accompanied by servants, hastily removed the body from its temporary burial place, which had been quickly chosen because of the approaching Sabbath (John 19:41–42). Indeed, if they were fearful that the body might be mutilated, there was precedent for removal of the body even on the Sabbath (B. T. Shabbat 30b, 43b). Afterwards, they may very well have had to flee the country, fearing reprisals from the authorities. In any case, it was propitious for them not to publicize what they had done.

Obviously, Joseph, described as a secret disciple (John 19:38), and Nicodemus had no contact with "the women" or the disciples either before, during, or after the crucifixion. This is clearly seen from the behavior of the women, who kept at a distance from the Friday-afternoon burial party, not daring to approach them (Matthew 27:61, Mark 15:47, Luke 23:55). They certainly would have approached them had they been on good terms with either Joseph or Nicodemus. When the women arrived at the tomb on Sunday morning, they did not even know that the body was already anointed (Mark 16:1; Luke 23:56, 24:1; cf. John 19:39–40). Afterwards, when the resurrection claim was made, Joseph and Nicodemus, if they heard of it, did not, it seems, advise the claimants of its absurdity. In any case, the early-morning visitors to the tomb saw the discarded linen wrappings and, in their guilt-ridden, highly emotional state, thought they must have belonged to the missing Jesus. Thus, a legend was born.

The first claim that Jesus appeared after the resurrection was made by Mary Magdalene. The early Christian myth-makers, seeking to substantiate the resurrection tale, needed more proof than the account of the hysterical Mary Magdalene, from whom Jesus is said to have cast out seven demons (Mark 16:9). Her story was not even believed by the apostles (Mark 16:11, Luke 24:11). This led to the development of other postresurrection apparitions. Forty days were added to Jesus' earthly stay, and they were then filled with a number of encounters between Jesus and his disciples.

Luke refers to a postresurrection appearance by Jesus to a man named Simon: "The Lord was really raised up, and has appeared to Simon" (Luke 24:34). This could not be a reference to one of the apostles by that name, for the two followers from Emmaus, who reported this apparition to the apostles, found the eleven surviving apostles gathered together (Luke 24:33). We are therefore left with a claim that an otherwise unidentified person named Simon saw Jesus. It would seem from the text that he may have been one of the two followers of Jesus who allegedly met him on the road from Emmaus (Luke 24:13, Mark 16:12) and later reported this sighting to the apostles. In any case, these two followers did not immediately recognize Jesus (Luke 24:16), and as soon as "their eyes were opened and they recognized him he vanished from their sight" (Luke 24:31). There was no verification from the person they met on the road that he was Jesus. Therefore, this report remains, at best, only their personal feelings as to the identification of the stranger. Matthew and John make no mention of these two men. This story is plainly unreliable evidence shrouded in legendary material.

It is stated by Mark and Luke that Jesus appeared to the eleven surviving apostles on the evening following the resurrection (Mark 16:14; Luke 24:33, 36). Contrary to this, John says that Thomas was not present and did not believe the other apostles' report when he heard it (John 20:24–25). Eight days later, John claims, Jesus appeared to the eleven apostles specifically to end Thomas' skepticism (John 20:26–27). Strangely enough, no other evangelist mentions this second incident specifically called for Thomas. It would certainly have been to their advantage not to omit an additional postresurrection appearance. But this is more than an omission on the part of the Synoptic Gospel writers, for they attest to Thomas' presence, contrary to John, at the earlier gathering. They speak of the eleven gathered together, which must include Thomas.

Where did the eleven apostles first see Jesus after the resurrection? According to Matthew, an angel instructs Mary Magdalene to tell the disciples that "he is going before you into Galilee, there you will see him" (Matthew 28:7). Matthew then states that when Jesus met the women, after they had departed from the tomb, and were on the way back to Jerusalem, he instructed them to "go, take word to my brethren to leave for Galilee, and there they will see me" (Matthew 28:10). Accordingly, the apostles "went into Galilee, into the mountain where Jesus had arranged for them. And when they saw him they worshipped, but some doubted" (Matthew 28:16–17). Mark states that it was an angel in the tomb, not Jesus, who informed Mary Magdalene and Mary that they should "go, tell his disciples and Peter, he is going before you into Galilee; there you will see him, just as he said to you" (Mark 16:5–7). Mark reports, contrary to Matthew's Gospel, that Jesus later changed his plans and "he appeared to the eleven themselves as they were reclining at the table, and he reproached them for their lack of faith and hardheartedness, because they did not believe those who had seen him after he had been raised up" (Mark 16:14). Luke's Gospel indicates that the women who came to the tomb were not informed by anyone about where Jesus would meet the disciples. Luke has the postresurrection Jesus first appear to the eleven disciples as they were gathered together in Jerusalem (Luke 24:33, 36). Later that same day, Luke writes, Jesus "led them out as far as Bethany" (Luke 24:50), which is near Jerusalem, where "he was parted from them [and was carried up into heaven]" (Luke 24:51).[4] According to John, Mary Magdalene, while standing outside the tomb, was commanded by Jesus to tell his disciples: "I ascend to my Father and your Father, and to my God and your God" (John 20:17). No mention is made to her about a forthcoming meeting with the disciples. Later, John has Jesus appear to them as they are gathered together in Jerusalem soon after Mary Magdalene had come to tell them what she saw that same day at the tomb (John 20:18–19). There is little or no agreement among the evangelists as to who was informed, when, and by whom, that Jesus would meet his disciples after the resurrection. The crucial question of whether Jesus' first meeting with his eleven disciples after the crucifixion was in Galilee, as stated in Matthew (Matthew 26:32; 28:7, 10, 16–17), or in Jerusalem, as in Mark, Luke, and John (Mark 16:14; Luke 24:33, 36; John 20:19), still remains.

John relates how a stranger appeared on shore to seven of the apostles as they were fishing on the Sea of Galilee (John 21:1–22). But mysteriously, the seven apostles did not actually recognize the stranger as being Jesus, even when they arrived back on shore. Then, instead of receiving confirmation from the stranger as to his identity, the Gospel of John says that they did not ask him who he was, "knowing that it was the Lord" (John 21:12). Again we have an instance where a stranger is said to have been an apparition of Jesus. With time the story was expanded still further to include a mythical conversation between Jesus and Peter. This is no surprise, since the later a Gospel was written, and John was the latest, the more details it contains concerning postresurrection appearances. This Gospel incorporated much of the increased legendary material concerning the postresurrection appearances that was created as the years passed.

Writing the first chapter of Acts many years after the ascension supposedly occurred, Luke incorporated a great deal of legendary material into his account. Comparing his description of events to parallel accounts in the Gospels yields evidence of disagreement and conflicting traditions concerning the ascension tale.

Matthew quotes Jesus as addressing the apostles, at what was, according to this evangelist, the only postresurrection meeting Jesus had with them: "Go therefore and make disciples of all the nations . . ." (Matthew 28:19). Similarly, Mark relates that prior to Jesus' ascension to a position at the right hand of God (Mark 16:19), he ordered the apostles to scatter throughout the world: "Go into all the world and preach the gospel to all creation" (Mark 16:15). This, the evangelist records, they pro-

---

ceeded to do: "And they went out and preached everywhere . . ." (Mark 16:20). The wording indicates that they did this immediately. No time is provided for a later meeting of Jesus and all the apostles. However, according to Luke's version, when the ascension took place forty days after the resurrection (Acts 1:3, 9), the apostles were still all gathered together in Jerusalem. How could the apostles travel the large distances needed to comply with the accounts of Matthew and Mark, and return to Jerusalem within that short space of time? It is impossible for them to have scattered as Matthew and Mark claim and yet be gathered back together in Jerusalem at the end of forty days. Travel conditions were just too difficult for that to have occurred. At the time of his alleged ascension Luke has Jesus instruct the apostles not to leave Jerusalem but "to wait for what the Father had promised" (Acts 1:4). Once the holy spirit came upon them they were to go out into the world (Acts 1:8). This conforms to what Luke says Jesus declared to the apostles at their first postresurrection meeting: "You are to stay in the city [Jerusalem] until you are clothed with power from on high" (Luke 24:49). In contrast to Luke's statement, Matthew (who has the postresurrection meeting take place in Galilee) and Mark assert that the apostles were already scattered throughout the world by the time forty days after the resurrection had passed. These variant Gospel traditions make it impossible to accept as serious evidence Luke's claim that the apostles saw Jesus forty days after the alleged resurrection.

Paul's references to Cephas (1 Corinthians 15:5) and James (1 Corinthians 15:7) seeing Jesus could not be verified to the Corinthians. Does Cephas refer to Simon Peter, who at times was referred to as Cephas? Paul's words indicate a chronological sequence of appearances after the resurrection, with first Cephas and then the surviving apostles meeting Jesus. However, at no time is the apostle Simon Peter, under any name, mentioned in the New Testament as seeing Jesus prior to the alleged appearance to the eleven apostles together. It may be that Paul was confused by a legend circulating in Christian circles, which Luke later incorporated into his Gospel, that someone named Simon saw Jesus (Luke 24:34). Paul, for un-specified reasons, may have claimed that this Simon referred to Simon Peter. However, it is evident from our earlier study of Luke 24:34 (above p. 247) that the Simon who allegedly met Jesus was not Simon Peter. It is conceivable that Paul may have inserted the claim that Simon Peter saw Jesus as a device to enhance his own doctrinal teachings concerning the meaning of the resurrection. It must be remembered that Paul did not know that his letters would be preserved and eventually widely circulated. Considering the time and conditions under which he wrote, Paul had nothing to fear if his exaggerated statements were challenged. Those who denied his claims he simply accused of being false teachers. As the years went by it became a case of his word against theirs, but since Paul had designed his teachings to appeal to Jews and Gentiles familiar with the pagan mystery religions of the Hellenistic world, he eventually won. As in the case of Cephas, the same vagueness and lack of interest in fact is found in the mention of James by Paul. There were at least three different men named James involved in the life of Jesus. Which one is supposed to have seen the resurrected Jesus? When and where did Cephas and James see Jesus? Can one truly base one's belief on such feeble evidence?

Paul writes in 1 Corinthians 15:6, without giving a geographic location, that "upward of five hundred brethren" saw Jesus and that most of them were still alive. No information is provided to indicate whether this experience was a visionary revelation or an actual appearance in the flesh. Moreover, Paul does not tell us whether he was among the five hundred, or whether he had heard the story from one of them, or whether it was merely a story that was circulating among certain Christians. This alleged postresurrection appearance is conspicuously omitted in both the Gospels and Acts. Had the Corinthians wanted to verify Paul's statement, it would have been, as Paul must have known, virtually impossible for them to do so, considering the primitive means of communication available in those days. Neither did he mention by name any of the five hundred for possible contact by the Corinthians, had they wanted to seek verification. The whole incident was either an unverifiable rumor utilized by Paul or simply the result of his overzealous missionary activity.

Stephen's alleged vision (Acts 7:55–56) was, at best, an hallucination and certainly not of divine origin. In fact, this was a legend created by the early Christians as a reward befitting their first martyr.

Paul, guilt-ridden and unstable, claims that while suffering from a seizure he heard Jesus (Acts 9:4–5, 22:7–8, 26:14–15; 1 Corinthians 15:8). Certainly, this is not the most reliable verification for an appearance.

What the author of the Book of Revelation records he experienced (Revelation 1:10–20) were, at best, the images of his own mind. The apparition described does not look or sound like the historical Jesus. The author's visionary experience does not confirm that Jesus was resurrected, merely that his mind was capable of conjuring up an image of the way he thought the heavenly Jesus should look. Again we find an identification which is based on unsubstantiated evidence.

The full extent of the questionable information associated with the above declarations of postresurrection appearances should not be underestimated. The sparse information provided by the New Testament has been retouched to give the impression that truthful accounts are being presented. But it is evident that from the burial on, the story is full of inaccuracies and inconsistencies. Despite what Christian missionaries may contend, the simple fact remains that the resurrection story is not based on any authentic historical evidence. There were no eyewitnesses. No one saw Jesus leave the tomb. There are only unsubstantiated third-hand reports. Significantly, the Gospels of Matthew and Luke diverge most from each other at exactly those points where they could not follow Mark, the first written Gospel, namely, in their accounts of the infancy and resurrection appearances of Jesus. The accounts of the resurrection and the encounters with the risen Jesus were developed after the events were supposed to have occurred. The belief in the resurrection existed first, but the stories surrounding this alleged event, and which are used to verify it, were later developments.

How can one trust such garbled and unreliable sources? No matter how the New Testament writers endeavored to enhance their extravagant claim, the truth shines through: The resurrection story is a fabrication. The notion that postresurrection appearances took place resulted from a combination of myth and highly emotional expressions stemming from the deep yearnings of disappointment and guilt that the followers of Jesus felt after his death. On the other hand, with the many discrepancies that appear in the story, it is no wonder that the overwhelming majority of the Jewish people dismissed the resurrection story as one more fabrication by Jesus' followers.

As to the final resting place of the body, there is a lack of reliable information for arriving at a definite answer. The body of Jesus is gone, but the many inaccuracies of the events surrounding the alleged resurrection remain. This distorted, mutilated, and misleading tale only calls into question the veracity of the other claims made on behalf of Jesus, especially the claim that Jesus can give everlasting life. There is, however, a promise of everlasting life that is not tied to the belief in the death and resurrection of a man. It is upholding the Torah, as promised in the Hebrew Scriptures: "It is a tree of life to those who take hold of it" (Proverbs 3:18). This is the glory of God's holy Torah, whose "ways are ways of pleasantness, and all its paths are peace" (Proverbs 3:17).

---

1. Friday is referred to in the Gospels as the Day of Preparation, i.e., for the Sabbath. (Cf. Matthew 27:62, Luke 23:54, and Mark 15:42 with Exodus 16:5. See also Josephus, *Jewish Antiquities,* vol. 8, Book 16, 163, p. 273, where an edict from Caesar Augustus says: ". . . and that they need not give bond [to appear in court] on the Sabbath or on the day of preparation for it [Sabbath Eve] after the ninth hour.") This particular weekly Sabbath was also the first day of Passover. It should be noted that although Passover is referred to as a sabbath in Leviticus 23:15, it is never called a sabbath in the New Testament. In the New Testament the festivals are always designated by their names.

2. The significance of the word *lestai* ("thieves," "brigands"), used by Matthew and Mark (Matthew 27:38, Mark 15:27), lies in the fact that it was a derogatory Roman term for the Zealots, who, by armed action, opposed Roman rule of the Holy Land.

3. Some of the oldest New Testament manuscripts omit Mark 16:9–20.

4. Some manuscripts add the words in the brackets.

53

DID JESUS MISREAD THE SCRIPTURES?

(Mark 2:25–26)

And he [Jesus] said to them: "Have you never read what David did, when he was in need and was hungry, he and those who were with him: How he entered into the house of God, when Abiathar was high priest, and ate the bread of presentation, which it is not lawful for anyone but the priests to eat, and he gave it also to those who were with him?"

(Mark 2:25–26)

Although Mark does not specifically say that David's companions also ate the holy bread, Matthew and Luke both state that they did eat it (Matthew 12:4, Luke 6:4). However, from the question put to David by the high priest, Ahimelech: "Why are you alone, and no man with you?" (1 Samuel 21:2), it is obvious that David came alone to the high priest. Moreover, as just indicated, it was not Abiathar who was high priest at the time this incident took place, but Abiathar's father, Ahimelech. Abiathar was the sole survivor of the slaughter of the priests at Nob, who were killed for having fed David. Matthew and Luke, in repeating this story, do not mention the name of the high priest (Matthew 12:3–4, Luke 6:3–4). We are faced with the question of determining whether Jesus or the evangelists was the source of this misreading of Scriptures.

254

54

A FAMILY'S VERDICT: "HE IS OUT OF HIS MIND"

(Mark 3:19–21, 31)

And he [Jesus] came into a house; and the multitude gathered again, so that they were not able even to eat bread. And when his relatives heard of this, they went out to lay hold of him; for they were saying: "He is out of his mind.". . . And his mother and his brothers came, and standing outside they sent in to him to call him.

(Mark 3:19–21, 31)

Is it not strange that Jesus' own family, including his mother, did not know that he was the Messiah and the Son of God? Not only did they not know this, but they believed him to be mentally unbalanced.

When Jesus was informed that his mother and brothers were looking for him, he displayed, in his response, hostile feelings toward them, denying the importance of familial relationships (Mark 3:31–35, Matthew 12:46–50, Luke 8:19–21). This was an expression of his resentment at their refusal to accept his messianic pretensions: "For neither did his brothers believe in him" (John 7:5). It is no wonder that Jesus declared: "A prophet is not without honor except in his home town and among his relatives and in his house" (Mark 6:4). How could Mary, the mother of Jesus, forget so quickly the visits of angels, magi, and shepherds, or the prophecies of Anna and Simeon in the Temple, and most of all her own impregnation by the Holy Spirit?

255

55

WHO DECLARED THE WORD OF GOD INVALID?

(Mark 7:9–13)

And he said to them: "You nicely set aside the commandments of God, in order that you may keep your own tradition. For Moses said, 'Honor your father and your mother'; and, 'He who speaks evil of father or mother, let him surely die.' But you say, 'If a man says to his father or his mother, anything of mine you might have been helped by is Corban (that is, given to God),' You no longer permit him to do anything for his father or his mother; thus invalidating the word of God by your tradition which you have handed down; and you do many things such as that."

(Mark 7:9–13)

Jesus, seeking to discredit the Pharisees, accuses them of negating the law of God and following instead an invalid tradition of their own making. According to Jesus' explanation of this alleged man-made Pharisaic tradition, a man who had devoted all his property to God is, in effect, prohibited by them from providing for his parents. But apparently, Mark's Jesus was not well-versed in the laws of the Torah. There it is written: "But any devoted thing which a man may devote to the Lord of all that he has, whether of man or beast, or of the field of his possession, shall not be sold, nor redeemed; every devoted thing is most holy to the Lord" (Leviticus 27:28). Actually, Jesus' quarrel is not with the Pharisees, but with the word of God as stated in the Torah. He is criticizing the Pharisees for their obedience to God's commandments, not for following a man-

256

made commandment. Jesus' attack is totally unjustified and is merely part of an early Christian polemic directed against obedience to God's commandments to Israel.

56

HOW KOSHER WAS JESUS?
(Mark 7:14–15, 18–19)

And calling the multitude to him again, he began saying to them: "Listen to me, all of you, and understand. There is nothing from outside the man which going into him can defile him; but the things which proceed out of the man are what defile the man. . . ." And he said to them [the disciples]: ". . . Are you not aware that whatever goes into the man from outside cannot defile him, because it does not go into his heart, but into his stomach, and goes out into the latrine?" Thus he declared all foods clean.

(Mark 7:14–15, 18–19)

Jesus negates the validity of the biblical principle that there is a distinction between clean and unclean foods, a distinction which is clearly spelled out in the Torah itself (Leviticus 10, Deuteronomy 14:3–21). Jesus says: "There is nothing from outside the man which going into him can defile him; but the things which proceed out of the man are what defile the man." This negation of the distinction between permitted and prohibited foods is of great significance. With this pronouncement, Mark's Jesus presumptuously demolishes a fundamental biblical precept. Moreover, this statement stands in direct contradiction to the various declarations Jesus made concerning the validity and permanence of the Torah (Matthew 5:17–19, Luke 16:17).

It has been claimed that what Jesus is stressing in his assertion is that there are many immoral things which proceed from within a person that defile him (Mark 7:20–23). This feeble attempt at denying the fact that Jesus' statement, as quoted above, refers to the dietary laws of the Torah is in vain. Mark is very explicit in declaring that Jesus meant specifically the nullification of the dietary laws of clean and unclean food. This the evangelist emphasizes by his editorial comment. Following his citation of Jesus' statement: ". . . whatever goes into the man from outside cannot defile him, because it does not go into his heart, but into his stomach, and goes out into the latrine," Mark adds: "Thus he declared all foods clean." Whether or not Mark is actually reproducing an actual saying of Jesus can never be known with certainty, but he certainly was expressing the view of at least a segment of the early church (Luke 11:41; Acts 10:15, 11:9; Romans 14:14; Colossians 2:16).[1] Although Mark's Jesus did not grant outright permission to eat unclean species, he did give his tacit approval. By denying the distinction between clean and unclean food, Jesus paved the way for his followers to declare invalid an important feature of God's Torah to Israel.

1. That there were those in the early church who opposed the nullification of the Torah is seen from Acts 15:5 and Galatians 2:11–12.

57

WHO IS A CHRISTIAN?

(Mark 16:16–18)

He that believes and is baptized will be saved, but he that believes not will be condemned. And these signs will follow those that believe: in my name they will cast out demons, they will speak with tongues, and with their hands they will pick up serpents, and if they drink anything deadly it will not hurt them at all. They will lay hands upon the sick and they will recover.

(Mark 16:16–18)

Who is the true believer in the teachings of Jesus? Roman Catholic, Greek Orthodox, Baptist, Pentecostal, Jehovah's Witness, Methodist, Latter Day Saint, Episcopalian, Seventh-Day Adventist, Lutheran, Quaker, etc.—each one belonging to a group claiming to possess the true teachings of Jesus. Who is correct? Who is actually a true Christian? The answer to this perplexing question appears to be given by Jesus himself in Mark 16:16–18.

According to this passage, the true Christian can cast out demons, speak with tongues, pick up serpents, drink anything deadly, and heal the sick. These are the promises made by Jesus to all the faithful, not only of his generation, but of all generations. The Christian, his Messiah informs him, possesses the ability to bring all of these miraculous deeds to pass. The formula for success is simple: "Believe!" Paul, realizing the emptiness of this promise to be able to do the miraculous, qualifies the words of Jesus. He declares that people are given different levels of ability to perform miraculous deeds, depending on the amount of grace bestowed upon them. All believers, Paul states, share in the miraculous works of the few since they are all part of "one body in Christ" (Romans 12:3–8, 1 Corinthians 12:4–31). It is a desperate and feeble attempt, on the part of Paul, at reinterpreting the promise of Jesus, in order to explain why his guarantee to *all* the faithful never came about. According to Jesus' words, however, *all* believers are given *equal* grace and ability to perform the miraculous. The believer himself performs the miracles; he does not share in them vicariously through a mystic union of the entire church body. The promise, coming directly from Jesus, vitiates any attempt to disavow or modify these deeds by any Christian spokesman.

But can the Christian actually perform these miraculous deeds? No, of course not! Yet everyone who believes Jesus is the true Messiah has been guaranteed by Jesus the power to cast out demons, speak with tongues, pick up serpents, drink anything deadly, and heal the sick. Even non-true-believing Christians are, according to Jesus, able to perform miracles in his name. "Many will say to me on that day: 'Lord, Lord, did we not prophesy in your name, and in your name cast our demons, and in your name perform powerful works?' And then I will declare to them: 'I never knew you, depart from me, you who practice lawlessness' " (Matthew 7:22–23). Thus, according to Matthew, even those individuals who claim to perform miracles in the name of Jesus are not necessarily following him. How then can one tell who is a real Christian? Neither those who are true followers of Jesus, whoever they may be, nor those whom Jesus would reject, according to Matthew, can do all the categories of miracles Jesus promised they would be able to do. Yet Jesus did promise that his followers would be able to do all of them.

What is the reason for the Christian inability to fulfill the words of Jesus? Obviously, Christians cannot perform these miraculous deeds because Jesus' claims have no validity. His own mouth testified against him. According to his own words, there is no such person as a Christian since a Christian should be able to do all the things enumerated in Mark 16:16–18. To continue worshipping Jesus is to stretch one's credulity to inadmissible limits.

58

THE CENSUS
(Luke 2:1–5)

Now it came about in those days that a decree went out from Caesar Augustus, that a census be taken of all the inhabited earth. This was the first census taken while Quirinius was governor of Syria. And all were proceeding to register for the census, everyone to his own city. And Joseph also went up from Galilee, out of the city of Nazareth, to Judea, to the city of David, which is called Bethlehem, because he was of the house and family of David, in order to register, along with Mary, who was engaged to him, and was pregnant.

(Luke 2:1–5)

It is not plausible that the Romans conducted a census in the manner described by Luke. There would have been no reason for them to demand that the people being enumerated return to the towns of their ancestors rather than register in the towns in which they actually resided. If information concerning the ancestral towns was essential to the Romans, they would merely have required the people to supply the names of their ancestral towns. If it were necessary to travel to one's ancestral town, the presence of the head of the household or someone making the trip as his representative would have been sufficient. There would have been no need to make a difficult situation worse by requiring a wife to accompany her husband, especially one in the last month of pregnancy.[1] It was obviously unnecessary for people to have to travel to a place often hundreds of miles away which they probably had never seen before.[2]

What Luke describes has the makings of a chaotic situation of unprecedented magnitude. The people involved would have had to travel throughout the length and breadth of the Roman Empire, clogging the roads and disrupting the smooth running of the imperial system in every province of the Empire. In the course of their journey, they would be traveling, for the most part, over extremely poor roads once they left the major Roman highways. Available services to travelers would be strained to the breaking point. Certainly in the eastern provinces, of which Judea was a part, such a census would present a serious military danger, for the Parthians, then Rome's strongest antagonist in the area, would have had an excellent opportunity to attack. Roman troops on the march would find it extremely difficult to compete with the tremendous mass of civilians on their way to or from registration. It is hard to imagine the Romans so incompetent or unrealistic as to throw the entire Empire into such a chaotic state by carrying out the census described by the evangelist.

It is unusual that an event of this magnitude should go unnoticed. Yet no contemporary writer mentions this disruptive census or the turmoil it would have engendered. Indeed, if this census took place in Judea it is strange that Josephus never mentioned it in any of his writings. It is obvious that Luke introduced the tale to explain still another legendary tale, that is, how it came about that Joseph and Mary went to Bethlehem at this time.

1. Luke states that Joseph and Mary were still "engaged," not married.
2. The alleged Roman demand presumes that the people all knew their ancestral origins. It would also have caused the disruption of normal family life in the many cases where husbands and wives had to set off in opposite directions in order for each to return to their "own city."

59

JESUS AND FORGIVENESS

(Luke 23:34)

Father, forgive them, for they do not know what they are doing.

(Luke 23:34)

This sentence is not found in the earliest manuscripts of Luke, and is, in all probability, an interpolation. That it is a later addition can also be shown from internal evidence. A careful reading of the Gospels indicates that this verse is not at all in consonance with Jesus' true feelings concerning forgiveness of enemies. Elsewhere, Luke records a statement by Jesus that is more in keeping with Jesus' true attitude toward his enemies: "But these enemies of mine who did not want me to reign over them, bring them here, and slay them in my presence" (Luke 19:27). Similarly, Matthew's Jesus expresses his feelings in a particularly merciless way when he says: ". . . so that there may come upon you all the righteous blood poured out upon the earth from the blood of righteous Abel to the blood of Zechariah son of Barachiah, whom you murdered between the Temple and the altar" (Matthew 23:35). Here Jesus condemns the Jews to suffering for "all the righteous blood poured out upon the earth" from a time even before the birth of Abraham, the father of the Jewish people. According to this passage, they are to suffer the penalty for the sins of murder of everyone else in the world since the dawn of human history, as well as to suffer the penalty for their own sins of murder. Is such an unforgiving attitude in accord with the allegedly benign and kindly soul of Jesus of Nazareth, the Prince of Peace?

60

A BONE OF CONTENTION

(John 19:33, 36)

But coming to Jesus, when they saw that he was already dead, they did not break his legs. . . . For these things occurred, in order that the Scripture might be fulfilled: "Not a bone of him shall be broken."

(John 19:33, 36)

It has been suggested by some Christian missionaries that this verse is a fulfillment of Psalm 34:21 (verse 20 in some versions): "He guards all his bones; not one of them is broken." However, the psalmist's words are simply too general in nature to have specific application to Jesus, and there is thus no proof that they constitute a typology of an event in his life. In fact, the author of John did not consider Psalm 34:21 the scriptural proof-text for the event he describes. He was referring instead to the scriptural sources which are much more specific and meaningful for his purposes. Psalm 34:21 just does not fit into the contextual framework constructed by the author of John. While he does not specify the exact scriptural reference to which he is alluding, it is quite evident that the thrust of his Gospel is not in the direction of Psalm 34 as the typology for the assertion that the soldiers did not break Jesus' bones. The author of John, in stating that the soldiers did not break Jesus' legs, is alluding to one of the restrictions regarding the paschal lamb (Exodus 12:46, Numbers 9:12), for he believes that Jesus was "the Lamb of God who takes away the sins of the world" (John 1:29). The author of John attempts to portray Jesus within the framework of the Passover celebration by representing him as the paschal sacrifice and, as

265

such, fulfilling a Scripture which deals specifically with the bones of the paschal lamb. He sees the death of Jesus, "the Lamb of God," which occurred just prior to the Passover festival, as the climax of his view of the paschal lamb. According to the author of John, the paschal lamb was sacrificed on the day before Passover as a prefiguring of Jesus, who, in his opinion, also died the day before Passover.

In the process of being turned into a sacrifice by which man can obtain atonement from sin, Jesus has been compared to the paschal lamb which was offered as a remembrance of God's passing over the Israelites when He slew the Egyptian firstborn (Exodus 12:26–27). But this analogy is fallacious because the paschal sacrifice is not at all offered for the atonement of any sin. More properly, Jesus should have been put to death not the day before Passover (according to John) or on the first day of Passover (according to the Synoptic Gospels), but rather on the Day of Atonement. On that day, the sacrifice was offered for the express purpose of obtaining forgiveness of sin for the entire nation (Leviticus 16:7–10, 21–22, 24, 29–30).

In his effort to show the literal fulfillment of the Hebrew Scriptures in the life of Jesus, the author of the Gospel of John informs us that not one bone of Jesus' body was broken. This was supposed to have occurred in conformity with the divine command not to break any of the bones of the paschal lamb (Exodus 12:46, Numbers 9:12). If we are to be literal, let us also be consistent. The most striking inconsistency in the hypothesis of Jesus' sacrificial death is the fact that the Hebrew Scriptures cry out with horror against the abominable practice of human sacrifice (e.g., Leviticus 18:21, 20:2–5). Even disregarding the unequivocal opposition to human sacrifice, there is the question of the commandment: "Whatever has a blemish that you shall not offer" (Leviticus 22:20). Any potential sacrifice that is maimed in any way is not qualified (Leviticus 22:19, 22). Just prior to his crucifixion, Jesus was whipped[1] and beaten (Matthew 27:26, 30; Mark 15:19; John 19:3). Moreover, Jesus was circumcised in the flesh, a practice which, according to Paul, constitutes "mutilation," *katatome* (Philippians 3:2). Indeed, he even likens circumcision to castration (Galatians 5:12). Therefore, although Jesus is depicted as an "unblemished and spotless lamb" (1 Peter 1:19), the most perfect of all sacrifices (Hebrews 9:14), his "mutilation" would disqualify him, as it would any sacrifice. Not only did the injuries just prior to his execution disqualify Jesus, but by disparaging circumcision in the flesh, Paul inadvertently rendered Jesus, almost from his very birth, as unfit for playing a sacrificial role!

Christian missionaries cannot pick and choose Scripture at their discretion, ignoring those facts that conflict with their claims. We cannot be satisfied with a claim to fulfillment of one random biblical commandment while totally ignoring another one. To accept John 19:33 as a fulfillment of prophecy, we must insist that Jesus fulfill all of the scriptural precepts regarding the fitness of a sacrificial animal. If the author of John insists on the unbroken state of Jesus' bones at the time of his death, as a fulfillment of biblical prophecy, then we must equally insist on the biblical requirement of the need for a perfect body with no mutilations or abrasions. This requirement could not be fulfilled because Jesus was neither "unblemished" nor "spotless." The body of Jesus was marred in such a manner that it could not symbolize, or actually be a substitutionary sacrifice in accordance with the Scriptures.

The point that Jesus was physically disqualified as a sacrifice cannot be countered by claiming that the author of the First Epistle of Peter was referring to the spiritual nature of Jesus, for he states that redemption was brought about "with precious blood, like that of an unblemished and spotless lamb" (1 Peter 1:18–19). Obviously, the mention of blood can only refer to the physical body of Jesus. So too, John is also referring to the physical nature of Jesus. Any attempt at spiritualizing either statement runs counter to the plain sense of the words.

Briefly reviewed: Being human, and moreover, wounded and mutilated, Jesus was not in a proper physical state to be suited for a sacrifice. To consider Jesus in a sacrificial role would violate the laws concerning sacrifices. In any case, treating Jesus as representing the paschal lamb does not bestow upon him any

268 / The Jew and the Christian Missionary

power to atone for sins since the purpose of the paschal lamb had nothing to do with the atonement of sins. All in all, there is no legitimate reason for identifying the death of Jesus with the atonement of sins.

---

1. The Roman soldiers often tied weights to the thongs of their whips to increase the impact.

61

CONFUSED ACTS

(Acts 7:14–16)

And Joseph sent and called to him Jacob his father and all his relatives,
seventy-five souls; and Jacob went down into Egypt. And he died, he
and our fathers, and they were removed to Shechem and were laid in
the tomb that Abraham had bought for a sum of silver from the sons of
Hamor in Shechem.

(Acts 7:14–16)

There are several errors to be found in the above verses:

1. Jacob's family that came down to Egypt, inclusive of Joseph
   and his sons, numbered seventy persons, not seventy-five
   (Genesis 46:27, Exodus 1:5, Deuteronomy 10:22).[1]
2. Jacob was not buried in the city of Shechem, but in the cave
   of Machpelah, which is located in the city of Hebron
   (Genesis 23:19; 49:29–30; 50:13).
3. The Hebrew Scriptures do not give any indication that the
   forefathers of the tribes of Israel were buried in Shechem.
   Only Joseph is said to have been buried there (Joshua
   24:32).
4. Abraham did not buy a tomb in Shechem. He bought the
   cave of Machpelah, which he used as a burial place, and
   which, as previously stated, is located in the city of Hebron
   (Genesis 23:19).
5. The cave of Machpelah was not bought from the sons of
   Hamor, but from Ephron the Hittite (Genesis 23:17–18,
   50:13).

6. It was Jacob, not Abraham, who purchased a piece of land near Shechem from the sons of Hamor. The author of Acts confused the two purchases (Genesis 33:19, Joshua 24:32).

1. The number seventy-five agrees with the Septuagint but not with the Hebrew text.

62

ABRAHAM AND FAITH

(Romans 4:9–16)

Is this happiness then upon the circumcised, or also upon the uncircumcised? For we say: "Faith was reckoned to Abraham as righteousness." How therefore was it reckoned? While he was circumcised or uncircumcised? Not while circumcised, but while uncircumcised. And he received the sign of circumcision, a seal of the righteousness of the faith which he had while uncircumcised, that he might be the father of all who believe without being circumcised, that righteousness might be reckoned to them; and a father of circumcision to those who not only are of the circumcision, but who also follow in the steps of the faith of our father Abraham which he had while uncircumcised. For it was not through law that Abraham or his seed had the promise that he should be heir of the world, but through the righteousness of faith. For if those who adhere to law are heirs, faith has been made void and the promise has been nullified. For the Law brings about wrath, but where there is no law, neither is there transgression. For this reason it is by faith, in order that it might be according to undeserved kindness, so that the promise may be certain to all the seed, not only to those who are of the Law, but also to those who are of the faith of Abraham, who is the father of us all.

(Romans 4:9–16)

It is Paul's conclusion that by faith alone, without any recourse to the Law, one can achieve righteousness. He bases his conclusion on the premise that Abraham attained righteousness without observing the Law of Moses: "And he believed in the Lord; and He counted it to him for righteousness" (Genesis 15:6). Since this statement preceded God's command to Abra-

271

ham to circumcise his household, Paul argues, even that practice is not needed. He reasons that Abraham was circumcised (Genesis 17:10–11) not in obedience to the Law, but rather as a sign of the faith which he had prior to circumcision. Paul states that God promised Abraham "that he should be heir of the world." He contends that since this promise was made prior to the command to circumcise, the true heirs of the promise are not the circumcised, but the uncircumcised, i.e., the church (Galatians 3:6–9, 29). Thus, Paul argues, it is faith, not works, which renders a man just before God (Galatians 2:16, 3:23).

There is a general lack of respect for the integrity of the Scriptures in the Pauline method. In his overriding desire to convert the masses to his beliefs, Paul is guided by the dubious assumption that the end justifies the means.

> And to the Jews I became as a Jew, that I might win Jews; to those under law, as under law, though not being myself under law, that I might win those under law. To those who are without law, as without law, though not being without the law of God but under the law of Christ, that I might win those without law. To the weak I became weak, that I might win the weak: I have become all things to all men, that I may by all means save some. (1 Corinthians 9:20–22)

The use of deception, by himself or others, in order to bring about belief in Jesus did not disturb Paul: ". . . whether in pretense or in truth, Christ is proclaimed; and in this I rejoice, yes, and I will rejoice" (Philippians 1:18). Since Paul did not hesitate to use deceit in his conversion process, it did not matter to him that he distorted the Scriptures. His assertion, for example, that Abraham was promised that he would be the "heir to the world," that is, he would inherit the world, is nowhere mentioned in the Hebrew Scriptures. Moreover, Paul conveniently overlooks the fact that God, in His inscrutable knowledge, knows beforehand whatever the future will bring. Hence, God's promises prior to Abraham's circumcision are posited on God's foreknowledge of Abraham's future actions. This is stated in the verse: "For I have known him, to the end that he may command his children and his household after him, that they may keep the way of the Lord, to do righteousness and justice; to the end that the Lord may bring upon Abraham that which He has spoken of him" (Genesis 18:19). Significantly, the promises given to Abraham were to be fulfilled, not through all the "multitude of nations" that would descend from him, nor through spiritual followers, made up of the uncircumcised, i.e., the Gentiles, but specifically through, and for, only one nation: Israel (Genesis 28:13–15).

The barrenness of Paul's outlook is seen from Genesis 26:3–5. There, God, after revealing some of the blessings that Abraham's descendants are to receive, states the reason for these blessings unequivocally, as follows: ". . . because Abraham obeyed My voice, and kept My charge, My commandments, My statutes, and My laws." Although the names of the particular commandments, statutes, and laws that Abraham kept are not given, it is made crystal-clear that Abraham did not live by faith alone. He earned his exalted position by practicing a good part of what was destined to become the divine Law as revealed to his descendants on Mount Sinai.

It was only with Abraham's circumcision and the establishment of the covenantal relationship that the promise to be "the father of a multitude of nations" (Genesis 17:5), made prior to circumcision, was able to be fulfilled. It is also indicated that it was through the circumcised Abraham that "all the nations of the earth will be blessed" (Genesis 18:18).

Did God demand of Abraham and his descendants faith alone without actual deeds? As previously stated, God Himself declares: "For I have known him, to the end that he may command his children and his household after him, that they may keep the way of the Lord, to do righteousness and justice; to the end that the Lord may bring upon Abraham that which He has spoken of him" (Genesis 18:19). Whatever God will command, in the way of works, the children of Abraham will do. As such, once the Law was formally given to Abraham's descendants, on Mount Sinai, it became binding upon every generation of Israelites. Paul certainly had no right or justification to abrogate the Law. In the last analysis, what was actually demanded of Abraham, and serves as an example for his descendants, was a balance of faith and works. Abraham's faith was reflected by means of positive deeds.

What Paul advocates is retrogression to a time before God revealed His will. He presumes that this lawless period is preferable to one in which God revealed His law. However, God's promise to make Abraham "the father of a multitude of nations," made prior to his circumcision, was actually contingent upon him and his descendants adhering to the act of circumcision. The fulfillment of all the promises God made to Abraham, both those made before circumcision and those made after, is contingent upon obedience to God's will, not simply to faith alone.

The Pauline viewpoint is totally discredited by the author of the Epistle of James. In contradistinction to Paul, who declares: "By works of law no flesh will be justified in His sight" (Romans 3:20) and "For if Abraham was justified by works, he has something to boast about; but not before God" (Romans 4:2), James clearly states that Abraham was measured by his works: "Was not Abraham our father justified by works, when he offered up Isaac his son upon the altar?" (James 2:21). He declares: "Faith without works is useless" (James 2:20); therefore, "a man is justified by works, and not by faith alone" (James 2:24). James goes so far as to say "faith without works is dead" (James 2:26).

Certainly, if all God ever demanded of Abraham was faith alone, He would not have commanded circumcision as a sign of the covenant between Himself and all generations of Abraham's Israelite descendants. Moreover, there would certainly be no reason for God to praise Abraham's obedience to His will (Genesis 26:5). Thus, Paul's analysis is faulty in its entirety and without merit whatsoever.

63

THE NEED TO BE SAVED

(Romans 5:12, 18–19)

Therefore just as through one man sin entered into the world, and death through sin, and so death spread to all men, because all sinned.

(Romans 5:12)

So then as through one transgression there resulted condemnation to all men; even so through one act of righteousness there resulted justification of life to all men. For as through the one man's disobedience the many were made sinners, even so through the obedience of the one the many will be made righteous.

(Romans 5:18–19)

Christian missionaries maintain that because of the sin of Adam, humanity has a sinful nature. By his disobeying God and eating of the Tree of Knowledge, Adam brought hereditary sin into the world, tainting all his descendants with what is called Original Sin. Thus, man is a sinner from birth, separated spiritually from a holy God. Consequently, man has to be saved from sin and reconciled to God. Left to himself, however, man can do nothing to overcome sin, for he is hopelessly involved in it. Atonement must be provided for him through means of a sinless sacrifice. Affirming that Jesus was the only permanent sacrifice ever provided by God, missionaries insist that the only way to achieve freedom from sin is by believing in Jesus as the mediating savior whose sacrificial death brings salvation to those who put their faith in him. The missionaries regard the death of Jesus as the only act of atonement which can redeem man from his sinfulness.

Whether man is a sinner by nature or not is immaterial. Recognizing that man does sin, the problem is how he attains salvation and rejoins the fellowship of God. In the Torah, the Law of God, two means of redemption are offered to the sinner: animal sacrifices, and prayer with a contrite spirit. Reconciliation through sincere repentance in which the sinner pledges to rectify his evil ways and lead a righteous life is one means that is open at all times to all of humanity. In opposition to this, missionaries claim that man is incapable of doing anything to gain his own salvation. To them no man is righteous, and thus man cannot justify himself before God. Man can receive salvation only through grace, by an unmerited act of kindness bestowed by God upon him. This undeserved kindness, the missionaries assert, can only be received by those who accept Jesus as their savior (Ephesians 2:8–9).

Christian missionaries cite numerous verses to adduce proof for their contention that no man is righteous and that man cannot justify himself before God. The missionary explanations of these verses, though specious in their reasoning, need to be examined because the verses lend themselves to misinterpretation. Among the verses cited is Psalm 51:7 (verse 5 in some versions): "Behold, I was brought forth in iniquity, and in sin did my mother conceive me." Missionaries claim that this verse indicates that man is born in a state of sin. This is without foundation. There is no reason to assume that David considers himself to be a sinner at birth. Rather, David's words are a hyperbolic expression of the deep sense of guilt which he felt as a result of his carnal sin with Bathsheba. Even if one is to insist that David is saying that he has been a sinner since his birth, not just prone to sin, the all-important concept in this psalm is that David and all Israel could approach God directly and ask for forgiveness. The repentant sinner may demonstrate his contrition through certain specified sacrifices and confession and prayer, or through confession and prayer alone. While sacrifices were a valid manifestation of repentance when the Temple was in existence, subsequent to its destruction the door to atonement was not closed to the sinner as he can still approach God in contrite prayer and ask for atonement.

Eager to justify their beliefs Christian missionary exegetes, referring to Psalm 53:3–5, argue that no one is righteous. There the psalmist states:

> God has looked down from heaven upon the children of men, to see if there is anyone who understands, who seeks after God. Every one of them is unclean, together they have become impure, there is no one who does good, not even one. Have the workers of wickedness no knowledge, who eat up My people as they eat bread, and call not upon God?

To really understand the message of this psalm, reference must be made to Psalm 14, which is another version of this psalm. In both psalms, the psalmist speaks of two groups. The first are "the workers of wickedness" who attack the second group, God's people. This second group, designated by God as "My people," is identified in Psalm 53:7 as Israel. The psalmist does not indicate, in either psalm, a universal unrighteousness on the part of mankind. This fact is illustrated in Psalm 14:5: "For God is with the righteous generation." What is described in these psalms is how widespread wickedness is in the world, and the difficulties Israel faces in a Godless world. Still, God looks down from heaven upon mankind and waits for those who truly seek Him. He never refuses those who approach Him with sincerity: "The sacrifice of the wicked is an abomination to the Lord; but the prayer of the upright is His delight" (Proverbs 15:8).

As a further illustration of their contention that no man is righteous, Christian missionaries make use of Ecclesiastes 7:20: "For there is not a righteous man upon earth, that does good, and sins not." However, a close look at this verse will show that it does not at all state that man is essentially unrighteous. On the contrary, it implies that there are many righteous persons, but that even the righteous may at one time or another fall prey to sin. In any case, he does not forfeit his status as a righteous person since the means for repentance are always available to the truly penitent, without recourse to anyone.

Endeavoring to prove their point of view, missionaries have

made reference to other biblical verses as well. Citing Isaiah, Christian missionary exegetes incorrectly contend that our sins have separated us from God: "But your iniquities have separated between you and your God, and your sins have hid His face from you, that He will not hear" (Isaiah 59:2). The prophet addresses himself here to a specific group at a particular time. If this was a general statement applicable to any and all sinners, who would then be exempt? Even the patriarchs and Moses sinned. If God will not hear the sinner, David's confession would have been for nought, and Hezekiah would have died fifteen years earlier than he actually did. There is no justification for assuming, on the basis of this verse, that anyone who sins is completely separated from God. God most certainly hears and accepts the repentant sinner.

As further evidence for their contention Christian missionary exegetes argue that no man can justify himself before God. In support of this allegation, they quote Psalm 143:2: "And do not enter into judgment with Your servant, for in Your sight no man living is righteous." But the Christian missionary understanding of this verse is faulty. The psalmist knows that if God judged mankind by the absolute standards of justice, no man could exist. That is why God always tempers justice with mercy. David, cognizant of this truth, does not despair, and is encouraged, despite his own insignificant status, in his appeal to God for vindication.

This entire psalm is a prayer for deliverance and guidance. In verse 2, David is asking God not to judge him by the rules of strict justice, for on that accounting, neither he nor anyone else could stand unacquitted. Instead, he asks God to judge him with mercy by answering him in His faithfulness and righteousness: "O Lord, hear my prayer, give ear to my supplications. In Your faithfulness answer me, and in Your righteousness" (Psalms 143:1). When compared with God "no man living is righteous," but it is not expected of man to be on the superlative level of God: "If You, Lord, should mark iniquities, O Lord, who could stand? But with You there is forgiveness, that You may be feared" (Psalms 130:3–4). The record of the Hebrew Scriptures is a testimony to God's boundless mercy by which the repentant sinner obtains forgiveness.

Job's friend, Eliphaz the Temanite, expresses a thought similar to that expressed by the psalmist in Psalm 143:2. Eliphaz says:

> What is man, that he should be clean or he who is born of a woman, that he should be righteous? Behold, He puts no trust in His holy ones; yea, the heavens are not clean in His sight. How much less one that is abominable and impure, man who drinks iniquity like water! (Job 15:14–16)

Christian missionaries argue that this indicates that man is totally unclean in God's sight. As a result, they insist that man cannot approach God directly for forgiveness. This construction contains a subtle change in the implication of the text. Again, what Eliphaz is saying is that, compared to God, nothing in the universe can be considered "clean," i.e., guiltless. Nothing can approach the perfection of God. But that does not mean that man cannot come directly before God. Eliphaz does not say that God has cast off humanity without any means of attaining forgiveness for sins committed. The biblical record consistently stresses that despite the damaging effects of sin, the sinner may personally approach God through sincere repentance: "Return, O backsliding children, says the Lord" (Jeremiah 3:14).

It has been argued by Christian missionary exegetes that Ezekiel 18:4: "The soul that sins, it shall die" is proof that man is left in a hopeless state of sin unless he accepts Jesus as the Messiah. The context of the verse and, in fact, the entire thrust of the biblical message, teaches us something entirely different. The biblical message is clear for all to read. Ezekiel teaches us that each man is responsible for his own sins. He does not merely say that "the soul that sins, it shall die" but adds: "The son shall not bear the iniquity of the father with him, neither shall the father bear the iniquity of the son with him; the righteousness of the righteous shall be upon him, and the wickedness of the wicked shall be upon him" (Ezekiel 18:20).

The remedy for sin is then clearly shown in the following verse: "But if the wicked turn from all his sins that he has committed, and keep all My statutes, and do that which is lawful and right, he shall surely live, he shall not die" (Ezekiel 18:21). Moreover, God says in verse 22: "None of his transgressions that he has committed shall be remembered against him; for his righteousness that he has done he shall live." But this is contingent on the person's sincere repentance as God says: ". . . he should return from his ways, and live" (verse 23). Since people will, at times, unwittingly sin, animal sacrifice and the contrite heart are offered by the Torah as a means of atonement, with the stipulation that the person resolve to live up to all of God's statutes. To keep "all My statutes" does not mean that remission of sin is contingent upon the future keeping of all the commandments on the part of the repentant sinner. What is meant by this requirement is that the repentant person must pledge to keep all the commandments in the future. By this pledge the repentant sinner sincerely resolves to make every effort to conduct himself thereafter in accordance with all God's laws.

"There is no man that does not sin" (1 Kings 8:46). Indeed, "Who can say: 'I have made my heart clean, I am pure from my sin'?" (Proverbs 20:9). That is why God provided us with the means of cleansing ourselves from sin through repentance. This calls upon the repentant sinner to undergo genuine remorse for his past misdeeds and to pledge himself to improve his ways in the future by making every effort to keep away from all his past transgressions. However, if righteous acts are done insincerely as an attempt to hide unrepentant iniquities, "all our righteousnesses are as a polluted garment" (Isaiah 64:5).

This last statement is distorted by Christian missionary theologians to mean that righteous acts are ineffective in bringing about atonement for sin. However, as indicated by the context, these words were only meant to apply to those who are insincere in the performance of good deeds. Since the verse is preceded by the verse wherein the prophet bemoans the disappearance of those "who joyfully performed righteous deeds, those who remembered You in Your ways" (verse 4), it becomes clear that in the contrasting verse that follows, the prophet describes graphically the insincere acts of those who act hypocritically. As an integral part of organic Israel, Isaiah includes himself among the sinners, as Moses did in the incident of the Golden Calf (Exodus 34:9). All Israelites, whether individually innocent or guilty, share in the collective responsibility of the nation as a whole (Daniel 9:4 ff., Ezra 9:6 ff., Nehemiah 1:5 ff.).

All the foregoing passages, which missionaries cite as proof that man is completely unrighteous and in a permanent state of sin, were put forth at a time when the divine means of atonement as set forth in the Bible were in full use and near to all who wanted to open the Bible and read. To claim that man has no power of initiating the process of atonement or that man's righteous deeds have no meaning to God is tantamount to saying God contradicts Himself. The missionary belief that atonement can only be effected through Jesus runs counter to the provisions for atonement prescribed in the Hebrew Scriptures.[1] First and foremost, God, and no one else, provides the means of reconciliation and fellowship (2 Chronicles 7:14), which precludes any claim for atonement through the death of Jesus. In contrast to the missionary concept that man is hopelessly entrapped in sin, the Hebrew Scriptures provide ample testimony that, although man may have an inclination towards evil (Genesis 8:21), the means of personal salvation are always at hand: ". . . sin is couching at the door; and it desires you, but you may rule over it" (Genesis 4:7). The missionary's question, "Are you saved?" is thus a question having no basis in the Hebrew Scriptures. Its origin lies in the New Testament and has no bearing on the spiritual life of the Jew.

Of Jesus it is said: "For because he himself has suffered and has been tempted, he is able to come to the aid of those who are tempted" (Hebrews 2:18). In contrast, the God of Israel does not need to be tempted and suffer in order to be able to understand and forgive man's sins, because He is the all-knowing creator of man. This is poignantly expressed in the verse: "And the Lord said: 'I have surely seen the affliction of My people that are in Egypt, and I have heard their cry because of their taskmasters;

for I know their pains' " (Exodus 3:7). God forgave sin before Jesus' appearance, and continues to forgive without any assistance from the latter. It is no wonder that many centuries before the time of Jesus, Isaiah declared: "Israel is saved by the Lord with an everlasting salvation" (Isaiah 45:17).

1. See above Chapter 5, "Sin and Atonement."

64

BORN UNDER LAW

(Galatians 4:4)

In Galatians 4:4 Paul claims that "God sent forth His Son, born of a woman, born under law." If we presume a birth without a man's assistance, we still have the problem that Jesus was not born in accordance with the Law. His birth, according to the New Testament, violates the laws of the Torah which specify what constitutes adultery. Mary, according to the New Testament, did not conceive by her betrothed, Joseph. Therefore, she committed adultery "under law" (Deuteronomy 22:23–24). As a result, the Christian missionary claim that Jesus was born of a woman engaged to a man, yet had God as his father, must be considered to refer to an illegitimate birth. God's law does not allow for Him to seduce a maiden, even through the medium of the Holy Spirit. What would be the worth of a moral code that is violated by God Himself? The seduction of a female by a god fits, at best, in the realm of pagan mythology. Such a statement made in reference to the God of Israel is an abomination.

65

WHO WAS MELCHIZEDEK?
(Hebrews 7:3)

Without father, without mother, without genealogy, having neither beginning of days nor end of life, but made like the Son of God, he abides a priest perpetually.

(Hebrews 7:3)

This verse refers to Melchizedek, priest-king of Salem (Genesis 14:18–20, Hebrews 7:1). There are some Christian missionaries who believe that Melchizedek was a manifestation of Jesus in human form. However, unlike Melchizedek, Jesus had a father, Joseph, a mother, Mary, and a genealogy, as found in Matthew's and Luke's Gospels. Most significantly, Jesus also had a beginning in time (Revelation 3:14, Matthew 1:18). Since Melchizedek is said to have been "made like the Son of God," he could not be identical with Jesus. There are Christian missionaries who believe that Melchizedek was a manifestation of God in human form, but then, how could God, the Father, be "made like the Son of God"? God cannot be made like anyone, nor can a father be considered to have been made like his son. Obviously, Melchizedek must be a completely distinct individual, different from either God or Jesus. The speculation of other Christian missionaries that Melchizedek was an angel is equally untenable. He could not possibly be an angelic being, because the angels were created by God, whereas Melchizedek is said to be without "beginning." The author of Hebrews indicates not just that Melchizedek's genealogy, father, and mother were not recorded in the Bible, but that he *never* had any of the ancestral requirements which an actual human being would have.

As we have seen, Melchizedek is stated to be without beginning and Jesus is said to have had a beginning. Therefore, while the two might have been conceived as similar in the perpetuality of their priesthood (Melchizedek is said to be "made like the Son of God"), the two represent two independent beings. What plainly results is a fourth member of the Christian godhead. Thus, what the author of Hebrews creates is a quaternity instead of a trinity.

66

NOAH AND BAPTISM

(1 Peter 3:20–21)

. . . when the patience of God was waiting in the days of Noah, during the constructing of the ark, in which a few, that is, eight persons, were saved through water. And corresponding to that, baptism now saves you.

(1 Peter 3:20–21)

The author of the First Epistle of Peter concludes that the great flood recorded in Genesis 6–8 is a foreshadowing of the rite of baptism by establishing the analogy that baptism saves the believer as water saved Noah and his family. However, reading Genesis correctly, we will quickly discover that Noah and his family were not saved *by* the flood waters, but *from* them. Such careless use of the Hebrew Scriptures obviously proves nothing.

67

THE MISSING TRIBE

(Revelation 7:4–8)

And I heard the number of those who were sealed, a hundred and forty-four thousand, sealed out of every tribe of the sons of Israel: Out of the tribe of Judah twelve thousand sealed; out of the tribe of Reuben twelve thousand; out of the tribe of Gad twelve thousand: out of the tribe of Asher twelve thousand; out of the tribe Naphtali twelve thousand; out of the tribe of Manasseh twelve thousand; out of the tribe of Simeon twelve thousand; out of the tribe of Levi twelve thousand; out of the tribe of Issachar twelve thousand; out of the tribe of Zebulun twelve thousand; out of the tribe of Joseph twelve thousand; out of the tribe of Benjamin twelve thousand sealed.

(Revelation 7:4–8)

The author of the Book of Revelation states that twelve thousand people were to be selected from each of the twelve tribes of Israel to make up a chosen group numbering one hundred and forty-four thousand. This group is to constitute the "first fruits" of Jesus' millennial reign (Revelation 14:1, 4). The author enumerates the twelve tribes as being: Judah, Reuben, Gad, Asher, Naphtali, Manasseh, Simeon, Levi, Issachar, Zebulun, Joseph, and Benjamin. The twelve sons of Jacob, from whom the tribes of Israel are descended, should have been listed, but one of the names listed is Manasseh, the son of Joseph and a grandson of Jacob.

In listing Manasseh, the text leaves out Dan, the son of Jacob, without offering any explanation for this omission. As a rule, when Joseph is listed as one of the tribes, it automatically includes Manasseh. Many unsatisfactory solutions have been suggested, by Christian missionaries to explain this discrepancy. It is contended, for example, that the Antichrist will come from the tribe of Dan, but no relevant scriptural proof for this assertion can be shown. It is also suggested that the use of the phrase *ek pases,* "out of every," signifies that the whole group is to be considered as an entity whether there is an omission or not.

According to this explanation, the author's intention is to indicate that he does not mean "out of *every one* of the tribes." This interpretation is not based on the plain meaning of the text, which shows that the author's intention is to list every one of the twelve tribes of Israel, which inadvertently is not done.

The fact remains, whether intentionally or not, that the tribe of Dan is omitted from the list, and there is no satisfactory reason for this error. Actually, the omission of Dan and the inclusion of Manasseh was the result of an error on the part of John or of some later copyist. Such an inaccuracy, found in a passage which plays so important a part in Christian theology, concerning the second coming of Jesus, destroys the credibility of the author of Revelation.

68

CONCLUSION

No appeal to faith can alter the fact that the Scriptures do not teach what the missionaries preach. Studying the Bible reveals that missionary Christianity actually disregards biblical teachings. Confronted with the inconsistencies of its contentions, the missionary movement claims that its beliefs are a matter of faith. Is this refusal to face the biblical reality the hallmark of true faith? The missionary movement often argues that Christian faith is not a rational process by which the believer comes to a logical conclusion that Jesus is the Messiah. It is contended that Christian faith is a gift from God by which the believer receives certain spiritual truths that the nonbeliever is incapable of believing. By using this apologetic device, the missionary movement hopes to stifle all criticism. It confounds emotion and ignorance with faith. Faith, however, does not preclude the proper understanding of the Scriptures.

Disregarding the biblical word in favor of reliance on what is said to be faith, the missionary movement distorts the Revelation of Sinai, presuming to know better than God what His intentions are for the people of Israel. These distortions of the message of the Torah can be traced back to the earliest Christian writings, the letters of Paul. Paul's antinomian statements, in which he extols faith in Jesus while deprecating the observance of the laws of the Torah, are actually only his own ideas and not those of God. They represent a futile effort to find fault where there is no fault, to substitute a new faith for that of the Torah, where no such requirement is necessary. By distorting the biblical word, Paul developed much of his teachings. How one came to faith, as he defined it, was of no importance. In fact, he considered deceit and pretense valid means for achieving his goal (1 Corinthians 9:20–22, Philippians 1:18).

The modern missionary movement still follows the traditional Pauline method of deceit and pretense. Its antirational faith-experience apology is an excuse in the face of the reality that the Jewish Scriptures do not show Jesus to be the Messiah. The Jewish convert to Christianity has been deceived by subtle mental manipulation into accepting Jesus as God, into thinking evil is righteousness, and into accepting the preposterous view that the observance of God's Law is against the will of God. Often that Jew is led to believe that he has experienced Jesus personally in his life. The Jewish convert should reevaluate the source of his experience. The experience on which a Jewish convert may base his faith is not the result of divine intervention in his life. A man's emotional experiences cannot take the place of the true biblical word, as found in the Hebrew Bible. The belief that Jesus can affect one's life is irrational and biblically untenable. Convincing oneself that something is true does not make it so.

The author of John, some seventy years after the crucifixion, alleged that the resurrected Jesus appeared to Thomas after the latter refused to believe the report of the other apostles that they had seen the risen Jesus. In the course of that meeting John's Jesus proclaimed: "Blessed are they who did not see, and yet believed" (John 20:29). This apologetic was contrived for the benefit of those who could not lay claim to having seen the risen Jesus and are now instructed to believe on faith alone. However, even this episode does not preclude the need for more tangible evidence beyond mere faith alone, for even John's Jesus urged the use of scriptural allusions to prove his claims (John 5:39).

To approach the Bible in a rational manner does not mean that by definition one is acting contrary to the Bible's teachings. Biblical faith is not belief without proof, but trust without reservation that God will never abandon Israel. The Hebrew Bible was given for the purpose of revealing God's will. That which is God's word cannot be false or based on falsehoods. In the study of the Scriptures there is nothing wrong with a person's not knowing all the answers to every question which arises. However, one must be honest enough to admit that it does matter when so many instances can be cited where the fundamental assertions of the Christian missionary movement are shown to be biblically unsubstantiated.

The potential Jewish convert to Christianity should ask himself whether the available information concerning Jesus can be properly used to identify him as the Messiah of Israel. However, the potential convert is confronted by a great difficulty. This is the fact that the information we have concerning Jesus comes from the New Testament, written many years after his death by men whose bias was decidedly in favor of representing him as the Messiah of Israel. These men often distorted the events in Jesus' life to fit what they viewed as proof-texts for the Messiah in the Hebrew Scriptures. Nevertheless, despite post-facto reconstruction of events so as to give the appearance of fulfilling prophecy, the diligent searcher for God's word can discern where the New Testament's contradictory teachings depart from the Hebrew Bible and from any claim to validity on the basis of that Bible.

The missionary movement's claim to reliance on pure faith is deceptive. Human history is replete with groups who believe fervently and with deep faith in false notions. Even the most apparent frauds, using faith alone or mixing it with signs and wonders, have inspired credulity in the trusting. But true faith is not credulity. Many individuals in history have, with varying degrees of sincerity, proclaimed that they were divinely inspired by God. Many systems of belief claim truth and authority. They insist that they could not be of evil origin because of all the good they are achieving. Would any Christian missionary who is not a Mormon agree that the martyred founder of the Church of Latter Day Saints, Joseph Smith, received divine revelations? Would any Christian missionary accept that Muhammad was visited by the angel Gabriel, who transmitted a divine revelation to him? The founders of these religious beliefs, and many other individuals like them, thought themselves to be the recipients of divine revelations. They also felt that by their pronouncements and deeds they were improving the world by bringing it the true worship of God. They too believed that through their sincere commitment to their new beliefs they were fulfilling the divine will. Although they believed fervently in what they may have thought to be God, faith alone did not make their beliefs divinely inspired.

It is for this reason that the Hebrew Bible is explicit concerning the conditions under which prophecy is validated (Deuteronomy 13:1–5, 18:20–22). Ultimately, one who studies the Scriptures will find that the reason uncritical faith is emphasized so heavily by the Christian missionary movement is because the Hebrew Scriptures lack the proof this movement needs for its contentions. Only by a superficial approach to the Scriptures can the missionary movement pretend to justify itself. It is no wonder the Scriptures warn that "the simple believe anything" (Proverbs 14:15).

The missionary profession that the Hebrew Scriptures are the true word of God means that the New Testament can be true only if it agrees with the Hebrew Scriptures. This is demonstrably not the case. The disagreement between these two books is not due to the unbeliever's lack of spiritual insight. The disagreement between them lies in their intrinsically contradictory contents. There is a basic truth concerning the New Testament message that no claim to faith can ever eradicate: "What is good is not new, and what is new is not good."

I firmly believe in the coming of the Messiah; and although he may tarry, I daily wait for his coming.
—*Thirteen Principles of Faith*

SCRIPTURE INDEX

(The figures in parentheses indicate notes)

THE HEBREW BIBLE

THE NEW TESTAMENT

INDEX OF NAMES AND SUBJECTS

(The figures in parentheses indicate notes)

305

Zealots, 221, 253(2)
Zechariah (son of Berechiah) 79, 82, 112, 220–221, 224, 264
Zechariah (son of Jehoiada), 220–221

Zelophehad, 180
zer'a, 10, 61–62
Zerubbabel, 184–185
Zerwick, Maximillian, 177(23)
Zeus, 20, 174